To Be of Use

Selected Papers

Vikki Reynolds

everything
is
connected

First published 2025 by
Everything is Connected Press
9-11 Main Street, Farnhill, UK, BD20 9BJ

British Library Cataloguing in Publication Data

A.C.I.P. for this book is available from the British Library

ISBN 978-1-7397733-6-6 (pbk)
ISBN 978-1-7397733-5-9 (ebk)

To Be of Use. Selected Papers. Vikki Reynolds

Cover image: Painting by Gail Mountain

www.eicpress.com

Endorsements

"justice-doing", "supervision of solidarity", "peopleing-the-room", "the zone of fabulousness". These phrases make complex ideas accessible and memorable. We find no puffed-up jargon here. Vikki's writing is poignant and direct, poetic and descriptive. At all times, Vikki does justice to the people she represents and the gravity of the circumstances they face. This is no small gift. It is wonderful to read a collection of essays about justice-doing. *To be of use* is written in an open and inviting style that "centres the people we work alongside". Justice is readable.

Sekneh Hammoud-Beckett, Registered Psychologist (MAPS) and Narrative Therapist, Dulwich Centre, Adelaide.

Vikki Reynolds has gifted us a collection that refuses the false comfort of neutrality. In *To Be of Use*, she weaves together decades of revolutionary love and solidarity work, offering a profound roadmap for practitioners who understand that healing and justice are inseparable. As a woman living on Gadigal land with Lebanese Muslim ancestry, I have witnessed firsthand Vikki's sacred struggle for justice. Her commitment and advocacy runs far deeper than the written word. I can attest that her wisdom and solidarity are not performative - they are lived, breathed, and embodied in every interaction. Vikki doesn't merely write about centering the most marginalised; she consistently shows up, especially when it is messy, uncomfortable, and demands that we all examine our own privilege and complicity. This book dares us to reject sanitised professionalism - the kind that too often abandons people at the intersections of oppression. Vikki invites us to ask not 'How can I help' but rather, 'What is the best use of me?' Her vision of justice-doing transforms therapy from a site of individual coping into a practice of collective resistance and care - a refusal to collude with the systems that wound us. Like the olive trees of my ancestral land - rooted deep, bending but never breaking -Vikki's work shows us how to sustain ourselves and each other through seasons of unimaginable loss. In a time when genocide is livestreamed and helpers are submerged in what she aptly names 'enraged grief,' she offers a 'believed-in-hope' and the 'Zone of Fabulousness' - spaces grounded in our collective ethics while acknowledging the struggle inherent in our pursuit of a more just world. Her work reminds us that we are all more than the worst thing we have ever done, and that our liberation is bound together. This book is *sadaqah* for the soul: a gift that continues to benefit our humanity and beyond. In the tradition of my ancestors, and Vikki's, who knew that hospitality and knowledge are forms of resistance, and that justice is carried through generations of struggle, this book is essential reading for anyone who refuses to separate their practice from their politics. For those who recognise that in the face of necropolitics, neutrality is complicity, *To Be of Use* is a love letter to our collective struggle and care. May we be useful - and brave enough to live into its vision.

Imelda McCarthy, Fifth Province Network, Ireland

'To Be of Use' is a red-hot book for this time in our history of chaos, 'panmorphiccrises' and madness. It invites, or rather confronts, us to re-encounter ourselves as Systemic practitioners who are committed to positions of justice, ethics and solidarities as well as to decolonising and anti-oppression practices while not forgetting love, hope, passion and joy. The lives and experiences of those who have been marginalised, abused, poisoned and colonised are not easy to read about. However, it is the courage 'to go on' in their lives and work that wraps itself around our hearts as readers and in turn gives us courage to resist individualising, pathologizing subjugations of already marginalised and colonised lives. All of the work presented in this book is held in the very passionate and tender embrace of a true warrior woman advocate who is of acknowledged White planter stock. However, she is also working class and from an ancestral lineage of colonised people in Ireland who were forced to flee due to starvation and great poverty at the hands of the English. In this book, as she stands with those who are brutalised in our Western societies, she carries the echoes of her ancestral people with her in a truly inspirational work. Thank you, Vikki.

marcela polanco, Professor, MFT & Spanglish Decolonial Healing, San Diego University

In "To Be of Use," Vikki delivers an unyielding provocation that disrupts indifference to genocidal and oppressive structures implicated in suffering; an invocation of relationships of resistance spirited by solidarity; and an evocation of "believed-in-hope" collective ethical commitments to justice—not as a concept, but as a verb—configuring practices inseparable from resistance and activism. An unwavering activist, Vikki positions herself as an implicated white settler and strategic-academic, "leaning in" to put to use her privilege to accompany, "show up," "shouldering each other up," and bear witness to stories of suffering, including political violence and torture, in therapy and supervision. At a time when mental health practices remain tightly gripped by capitalism—driven by institutional ethics, outcome-measured interventions, and therapists academically trained to be preoccupied with productivity, Vikki's selected writings written over time, provides an alternative path guided by solidarity and a politics of "imperfection." She problematizes depoliticized frameworks of trauma, suicide, pathology, self-care, transphobia, and individualism by opening a relational path of hope that cracks through the rhetoric of practitioner's burnout, complacency, optimism, and innocence. Furthermore, Vikki's writing also inspires a collective ethics of care. She betrays the illusion of the single author depicted in the cover of the book when her collaborators—geopolitically diverse poets, scholars, activist, her extended family and family of choice, and communities—break away from the parenthesis of academic citations or order of authorship to have an active voice in her writing, collaborating with her, accompanying, critiquing, and teaching her. She calls on our re-imagining when we engage her body of work from our own diverse contexts, not to replicate her, but to further expand practices of solidarity as a living stance of justice-doing. Vikki offers this invitation while, at once, marking the continuation of her work but bringing her publication journey to a close.

Donny Riki, Māori Clinical Psychotherapist (Indigenous to Aotearoa)

The intersections of power and struggle are situated on Indigenous land, which continues to be occupied and commodified by colonial settlers. The effects of colonial violence have endured through generations of Indigenous peoples under the guise of "progress," resulting in a forced disconnection from our sacred relationships with mother earth, father sky, our ancestors, our communities, and our most intimate selves. *"To be of use"* invites deep reflexive conversations about ethical courage and reminds us that in every encounter with another, we make conscious choices to actively participate in systems of colonial violence and oppression or disrupt them. There is no neutrality. Vikki shares personal vignettes that illustrate acts of social justice, fierce resistance and courage, as well as moments of humility and vulnerability. *"To be of use"* serves as a compelling call to action. It functions as a textbook, self-help guide, and therapist's tool kit for sovereigntists, social change makers, visionaries, and justice advocates within the social service, health, justice, and education sectors.

Riel Dupuis-Rossi, Two Spirit Onkwehón:we/Indigenous therapist (Kanien'kehá:ka/Mohawk, Algonquin & Italian descent from Great Turtle Island)

In social contexts overdetermined by settler colonialisms, ongoing attempted genocide of Indigenous peoples, occupational land theft and the relentless ecocidal attacks on our unceded Homelands, it is more important than ever for those who benefit from state-based colonial violence to adopt an ethic of collective accountability in actively righting these, and other, injustices. Creating an opening for genuine solidarity in disrupting multiple systems and structures of colonial oppression, one of the most salient and hopeful messages of this book is for the settler and non-Indigenous reader to "stay implicated in the ongoing catastrophes of white supremacy, colonization and genocide" (p. 262). *To Be of Use* invites a way forward, details important steps and reaffirms the importance of social justice activisms that are accountable to Indigenous sovereignties and land. Amid deeply heartfelt, moving, vulnerable, humanizing and powerful relational accounts of political resistance to injustice, *To Be of Use* serves as a timely reminder of how crucial transforming oppressive political, social and economic structures truly are.

Sheila McNamee, Professor Emerita, University of New Hampshire & Vice President, Taos Institute

I am so delighted to be asked to endorse Vikki Reynold's collection of essays, *To Be of Use*. The power of her voice and the message she offers should be required reading for anyone in the service of others. The offerings here are critically important, particularly in the present context where ignoring social injustices has become more challenging. There are many professions – therapy being only one – that claim neutrality in an attempt to help others. A stance of neutrality divorces us from acknowledging (or even noticing!) the very real institutional and professional harm we perpetuate as we engage with others. Largely, the social justice work that Vikki engages and writes about rises above neutrality by acknowledging that the hardships, the trauma, the violence, and the isolation that we feel is not our own problem and is certainly not a psychological problem. Our hardships are the byproduct of institutionalized discourses – ways of being – that persist and remain unquestioned. Thankfully, Vikki questions these institutionalized discourses. She provokes us to consider if we can discern what is unsafe from what is uncomfortable? If we can act in solidarity with others rather than step in as their ally? If we can describe what solidarity looks and feels like?

Or, if suicide among trans youth is a sign of their mental illness or a result of a transphobic culture? Question such as these are only a small sampling of the big issues this collection addresses. This volume provides not only food for thought but – more important – calls to action.

Johnella Bird, Co-founder of the Family Therapy Centre, Auckland, NZ

This book of selected writing reflects Vikki's Reynolds lifelong dedication to 'practice based activism'. Those of us who are interested in heeding her impassioned call to action will find support, challenge and companionship within these chapters. Each chapter provides inspiration while affirming the importance of acting collectively. Acting collectively may sounds obvious yet increasingly this aspiration is undermined by those complex forces generating wide-ranging divisions within communities. Through-out this book Vikki invites us to resist those divisive strategies by joining her in refusing to be cowed or intimidated by experiences of fear, tension and distress. This invitation goes beyond rhetoric as Vikki offers readers both theoretical inspiration and the practical processes she uses to engage with complexity.

Ramón Karamat Ali, Systemic Centre for Professional and Personal Development, UK & Netherlands; Research Lead, MSc Systemic Psychotherapy, Manchester

I unreservedly endorse this book. My support for it, my admiration of it, and my solidarity with it, seem to make it almost impossible to find the words to describe its usefulness. Reading some chapters for the first time, and re-reading others at this point of my professional life has truly been 'sensational'; all my senses being called upon to create the fullness of the experience. As a seasoned therapist, supervisor and trainer, I feel that when Vikki Reynolds writes she is able to reach the readers beyond the semantics. Working with individuals, families and other groupings who experience trauma responses to circumstances of inequality and who are often at the receiving end of oppressive practices, including those of the systems we as professionals work in, the experience of wanting to "be of use" can seem an obvious one. Her writings about positioning ourselves ethically in the work and about *"building communities and creating rooted and fortifying connections"* are not only inspiring and feel sustaining, but they can also have a direct impact on the practicing professional. I want to acknowledge Vikki's bravery and commitment to continue to step forwards outside of her comfort zone; to continually challenge any taken for granted ideas and practices. The Introduction she wrote to the collection of her work offers clarity of vision and is written with absolute integrity. This collection of papers I recommend to therapists and supervisors, and to the trainers and their students so that they can learn, challenge, and grow in solidarity with one another. In a world that currently seems to be 'out of control' in so many ways, politically, climatologically, ideologically, existentially, ethically, and most of all spiritually, *"To Be of Use"* offers professionals a space to critically consider one's own values and re-connect with what keeps us wanting to be of use to our fellow travellers on this journey we call life.

Travis Heath, Department Chair of Counseling and School Psychology, San Diego State University

When I first met Vikki several years back she noted that a question she asked those who consulted her was, "How can I be useful?" It had a simple brilliance to it, and it's one I've adopted in my own work. And I have no doubt this collection of writings will be of use for many years to come for those of us who strive to welcome solidarity, resistance, accountability, and critique into our work. These writings are as inspiring as they are unsettling and are mandatory reading for the advancement of justice-doing in community work.

Kenneth J. Gergen, President of the Taos Institute

The publication of these exhilarating essays is a banner event. Vikki Reynolds is an international leader in social justice activism, and *To Be of Use* is an invaluable sharing of her experience and thought - challenging, inspiring, and pointing the way forward.

About the book

Vikki Reynolds' book inspires practitioners working collaboratively for social justice. Vikki shares experience of working with communities in crises imposed from without by systematic misuse of power manifesting as structural violence. Many of the papers, some co-authored, speak to the concerns and responses of First Nations People, community members and allies. Vikki not only asks the question "how can I be of use?" but "how can I be of use ethically?" We can see how she considers power and ethical positioning in professional relationships to avoid recreating colonial acts of violence.

About the author

Vikki Reynolds (PhD) is an activist/ therapist and community organizer who works to bridge the worlds of social justice activism with community work and therapy. Vikki is a white settler on the territories of the Squamish, Tsleil-Waututh and Musqueam nations. Vikki's people are Irish and English folks, and she is a heterosexual woman with cisgender privilege. Her experience includes supervision and therapy with People with Lived/Living Experience and other workers responding to the drug poisoning catastrophe, refugees and survivors of torture - including Indigenous people who have survived residential schools and other state violence, sexualized violence counsellors, mental health and substance misuse counsellors, housing and shelter workers, activists and working alongside gender and sexually diverse communities. Vikki has taught as an Adjunct Professor and has written and presented internationally. Articles & speaks free at: www.vikkireynolds.ca

For Johnella Bird

Whose profound influence, moral courage, generosity, and brilliant relational language practices generatively welcomed all of me (and so many others) into our work in ethical, spirited, and embodied ways.

Contents

Section 3:   Solidarity, Collective Care and Sustainability: Resisting Burnout

Permissions

Section 1
Working in Solidarity

Reynolds, Vikki (2013). **"Leaning in" as imperfect allies in community work**. Narrative and Conflict: Explorations in theory and practice, 1(1), 53-75. https://doi.org/10.13021/G8ncetp.v1.1.2013.430. This work is licensed under a Creative Commons Attribution-NonCommerical-NoDerivs 3.0 Unported License. Copyright and usage rights Vikki Reynolds.

Reynolds, Vikki (2010). **Fluid and Imperfect Ally Positioning: Some Gifts of Queer Theory.** *Context.* October 2010, Association for Family and Systemic Therapy, UK, 13-17. Permission for this re-print granted by Ged Smith, Editor of Context.

Reynolds, Vikki & Kelly, James (2018). **Beyond trans tolerance and trans exclusion: Contributing to transformative spaces in an all-genders youth, live-in, substance mis-use programme.** *Context.* February 2018, Association for Family and Systemic Therapy, UK, 37-40. Permission for this re-print granted by Ged Smith, Editor of Context and agreed with co-author.

Reynolds, Vikki, (2011). **The Role of Allies in Anti-violence Work.** *Ending Violence Association of BC Newsletter.* (2) 1-4. Permission for this re-print granted by Samantha Matute Arrieta, Ending Violence Association of BC.

Reynolds, Vikki (2014). A solidarity approach: The rhizome & messy inquiry. In Simon, G. & Chard, A. (Eds.) *Systemic Inquiry: Innovations in Reflexive Practice Research.* London, UK: Everything Is Connected Books. Permission to re-print granted by Everything is Connected Press.

Section 2
Solidarity in Action: Addressing complexity and holding tensions

Richardson, Cathy, & Reynolds, Vikki (2014). **Structuring Safety in Therapeutic Work alongside Indigenous Survivors of Residential Schools**. Canadian Journal of Native Studies, XXXIV (2), 147-164. Permission for this re-print granted by Velvet Maud, Editor of Canadian Journal of Native Studies and agreed with co-author.

Reynolds, Vikki (2016). **Hate Kills: A social justice response to "suicide".** In White, J., Marsh, J., Kral, M., & Morris, J. (Eds.) Critical Suicidology: Towards creative alternatives. Vancouver, B.C.: University of British Columbia Press. Approval to reprint granted by UBC Press.

Reynolds, Vikki (2013). **The problem's oppression not depression.** In M. Hearn & the Purple Thistle Centre, (Eds**.), **Stay Solid! : A Radical Handbook for Youth. Oakland, CA: AK Press. Copyright author.

Reynolds, Vikki (2014) **Resisting and transforming rape culture: An activist stance for therapeutic work with men who have used violence**. The No To Violence Journal. Spring, 29-49. Permission for this re-print granted by David Sutherland at No To Violence.

Reynolds, Vikki (2020), **Trauma and resistance: 'hang time' and other innovative responses to oppression, violence and suffering**. *Journal of Family Therapy*. https://doi.org/10.1111/1467-6427.12293 Licence to reprint granted by Wiley Publishers.

Reynolds, V. & Hammoud-Beckett, S. (2018). **Social Justice Activism and Therapy: Tensions, Points of Connection, and Hopeful Scepticism**. In *Social justice and counseling : discourse in practice*, edited by Cristelle Audet and David Par. Abingdon, Oxon: Routledge.

Section 3
Solidarity, Collective Care and Sustainability: Resisting Burnout

Reynolds, Vikki & polanco, marcela (2012). **An ethical stance for justice-doing in community work and therapy.** *Journal of Systemic Therapies,* 31(4), 18-33. Licence to reprint granted by Wiley Publishers.

Reynolds, Vikki (2011). **Supervision of solidarity moving into supervision practices.** Context, 116, August 2011. Permission for this re-print granted by Ged Smith, Editor.

Reynolds, Vikki & Natasha Sanders-Kay (2023).**The F Word: Vikki Reynolds on the Politics of Forgiveness.** Interview conducted by Natasha Sanders-Kay, *subTerrain,* 92, 44-47. Permission for this re-print granted by Magazine Editors.

Reynolds, Vikki (2019). **The Zone of Fabulousness: Resisting vicarious trauma with connection, collective care and justice-doing in ways that centre the people we work alongside.** *Context.* August 2019, Association for Family and Systemic Therapy, UK, 36-39. Permission for this re-print granted by Ged Smith, Editor of Context.

Reynolds, Vikki, Riel Dupuis-Rossi, R & Heath, Travis (2021). **Inspiring Believed-in-Hope as an Ethical Position: Vicarious Resistance & Justice-Doing.** *Journal of Contemporary Narrative Therapy,* 2021, Release 1, 2-18. Permission for this re-print granted by Journal Editors and agreed by co-authors.

Foreword

Leah Salter, DProf

Co-Director, Centre for Systemic Studies, Wales

I was introduced to Vikki's work just over a decade ago. In the midst of my doctoral research, I was talking with people with lived experience of abuse and structural violence; and writing about solidarity and justice doing. I was speaking into an existing and evolving body of work that would become a cornerstone of my research and practice. My practice was and is embedded in community work, depathologising practices and resisting narratives that maintain elitist, colonial structures of power. Connecting with Vikki and other community activists at that time was vital. It shored me up and enabled my research and practice to stay responsive and "of use" to the communities I was working with. With some similarities to Vikki (and some important cultural and practice differences) I come from a place of working directly with communities impacted by economic deprivation, marginalisation, oppression and violence who were/are blamed for the oppression and violence that is targeted against them. Vikki is a networker, driven by her desire to support activist community. She introduced me to the work of Allan Wade, Cathy Richardson, Linda Coates and others engaged in response based practices. It helped give language to what I felt I was trying to do; to re-centre people as living with dignity, agency and resourcefulness; putting that to use to resist violence and abuse. Engaging with Vikki and her work meant I felt connected, understood and buoyed up. Writing about my research started to feel an integral part of the community and activist work I was part of. It was feeling less separate to it, less of an after-the-fact capturing of the "real work". It, too, *was* the work. A call to action actually. Writing *as* practice *as* action, to paraphrase Gail Simon. Research and writing matters. Education matters. Reading matters. They are all forms of action. bell hooks is one of many people who has inspired me in my work as an educator and her voice reminds me that education can be and needs to be more than state-controlled transmission and acquisition of knowledge. Learning is not a transaction. Education can, and should be, a relational process and a call to action on oppression and injustice. A pathway to liberation. Never has that felt as relevant as it does today. Today, when books, journals, papers, *words* are being systematically taken offline, taken off shelves, banned from use; and fake news is being promoted to reinforce oppressive practices.

Voices of marginalised groups, and their allies are being silenced. Again. On our watch. We cannot just watch. We need to feel invested in what we are reading and writing about; alongside our other practices and doings. We need to feel invested in the communities we live in and the communities we work with and speak with. We need realistic hope to inform our practices and our ways of living. Vikki's work absolutely does that. Her work reaches out from a place of direct action and reaches into our everyday practices via carefully crafted and ethically grounded writing. Vikki's writing, and her being in the world, helps us all feel connected in ways that can honour the people we are collectively working with. Vikki has hosted workshops for one of the practice communities I am part of in South Wales- The Centre for Systemic Studies; and has visited us in person. She has been generous and supportive of the overlapping areas my colleagues and I are involved in- sustaining social justice-led systemic practice and training- and we have forged a strong connection from across the water.

I cannot remember which paper or chapter I first read of Vikki's, they all feel like old friends now, but I continue to be blown away by the passion and honesty within them; and the breadth of experience they capture. You can feel the relational ethics in every page and you can hear Vikki's voice speaking into power and oppression- helping us to carefully consider how we position ourselves and why; whose voices we are able to hear; and why; and what's happening to our communities and why. Many of the papers that have become companions to me over the years are reproduced here in a collection for our time. You will find something in these pages, and in Vikki's and her co-author's words, to hold onto in times of trouble. We are not short on trouble right now. Wherever we are located geographically we are likely to be faced with injustice, and struggles in the face of injustice, that call for a response. Vikki's work gives us hope that we can collectively, collaboratively form a response that can put our trainings and lived experience to use. Her experiences working with men on death row, working with survivors of torture, working with communities oppressed by hate and state-sanctioned violence is hope-full and humbling. She shares what she has learnt through her work in ways that inspires others and respects the dignity of all involved.

This book represents a collection of previously published papers and chapters and a thoughtfully written introduction that speaks to the overall collection; looking back on the times when they were written and acknowledging changes and evolving ethical considerations over that time. The three sections flow into one another and offer a sense of overlapping concerns that Vikki's work speaks to; rather than distinct areas of practice. In the first section the theme of *Working in Solidarity* captures the essence of direct work in and with differing communities who have faced acts of violence and oppression. The second section, *Solidarity in Action: Addressing Complexity and Holding Tensions,* speaks to the complex nature of working in solidarity and how imperfect a project this is. The third section, *Solidarity, Collective Care and Sustainability: Resisting Burnout* leads the reader into a place of grounded hope and gives practitioners an insight into how Vikki has kept hope alive in the work. It also offers a guide to how you/we may resist the invitation to pathologise ourselves or the people we work with; as if it *must* be true that at least one of us is damaged, and at least one of us *must* be to blame. This idea needs multi-faceted resistance; resisting the commercialisation of care and the pathologising of people who care.

Working with Vikki on the book has been re-energising, refreshing and provoking. Everything is Connected Press wants marginalised voices to be heard, and relational practices to be centralised. A collection of Vikki's work is an obvious fit. It epitomises collective care. The decisions about the flow of the book, the consents and permissions required, the art material on the cover (painted by a dear friend of Vikki's) were made ethically, with love and a commitment to upholding the dignity of others. And the writing that is so well grounded in social justice practices is completely inspiring.

Introduction

Vikki Reynolds, PhD

Paths towards Justice-doing

This writing and work took place on the occupied traditional and unceded ancestral lands and territories of the Coast Salish – (xʷməθkwəy̓əm [Musqueam], Sḵwx̱wú7mesh [Squamish], and Səĺílwəta? [Tsleil-Waututh] – nations, which were never surrendered.

In the before times, before I was a therapist or had graduate education, I was a direct-action activist and community organizer, and that is and continues to be the heart of my work. I have been informed and transformed by the revolutionary love and solidarity of activists and social movements over four decades of anti-authoritarian and anti-imperialist struggles.

I responded to the struggles that intersected my life. My people are from Ireland and England. Early on, as a white working-class young woman, my primary struggles were with misogyny, gender-based violence and class. I became involved in issues of Reproductive Freedom and Choice and attempted to address issues of class and access as part of the Student Union at university. In the mid 1980's I was teaching in Botswana, Africa, for four years on the border of the apartheid state of South Africa. Nelson Mandela was still imprisoned on Robbin Island, and the white South African government had declared a State of Emergency. This was an education in political analysis and a call to solidarity, which required I make connections from there to understandings of, and resistance against, genocide and colonialism in my own country, Canada. This analysis led to profound expansive teachings on abolition, which I was led to by Black Panther and former political prisoner, Angela Davis, who made the connections for me of apartheid states of South Africa and Israel; and open prisons. Davis speaks of abolition meaning against all police, surveillance, family policing, executions, prisons and people in cages (2022). It was in dialogue with beloved friends in Botswana that my own white privilege and participation in, and benefit from, both colonization and white supremacy became visible to me. I was informed and transformed specifically by Ngugi wa Thiong'o's (1986), 'Decolonizing the Mind' and Black Consciousness' assassinated leader Steven Biko's (1987) collected articles in 'I write what I like'.

Because AIDS ravaged Botswana, I became involved with AIDS activism in the late 1980's and early 90's, and was hugely educated by the street theatre and brilliance of queer activism, especially ACT UP and Queer Nation. I am heterosexual and cisgendered and so this invitation into queer and non-binary resistance was a gift to me that has offered many networked community connections of love and solidarity, and created much of my family of choice.

In the late 1980's California was moving towards implementing the Death Penalty after over twenty years without an execution. I became involved in the international abolition movement with many community organizers, organizations and some beautiful humans who shaped my activist identity. I spent a decade of my life focused on resisting the Death Penalty worldwide, especially in Iran, and specifically the executions of over twenty men on Death Row in the USA. Every one of these men was murdered by their government- only one had been innocent. That was not the point. I do not believe any government should kill people. The men on Death Row taught me a famous abolitionist adage 'Everyone is so much more than the worst thing they have ever done'. That is our mantra, and that teaching has shouldered me up as a therapist and supervisor, as I was taught by these men to see the humanity in all people. This has resourced me in my work as a therapist to be of use to people of all genders who have used violence.

When I became the therapeutic supervisor of a centre for refugees and asylum seekers who had survived torture and political violence it was, for me, an extension of my work with men on Death Row. The Death Penalty is torture. Working as an activist with a witnessing stance to honour the resistance and dignity of people on Death Row profoundly informed my approach to therapeutic work with people who experienced torture and political violence. In many ways it is the same work. My qualification for this work addressing torture and political violence was not academic or particularly psychological. I position myself in solidarity as an activist and a witness to the person's acts of resistance, uphold their dignity and humanity, invite collective care and 'people-ing-the-room' in ways that resist isolation and terror. This I learned from men on Death Row.

Working alongside Tibetan survivors of torture connected me relationally with activists, including the Canada Tibet Committee, organizing around resistance to occupation and genocide in Tibet by the government of China. This led to a visit to the Tibetan community in exile in Dharmsala India, and engaging in lateral mentorship alongside monks working at Gu Chu Sum, the centre for survivors of torture. Here a Tibetan Buddhist Monk shared a teaching that accompanies me now in struggles- to hold onto believed-in-hope. Roughly it goes like this, 'things are not so awful because we are doing nothing. Things are this horrific and no worse because we are doing everything humanly possible to keep things from being worse'.

When the 1997 APEC conference was coming to Vancouver, we were required to create solidarity connections with the struggle against the government of Indonesia's genocide in East Timor, as Vancouver welcomed the dictator Suharto. We organized around a citizen's arrest of Suharto for genocide in East Timor. This organizing and lateral pedagogy led me to see how I was personally and collectively implicated as a settler in Canada.

As a settler-activist it is ethically imperative for me to acknowledge where I stand. The context of the work that I am involved in, dedicated to, and in solidarity with, occurs on occupied, stolen and unceded traditional and ancestral lands and territories of Indigenous peoples. As a white settler to these territories, I work to stay implicated in the ongoing catastrophes of white supremacy, colonization and genocide. Here I am ever-mindful of the teachings of Riel Dupuis-Rossi (2018) who informs me that genocide by the Canadian state is ongoing, in current necro-practices and policies, but also only attempted, as resistance from Indigenous peoples is as long as colonization on Turtle Island. As a white settler I am also required to act in solidarity with the Palestinian people in resistance to settler colonialism and genocide. It is essential that I take this position at a time when many people at the intersections of oppression and subjugation are being punished, silenced, and erased for their resistance to ongoing genocide in Palestine. In similar ways, many Indigenous people, especially land defenders (for example Unist'ot'en Camp, n.d.) and people acting in solidarity with them have experienced, and are still experiencing, tactics of erasure, criminalization and punishment for naming and resisting the ongoing colonial violence of Canada's nation building, especially 'residential schools', as political violence, torture and genocide.

Our solidarity as activists and workers is framed on the intersections of our struggles, as Angela Davis (2015) teaches, not only the intersections of our domains of identity (Crenshaw, 1995). Justice-doing requires that we locate our relational work and solidarity in the socio-political context which frames it. Workers I am committed to shouldering up struggle in contexts of both necropolitics (Mbembe, 2003, 2019) and structural and targeted abandonment (Gilmore, 2022). Mbembe created the language of necropolitics, necro meaning death, to more accurately describe mean spirited policies that actually kill people. In my country, at the time of writing, over 50,000 people have died from drug poisoning deaths that are facilitated by bad drug policy, which means they are political deaths connected directly to the drug war of the USA. In Canada, over twenty people die each day of this preventable poisoning. The number of people killed in this catastrophe would be unimaginably higher without the resistance and mutual aid of drug users and folx working in solidarity alongside them to overturn these deaths, at Overdose Prevention Sites and Safe Consumption Sites. These sites are being systematically closed down by right-wing, populist, hateful governments demonizing people who use drugs for political gain. The people who have died in this catastrophe of morally bankrupt governance did not simply 'slip through the cracks' or get caught in 'gaps in services'. These folx were targeted for abandonment, as abolitionist Ruth Wilson Gilmore teaches, because they are at the intersections of power, are poor, underhoused or shelter folx, and drug users. Certainly, a disproportionate number of these people who have died are Indigenous, leading some Indigenous activists to name the drug poisoning catastrophe a weapon of genocide. It is hard to shoulder up these workers when the people are dying in what Harm Reduction activist Zoe Dodd names as "carnage" (quoted in Riete, 2017).

There is nothing natural about these deaths. Workers are immersed in mourning amidst atrocity and are experiencing embodied responses I understand as 'enraged-grief'. Anger, as Audre Lorde (1984) teaches is an outlaw emotion, and workers with lived and living experience can experience stigma and judgments of being 'unprofessional' when they, of necessity, out their rage. The gas-lighting of workers and people with lived and living experience who carry the greatest burdens of this weight for communities and society dictates that workers are experiencing vicarious trauma, and burnout. Self-care is weaponized against workers, as if a massage, sauna, swim, would erase the spiritual and ethical pain workers experience when we are not able to enact justice-doing and dignity with people we struggle alongside. If self-care makes workers okay with these deaths by necropolitics, they are probably in the wrong work. I also believe we have put workers in an existential crisis, saying this is not the new normal, these deaths are not natural but political, and, be prepared to work responding to this carnage every shift.

Queer theorist Judith Butler's (2009, 2015) ideas of precariousness and grievability are meaningful here. Butler speaks of precarious lives, and people who are 'ungrievable', whose lives are not worthy or capable of being grieved because they have not been allowed to live. I am reminded of a tender conversation I had with a mother whose adult child died of drug poisoning. She explained how friends were devastated to hear how she, as a mother, had lost a child, but when the cause was understood as 'addiction' and 'overdose' the compassion was 'fatigued', and the ethical space to grieve was rescinded. This is an ungrievable life, abandoning this bereaved mother to disenfranchised grief. In response, this mother helped form Moms Stop the Harm (n.d.) a beautiful spirited movement of parents advocating for dignity and an end to the drug war and the poisoning deaths of other families' beloveds. I celebrate, honour, and am humbled by the acts of resistance they have co-created in response to the harrowing deaths of their children by necropolitics.

As a direct-action activist, informed by Paul Ricoeur's (1970) hermeneutics of suspicion, I held a hopeful skepticism about engaging in academia. I was aware a graduate degree would potentially elevate me both economically and professionally. I entered a Masters Program strategically to become qualified, as deemed by professionalism, to work with asylum seekers and refugees who had experienced torture and political violence. I have been ever led by Marge Piercy's (1982) poem, "To be of Use", and recursively reflected on the best use of me, my locations, resources, relational connections and lived experience. My 'career path' doesn't make sense when viewed through a lens of hierarchy, upward mobility, capitalism or success narratives. But I have been guided and accompanied by Marge Piercy's gorgeous provocation: *what is the best use of me?* This better explains my lateral, often circuitous and fluid attempts to move to sites and connections where I am more of use. I think I bring this recursive provocation to every supervision dialogue I engage in with workers. I never expect to answer or silence this question, and I engage with it as an anti-perfection project. Johnella Bird's profound influence on my own path and relational language practice and supervision leads me to be ever in relationship with this inquiry: *what is the best use of me?*

bell hooks offered a way forward for me in my fraught relationship with academia, when she honoured that theorizing is part of the struggle. There is a role for participation in academia in movement work, held in a tension alongside an analysis of the intersectional abuses of powers academia is both created by and perpetrates. I felt accompanied by hooks words: "I came to theory because I was hurting— the pain within me was so intense that I could not go on living. I came to theory desperate, wanting to comprehend — to grasp what was happening around and within me. Most importantly, I wanted to make the hurt go away. I saw in theory then, a location for healing" (1994, p. 59).

The articles so carefully and intentionally chosen for this book by Leah Salter and Gail Simon are my answer to the questions I was responding to at the intersections of power. My theorizing is part of both my resistance against the oppressive contexts of problems, and my hope to be of use to other workers facing up to similar struggles alongside participants.

Section 1: *Working in Solidarity*

"A story from the 20 Bus", included in the first paper, describes a ride through the harsh centre of Vancouver's downtown east side, and a re-telling of collective creative responses to a racist attack on an elder Chinese woman by a large, angry, drunk white man. The story witnesses the love, collective care, resistance and solidarity of various residents of Canada's poorest urban neighbourhood. The story was originally written as part of a newsletter from a rape crisis centre, now called Salal Sexual Violence Support Centre (n.d.), where I was the therapeutic supervisor. I am indebted to the brilliance of Jon Winslade, who edited the article, *"Leaning In as Imperfect Allies in Community Work"* and suggested the possibility of starting with this 20 Bus story and then bringing all of the theory and practices of 'Leaning In' to relate to the tale. Leaning In is my response to both calling out and calling in, and differs as it requires us, as practitioners with an ethic of justice-doing, to create pre-existing relationships of respect and dignity that can invite, not just tolerate, the moral courage of critique, discern feeling uncomfortable from being unsafe, and welcome critique as a performance of collective care.

Re-reading this article I was discomforted by the use of the word ally. In my own writing I have critiqued the use of ally as an identity. Claiming the identity of ally can enact what Eve Tuck and K. Wayne Yang (2012) speak of as a settler move to innocence, referring to settlers' strategies to avoid acknowledging their culpability and benefit from colonialism and genocide, hiding behind understandings of individual innocence. Like many organizers, I now use the language of acting in solidarity, acknowledging the fluidity of accountabilities in moment-to-moment analysis. I say more about this in the article *"Fluid and Imperfect Ally positioning; Some Gifts from Queer Theory"*, which is my homage to multiple ways I have benefited as a heterosexual cisgendered woman from Queer Theory and community.

It addresses the teachings on fluidity in working in solidarity with each other, and the ever-moving nature of accountability. Ethical practice requires we track vulnerability and then centre the person most vulnerable in any interaction. This is a fluid process, and requires us to move nimbly and smoothly from positions of needing solidarity to showing up in solidarity for others when our privilege is of use. This writing and analysis suggest 'acting in solidarity' as differentiated from claims to 'being' an ally.

"Beyond trans tolerance and trans exclusion: Contributing to transformative spaces in an all-genders youth, live-in, substance mis-use programme"' is co-authored with James Kelly, a transgender man who is the program's Executive Director. The dialogue tracks the space-making practices that move beyond inclusion. Most meaningful in this article for me is the acknowledgment that the youth who are transgender, Two-Spirit, nonbinary and gender diverse, are the ones that lead the change. In re-visiting this writing, I was profoundly saddened and called to account by the dedication: "We honour the strength and moral courage required to trust us enough to share their identities with us, and acknowledge the silencing pain we contribute to for all of the youth for whom we were and are not safe-enough to be out with".

'Transphobia' as a term, doesn't do the work of describing current attacks on transgender communities. Here, again, Judith Butler (2024) lays the hateful path out clearly, "Once you decide that a single vulnerable minority can be sacrificed, you're operating from a fascist logic, because that means that there might be a second one you're willing to sacrifice, and a third...". At the time of writing the UK Supreme Court has delivered a decision that erases transgender people, and their rights, declaring that there are officially and legally only two genders as assigned at birth (Carrell, 2025). In this present context of political warfare, fuelled by the global far right on transgender and non-binary people, especially youth, this article offers more of a provocation and call to solidarity and action, than any actual answer.

Caution of transgressions and causing harm while attempting to act in solidarity is part of the focus of the article "*The role of allies in anti-violence work"* which I wrote at the invitation of EVA (Ending Violence Association of BC. n.d.). In profound ways being an 'ally' is a site of privilege, not a badge of honour, as people require allies because of oppression. Allies are not necessarily worthy of trust, but are invited to act in solidarity because of necessity in contexts of oppression and abuses of power. Working in solidarity requires critique, accountability and at times strong disagreement. Discord has an important place in our movements, discomfort is at times required, and critique shouldn't be understood as attack. These tactics speak to the messiness of solidarity in action, where we search not for unity, but for points of connection. America Bracho (2000) teaches that in building solidarity we do not want to annihilate our important differences.

Gail Simon approached me to write a chapter about my PhD research methodology for a book she was editing, alongside Alex Chard, entitled 'Systemic Inquiry: Innovations in Reflexive Practice Research'. This baffled me, because I didn't really think I had a methodology that would be of use to anyone. Gail thought that I had come up with a way of approaching inquiry that could be useful to graduate students struggling, as I did, to be both ethical and accountable in their work. In the chapter *"A solidarity approach: The rhizome & messy inquiry"'* I lay out my strategy to hold all of my 'research' and writing accountable to the ethical stance I have for my activism and therapeutic work; A solidarity approach included solidarity teams and community accountability practices. I didn't want to replicate any oppression my work was striving to resist. In her most fabulous book, "Decolonizing Methodologies", Māori scholar Linda Tuhiwai Smith (1999) says this: "'research' is probably one of the dirtiest words in the indigenous world's vocabulary...It stirs up silence, it conjures up bad memories, it raises a smile that is knowing and distrustful..." (p. 1).

I am ever-led by Linda Tuhiwai Smith's praxis throughout all facets of my practice and writing. When I was in Aotearoa, New Zealand, in 1990-something I was doing a practicum with the Just Therapy Team at the Family Centre in Wellington. I was there to address white supremacy, colonization and racism in my work, and was impacted in seriously meaningful ways, most especially around critiques of white feminism, by both Flora Tuhaka, the head of the Māori Section at the Family Centre, and Kiwi Tamasese, the head of the Pacific section of the Family Centre. A few years later Kiwi gifted me with Linda Tuhiwai Smith's book. I said I had no intention of further graduate studies and was not intending to publish anything. Kiwi looked knowingly at me saying something like, 'well, when you *do* do a PhD, because you will, be sure to read this first'. So, I guess Kiwi and Gail are co-creators of this one.

Section 2: Solidarity in Action: Addressing complexity and holding tensions

"Structuring Safety in Therapeutic Work alongside Indigenous Survivors of Residential Schools". Around 2008 the Truth and Reconciliation Commission was created under the stewardship of the brilliant Murray Sinclair of the Peguis First Nation in Manitoba. They began taking testimony from over 6,000 Indigenous people who had experienced violence and abuse in Canada's Residential School System, which ran for 150 years. I was called to act in solidarity alongside Cathy Richardson/Kinewesquao, a Metis professor, who was despairing that white settler therapists were going to be part of the process for Indigenous people giving testimony in this action. We shared a deep fear that white settler therapists could do much harm and violence to Indigenous people who sought to give testimony, especially as the qualification was academic degrees, not understandings of acting in solidarity and working in ways that structure safety for Indigenous people who have experienced not only 'trauma' but violence and torture from the Canadian state. Cathy Richardson/Kinewesquao wrote an outline of the atrocities of the 'schools' she names as "prison camps or internment centres" (p. 149) given the large numbers of preventable deaths that occurred. She invited me to offer teachings from my work alongside refugees and asylum seekers who experienced torture and political violence. In the article I outlined practices of structuring safety that were co-created alongside people who had survived torture. This article has applications for any therapist or worker with an ethical stance for justice-doing to structure safety in contexts of necropolitics and oppression. In its

final report The Truth and Reconciliation Commission of Canada (2015) described the residential school system as a cultural genocide.

Professor Jennifer White invited me to speak at a national conference addressing suicidality because she heard me critique the language of suicide as unjust, abusive and inaccurate language. I called my keynote: *"Hate Kills: A social justice response to 'suicide'"* and said that people don't kill themselves. Hate kills. From a perspective of justice-doing I see the language of suicide as psychological language that blames people for their own suffering and deaths, when we have collectively failed to join them to the human community with an ethic of belonging. Huge numbers of transgender and gender questioning youth attempt 'suicide' every year, and this is used as evidence that the transgender community is mentally ill - when we know it means transphobia kills. In my work with people who have survived torture I don't believe they take their own lives. The torturers, the governments benefiting from the torture, the imperialist nation sponsoring the torture are the killers- not the person. 'Suicide' also obscures the person's many acts of resistance to stay on the planet. I have heaps of gratitude for Jennifer White teasing this small sentence out of a talk, and creating space to bring my analysis and work to her broader international community addressing suicidality ethically and with care. I am humbled this chapter sits alongside Jennifer's own writing and the excellent work of Ian Marsh in their book on Critical Suicidality (2016).

Matt Hearn and the Purple Thistle Collective invited about a hundred 'elder' activists, including me, to write a one-page rant to offer solidarity to a younger generation of direct-action activists resisting oppression on all fronts. Too large for a 'zine', but in the spirit of punk aesthetics and actions, the book is called "Stay Solid! A Radical Handbook for youth". I ranted about resisting the over diagnosis and medicalization of youth activists who are involved in movement work. *"The problem's oppression not depression"* is a succinct love letter to a younger community of radical activists, and was a heartfelt joy to write. In this writing I use the term 'paralyzing'. Later, in the chapter "Social Justice Activism and Therapy: Tensions, Points of Connection, and Hopeful Scepticism" we use the ableist term 'ethical blindness'. These transgressions invite a wave of shame as they are such a failure to aims of disability justice. This reminds me of a later experience when I used this term while I was presenting in a large public workshop. A participant in a wheelchair took the space, and with moral courage, taught me and the community of learners that I was not paralyzed, I was stuck, and asked that we all consider the inherent harm and privilege of this ablest language. Re-reading this boisterous rant brought that generous and painful teaching to my mind.

"Resisting and transforming rape culture: An activist stance for therapeutic work with men who have used violence" offers an approach to the work that is overtly political and resists carceral logics and individuating violence and moves towards not only personal accountability but actually transforming rape culture. There is complexity in addressing the tension of holding the dignity and safety of women, transwomen and children at the centre while working to hold men responsible for their violence - while also maintaining the dignity and humanity of these men. Here the teachings of men from Death Row, reminding me everyone is more than the worst thing they have ever done, shoulders me up. This article was invited for the No to Violence Journal (n.d.), who are part of a "movement to end men's use of family violence". My connection with these ethical and accountable humans amplifies my hopes for gender-based resistance and safety.

The heart of my work with people who have survived political violence and torture is not trauma based, but centred on positioning myself as a witness, looking for sites of resistance, and asking people to teach me how they resisted and stayed human in these situations outside of human understandings. Here I refer to witnessing from activist cultures, and specifically the work of Ignacio Martín-Baró (1994) who believed all political violence is social and requires social responses and mobilization, what I refer to as collective care and a spirit of solidarity. Martín-Baró taught that in order for there to be liberatory psychology first we must liberate psychology itself. In the article *"Trauma and resistance: 'hang time' and other innovative responses to oppression, violence and suffering"* I offer theoretic underpinnings of the work from an activist stance, centering the work in resistance to violence, suffering and oppression and resist psychological orientations to understand behaviour. The practice example is from my work with youth in substance misuse programs, which requires a political analysis of suffering as contextualized in oppression, and not the usual suspects of addiction, trauma and mental illness. I believe that across more than three decades, my orientation to witness people's acts of resistance and honour their moral courage, intelligence, sacredness and creativity has led to my sustainability in the heavy lifting work we do.

"Social Justice Activism and Therapy: Tensions, Points of Connection, and Hopeful Scepticism" is a chapter I am honoured to have co-authored with Sekneh Hammoud-Beckett. We were invited to write about the presence of social justice in our therapeutic work, but in dialogue we found we were drawn more to interrogating whether we were actually enacting justice-doing. The chapter invites a rigorous critical investigation with our ethical stances for justice-doing, and problematizes our practices to unsettle our complicity and make our limitations more apparent to us. Our aim was to bring a hopeful skepticism to our practice as therapists who work towards justice-doing in our work. Sekneh and I offer provocations to problematize and unsettle our relationship to: addressing power and privilege, resisting neutrality and taking overt positions for justice-doing, naming and responding to white supremacy and colonization, doing social change work, and resisting affronts on solidarity. Re-reading this chapter in the present context invited a humility about my commitments across time to abolition and decarceral practices. Problematizing our co-option with social control and direct reporting as participation in family policing was not language Sekneh and I had at the time of writing. I believe the Black Lives Matters movement, amongst others, offered me a language and analysis to more clearly bring an abolitionist stance to my work. Resisting neutrality is particularly important in the present historical moment, where universities, therapeutic training organizations and professional bodies have remained, for the most part, and at best, neutral about genocide.

Section 3: Solidarity, Collective Care and Sustainability: Resisting Burnout

"An ethical stance for justice-doing in community work and therapy" was initially a keynote address I was invited to deliver by David Paré, for the Winds of Change Conference, which was an excellent home for the words

as they received a gorgeous, embodied and spirited welcome. I believe our community was hungry for ethics and justice-doing to be acknowledged and centered. The response spoke to our collective world-building and commitments to a just society and the wee role in it for therapy and community work. Jim Duvall asked me if the Journal of Systemic Therapies could publish the keynote, and they did so without depoliticizing or smoothing over any of the politics, fierce and just anger, and naming of white supremacy and genocide. I asked marcela polanco to offer a reflection as I was mindful that I spoke as a white settler and needed to be open to critique. marcela wrote a beautiful reflection that was expansive, connecting in a strained solidarity with me across the intersections of power that separate us, and moving to name colonization and resistance. This co-authoring with marcela became a new strategy for me and I expanded my writing practice to more co-authoring and inclusion of often critical and silenced voices. I believe we co-visioned this writing in the bar after the keynote, shouting loudly over the community's music fest! Joyful. This keynote and article were important in me finding my voice in our community and I have profound respect and gratitude to the folx who carved out and held this space for me, and those who edited these words in courageous ways.

I approach supervision as community organizing. I call my work a Supervision of Solidarity, and in *"Supervision of solidarity practices: Solidarity teams and people-ing-the-room"*, I lay out some of the practices for putting the ethics of solidarity into action. The article includes an expansive set of questions, inviting an inquiry, for creating Solidarity Teams. People-ing-the-room was a strategy I co-created alongside refugees and asylum seekers who had no one from their community and former life available to them in person to bear witness to the meaning of their acts of resistance. I morphed Karl Tomm's (1985) ideas of internalized others as a useful construct to try to bring people who were the appropriate and authentic witnesses to the person's life into the dialogue. In this writing a Nigerian man who survived torture finds himself in a context of disconnection and dislocation, and loses track of the meaningfulness of his political activism which led to his torture and necessity to seek asylum. He is disconnected by despair from his courage. Embracing people-ing-the-room we bring his mother and grandmother to his service to re-member him back to lost pieces of his resistance and identity. In re-reading this article I was transported across time back to that sacred space when we experienced his grandmother's spirited presence, love and wisdom.

Natasha Sanders-Kay, a writer and journalist at subTerrain, had heard me speak somewhere about forgiveness being the F word in therapy. She told me she was moved by that language in ways Aotearoa/New Zealand therapeutic supervisor Johnella Bird (2004) might name 'Talk that sings'. When the journal decided to have an edition committed to forgiveness, Natasha approached me for an interview, which she succinctly and thoughtfully crafted into the article, *"The F Word: Vikki Reynolds on the Politics of Forgiveness"*. I am concerned about the coercive nature of forgiveness, especially in the therapeutic context when primarily people who are harmed and oppressed are coerced into working on forgiveness. In early days of my therapeutic training, I heard Johnella Bird (n.d.) problematize the normalization of forgiving and forgetting, and conversely hold up practices of forgiving with re-membering. This teaching stayed with me. Forgiveness can be weaponized by people at the intersections of power against people they harm. From a justice-doing lens forgiveness can be a bad tactic, especially if it occurs without the person perpetrating the harm taking responsibility and working through an accountability map to actually make change and centre the person who experienced the harm's needs. Authentic apologies that promote morally courageous and relational forgiveness can be transformative and part of world building, imagining spaces of justice we can live into. I strive to co-create networked relationships in our movements where, as transformative justice and disability justice activist Mia Mingus (2019) teaches, accountability isn't scary.

"The Zone of Fabulousness: Resisting vicarious trauma with connection, collective care and justice-doing in ways that centre the people we work alongside" is my attempt to make sense of the harms workers experience without pathologizing them or demonizing clients as the cause of hopelessness. I offer alternative ways to understand worker burnout,

where instead of focusing on the mental issues of the worker we focus on how we are treating people. Harms workers experience are better understood, not as vicarious trauma or other mental issues, but as spiritual pain, the embodied pain we experience when we are not acting in accord with our collective ethics for justice-doing. I borrow inspiration from Queer community in naming the Zone of Fabulousness, in an attempt to defy pathology and embrace something playful, joyful, effervescent and necessary. This article lays out the moves to disconnection and enmeshment workers make when we experience spiritual pain, when we are exhausted, heart broken and responding to necropolitics and structural and targeted abandonment. Conversely there is the Zone of Fabulousness, where we resist enmeshment and disconnection, we are in solidarity with our co-workers, enacting our collective ethics, and engaging in a culture of critique with moral courage that keeps the person at the centre.

Around my sixth decade on this planet lots of folx were asking me how I had stayed alive in the work and struggle so long, and frankly, to throw my own language back at me, how I was resisting burnout across decades amidst heart break and devastating politics and violence. Sally St George was particularly useful in articulating my responses to these provocations, and my response became this writing: *"Inspiring Believed-in-Hope as an Ethical Position: Vicarious Resistance & Justice-Doing"*. I invited Riel Dupuis-Rossi and Travis Heath to offer reflections alongside my words, and their spirited critical voices reached out in solidarity to make space for my voice in accompanied ways. I had planned for this article to be my last publication, as I believe my body of work is out there in different ways. I'm more interested now in making space and being informed by the voices of others, especially workers with lived and living experiences: This wee introduction is an exception.

Everything I offer in these writings is profoundly collaborative and co-created. I have been in generative therapeutic and supervisory relationships with people with lived/living experience and other workers responding to the drug poisoning catastrophe; refugees and survivors of torture - including Indigenous people who have survived residential schools and other state violence in Canada; gender-based violence counsellors;

mental health and substance misuse counsellors; housing and shelter workers; activists and gender and sexually diverse communities. I aim to work towards a decolonising practice and justice-doing for all of my paid and unpaid work, and honour all of the learnings I have benefited from that have come at a cost to people at the intersections of power. Diverse communities of activists, workers, clients, teachers, colleagues, family and family of choice, have inspired, critiqued, provoked and taught me this work.

The value of the ethical stance and practices of justice-doing ensconced in this collection of papers lies in how they might be re-imagined in a diversity of contexts, in the specificity of practitioners' own and collective struggles at the intersections of power, and how they are moved to action. Patti Lather teaches that research is useful not for what it measures, but for what it can do (1993). It has been increasingly sustaining for me to hear back from community workers who have taken up this invitation and furthered the diversity of possible dignifying practices that share this spirit of justice-doing. Like "rhizomic organisms growing horizontally into new terrains, establishing connections just below the surface of every day life, eventually bursting forth in unpredictable ways" (Uzelman, 2005, p. 17).

I want to acknowledge with heartfelt appreciation and gratitude the beautiful humans connected in webs of revolutionary love across time who have collaborated in these writings. My primary teachers have been the participants who have taught me this work off of their backs and to my benefit. Also, co-collaborators from the Solidarity Groups and community gatherings we've manifested over the decades: community workers, activists, community organizers, therapists, people with lived and living experience, and clinical supervisors. Also, beloved activists in our Abolition Action Circle, especially Nicole Kief, Stephanie Saville, Andrea Lofquist and Abby Chow, who expand my analysis and move theorizing to actions. My Solidarity Team: Tara 'Danger' Taylor, Cori Kelly, Jill Faulkner, Riel Dupuis-Rossi, Donny Riki, Sekneh Hammoud-Beckett, Michael Boucher, Janet Newbury, Brian Gilligan, Nancy Holman, and Wendy Wittmack, and the men from Death Row who still shoulder me up. Mentors and teachers and folx who have continually made room for my work and analysis, as part of the larger project of making room for justice-doing: especially Cathy Richardson/Kinewesquao, Allan Wade, Cheryl White, David Denborough, Johnella Bird, Gail Simon, Colin Sanders, and Imelda McCarthy. Gratitude, humility and revolutionary love to Leah Salter and Gail Simon who envisioned this writing project, with committed, skilful, spirited effort and tender care for the work and for me. My dear one, Gail Mountain, painted the cover. Mr. Peaslee helped again.

I will leave this welcome with a witnessing of one of the most meaningful acts of believed-in-hope that I have encountered in this life. After over five decades of resistance to being wrongfully accused, caged, incarcerated, tortured, and in isolation, political prisoner and American Indian Movement leader Leonard Peltier is free, though under house arrest. Leonard's ability to stay human, in these situations outside of human understanding, confound and inspire me. Leonard Peltier (1999) refuses to be put on a pedestal, even though he has given his life to the cause of Indigenous sovereignty and liberation and is held up by many as a hero. In his autobiography, "My Life is my Sundance", Leonard offered this humbling teaching to all activists, community organizers, and to his fellow Indigenous warriors:

> "You must understand.... I am ordinary. Painfully ordinary. This isn't modesty. This is fact. Maybe you're ordinary, too. If so, I honor your ordinariness, your humanness, your spirituality. I hope you will honor mine. That ordinariness is our bond, you and I. We are ordinary. We are human. The Creator made us this way. Imperfect. Inadequate. Ordinary...We're not supposed to be perfect, we're supposed to be useful" (p. 10).

In Imperfect Solidarity & Revolutionary Love,

Vikki

References

Biko, Steve (1987). *I Write What I Like: A Selection of His Writings*. Oxford: Heinemann.

Bird, Johnella (2004). *Talk that sings: Therapy in a new linguistic key.* Auckland NZ: Edge Press

Bird, Johnella. *Forgiveness: A work in progress.* (unpublished manuscript).

Bracho, America (2000). An Institute of Community participation. *Dulwich Centre Journal*, No. 3. Adelaide, Australia: Dulwich Publications.

Butler, Judith (2009). *Frames of war. When is life Grievable?* London: Verso Books.

Butler, Judith (2015). *Precarious Life: The Powers of Mourning & Violence.* London: Verso Books.

Butler, Judith (2024). Interview in El Pais. https://english.elpais.com/culture/2024-12-15/judith-butler-philosopher-if-you-sacrifice-a-minority-like-trans-people-you-are-operating-within-a-fascist-logic.html

Carrell, Severin, (2025). The Guardian. *Legal definition of woman is based on biological sex, UK supreme court rules.* 16th April 2025.https://www.theguardian.com/society/2025/apr/16/critics-of-trans-rights-win-uk-supreme-court-case-over-definition-of-woman

Crenshaw, Kimberley (1995). Mapping the margins: Intersectionality, identity politics, and violence against women of colour. In K. Crenshaw, G. Gotanda, G. Peller, & K. Thomas (Eds.), *Critical race theory: The key writings that formed the movement* (pp. 357-383). New York: The New Press.

Davis, Angela Y., Meiners, Erica R., & Richie, Beth R. (2022). *Abolition. Feminism. Now.* Chicago: Haymarket Books.

Davis, Angela. (2015). *Freedom is a constant struggle: Ferguson, Palestine and the foundations of a movement.* Chicago: Haymarket Books.

Dupuis-Rossi, Riel. & Reynolds, Vikki (2018). Indigenizing and Decolonizing Therapeutic Responses to Trauma-Related Dissociation. In Arthur, N (Ed.) *Counselling in Cultural Contexts Identities and Social Justice.* Switzerland: Springer, pp. 293-315.

Ending Violence Association of B.C. https://endingviolence.org

Gilmore, Rachel Wilson (2022). *Abolition Geographies. Lessons towards liberation*. London: Verso Books.

hooks, bell (1994). *Teaching to transgress: Education as the practice of freedom*. New York: Routledge.

Lather, Patti (1993). *Fertile obsession: Validity after poststructuralism*. The Sociological Quarterly, 34(4), 673-693.

Lorde, Audre (1984). *Sister Outsider*. CA: Crossing Press.

Martín-Baró, Ignatio (1994). *Writings for a Liberation Psychology*. Cambridge: Harvard University Press.

Mbembe, Achille (2003). Necropolitics. *Public Culture,* 15, 11-40. https://doi.org/10.1215/08992363-15-1-11

Mbembe, Achille (2019). *Necropolitics*. Durham NC: Duke University Press.

Mingus, Mia. Dreaming Accountability. *Leaving Evidence.* May 5th 2019. https://leavingevidence.wordpress.com/2019/05/05/dreaming-accountability-dreaming-a-returning-to-ourselves-and-each-other/

Moms Stop the Harm. https://www.momsstoptheharm.com/

Ngugi wa Thiong'o (1986). *Decolonising the Mind: The Politics of Language in African Literature*. London: Heinemann.

No to Violence. https://ntv.org.au

Peltier, Leonard (1999). *Prison writings: My life is my Sundance*. New York: St. Martins Griffin.

Piercy, Marge (1982). *Circles on the Water*. New York: Knopf.

Riete, John (2017). CBC News: Activists warn of 'carnage' if city can't keep Moss Park overdose prevention tent open. 1st November 2017. https://www.cbc.ca/news/canada/toronto/overdose-prevention-site-1.4381016

Ricoeur, Paul (1970). *Freud and philosophy: An essay on interpretation*. New Haven, CT: Yale University Press.

Salal Sexual Violence Support Centre. https://www.salalsvsc.ca/

Tomm, Karl (1985). Circular interviewing: A multifaceted clinical tool. In D. Campbell & R. Draper (Eds.), *Applications of systemic family therapy: The Milan approach* (pp. 33-45). Orlando, FL: Grune & Stratton.

Truth and Reconciliation Commission of Canada, (2015). *Honouring the Truth,*

Reconciling for the Future: Summary of the Final Report of the Truth and Reconciliation Commission of Canada. https://web.archive.org/web/20200611001013/http://nctr.ca/assets/reports/Final%20Reports/Executive_Summary_English_Web.pdf

Tuck, Eve, & K. Wayne Yang (2012). Decolonization is not a metaphor. In *Decolonization: Indigeneity, Education & Society.* 1(1), 1-40.

Tuhiwai Smith, Linda (1999). *Decolonizing methodologies: Research and indigenous peoples.* London: Zed Books.

Unist'ot'en Camp. https://unistoten.camp

Uzelman, Scott (2005). Hard at work in the bamboo garden: Media activists and social movements. In A. Langlois, & F. Dubois (Eds.), *Autonomous media: Activating resistance and dissent* (pp. 17-27). Montreal, QU: Cumulus Press.

White, Jennifer., Marsh, Ian., Kral, Michael. J. & Morris, Johnathan (Eds.) (2016). *Critical Suicidality: Transforming suicide research and prevention for the 21st Century.* Vancouver: UBC Press.

SECTION ONE

WORKING IN SOLIDARITY

ONE

"Leaning In" as Imperfect Allies in Community Work

Abstract

The work of allies in community work is informed by justice-doing and decolonizing practice. A brief description of being an ally is outlined here, as well as understandings of the importance of the concepts of fluidity and groundless solidarity in ally work. "Leaning in" is described and offered as a way to invite accountability while resisting righteousness. "Leaning in" invites collective accountability, which is a more useful concept than personal responsibility, which sides with individualism and the idea we are only held accountable for our personal actions. Strategies for being an ally are considered, including engaging with a hopeful skepticism while reflexively questioning whether we are "walking the talk". The limitations of allies are discussed, as well as the need to make repair for our failures as allies. Strategies for resisting both unity and division are addressed, as is the possibility of creating cultures of critique that allow for something other than attack and division. Imperfect solidarity based on points of connection is offered as a useful strategy for maintaining good-enough and required alliances across time. Finally, some exercises are offered for readers to engage with: an inquiry into their histories and imperfect practices of being and needing allies, and some invitations to step into domains where they have previously not served as allies.

Keywords

ally, community work, leaning in, power, privilege, fluidity, imperfect solidarity

Authors' Note

This work is profoundly collaborative and owes much to a diversity of activists who have been in imperfect solidarity with me across time. Graeme Sampson and Sherry Simon, practicum graduate students from the Adler School of Professional Psychology, critiqued the ally exercises and contributed to their usefulness. Thanks to WAVAW for allowing me to reproduce a version of "Story from the 20 Bus," which originally appeared in their newsletter. Andrew Larcombe, Paka Ka Liu, Aaron Munro, Tod Augusta-Scott, Jeff Smith, Allan Wade, and John Winslade offered generative and expansive critiques that improved this work. Mr. Peaslee helped again.

****

The story that follows illuminates an experience of messy and imperfect ally work on the number 20 bus that goes through the Downtown East Side, the poorest part of Vancouver, and the poorest off-reserve part of Canada.

I get on the 20 bus late at night, and like most women, I can tell you exactly how many drunk men are on the bus. But there is one guy that requires all of my attention because he's loud, he's standing up and he's shouting racist things at an elder Chinese woman. I stand still, not moving, looking and listening. I think what am I going to do? The first thing I think about is, I can't take on a great big, drunk man. I've tried this in my life, it hasn't worked for me and I'm scared of great big drunk men. I'm not required as an ally to take on that guy, unless I have the power to do it. I am required to be an ally to this woman.

I look at the Chinese elder woman and I kind of throw my love at her. I want her to know I'm here, I'm with her. I'm going to try to figure out what I'm going to do. She's got her head down, she's got her groceries on her seat next to her and she's tucked in tight. She's not looking at my love that I'm throwing at her. This is a good tactic, but it's not working.

While I'm trying to figure out how the heck I'm going to respond, a young, sweet, lovely person who I could not tell the gender of slips by me, Aikido

2

style, and picks up the groceries, puts them on their lap and sits next to her. What I saw as a full seat, this person saw as a seat without a person in it.

Beautiful! What a beautiful thing! So now, there is a body between this elder Chinese woman and this man who is attacking her with racism. The Chinese woman doesn't thank this person. I can tell this person is looking to say, "Should I put my arm around you? Should I talk to you?"

And the Chinese woman is letting them know she's not engaging with them either.

There's a whole bunch of us on the bus that are thinking, "OK. What's the next thing we should do?"

This guy is still going. Now I'm rooting for this young person, and I'm worried for them. My read is that they are possibly trans, or gender-variant and maybe they are queer[53], so they could be next to be attacked. Why should they be in front of this big angry guy? This is not good.

---

[53]   'Queer' has been adopted by groups of people I work with, both workers and clients, who do not identify as strictly heterosexual. Using queer as an umbrella term to include folks who self-identify as lesbian, gay, bisexual, Two Spirit, questioning and queer, is problematic for many reasons (Fassinger & Arsenau, 2007). Primarily people who self-identify as lesbian, for example, may not resonate with queer theory or politics at all, and be subsumed by that term. As well, some folks who do identify as queer mean specific things by it, such as resonating with queer theory in ways that do not align them with gay or lesbian identities, and find using the term queer as an umbrella term mystifies and erases the queer politics and ethics that are at the heart of their preferred ways of identifying (Aaron Munro, personal communication, 2012). People I work alongside who identify as queer primarily identify outside of heterosexual normativity, which refers to discourses that promote heterosexuality as normal. People I work alongside who identify as transgender or trans do not identify strictly with the gender they were assigned to at birth, and may transition culturally, socially and/or physically to a gender in which they feel more congruent, which could be something other than male or female (Nataf, 1996; Devon McFarlane, personal communication, 2011). Many people do not identify their gender in any way, and others identify as gender-

There's a really large First Nations guy on the bus. I can't tell whether or not he's had a few beers or he's doing performance art because he's by the window, and he slips by the person on the aisle seat, puts his hand on the bar and swings around, you know, takes all the room on the bus.

In my head I'm thinking, "Oh man! Big guy stuff, there's big guy and big guy; this is going to be bad."

But no, I totally misjudged this guy. He's being an accountable man, what he's saying is bring it on, bring it over here.

One of the nasty things the white guy had said to the Chinese woman was, "Get back on the boat. Go back to China."

And the big First Nations guy says to the white guy, with humor, "Hey man, you are the original boat person. Christopher Columbus was your captain. Get back on your own damn boat," and he's laughing as he says this.

Everyone on the bus exhales, because we know we are going to be OK-enough, and then everybody leans in, and the guy looks at me, and though I do seem inept, I am available to be an ally. He looks at me and, with a smile, he asks, "What the hell boat did you come from?"

I timidly say, "Ireland, Newfoundland, a little bit of England."

He says, "You can stay, you know your boats."

He starts holding court, inviting other folks into the fray.

As all this is going down, I notice the elder Chinese woman picks up her groceries and slips out the door at the next stop. I go out with her. The bus

---

variant, gender non-conforming or gender queer, meaning something different than trans and outside of the normative gender binary (Janelle Kelly, personal communication, 2011). All of these terms are problematic, contested and evolving. I am using these terms for clarity and because groups of folks I work alongside have settled on this imperfect phrasing for now (Reynolds, 2010b).

goes on. I don't get to see the rest of this lesson in 500 years of resistance to colonization, but I envision it: it makes me happy.

But I'm left on the sidewalk with the Chinese woman, and I'm wondering if she wanted me to accompany her, does she feel safe-enough to go to her home. She puts her head down and she kind of runs, dragging her groceries behind her. She's probably not new to this. She probably has really good reasons to not trust me either. I'm not a perfect ally to her, she doesn't love me, she doesn't thank me: she takes off.

I realize I cannot follow her. A big white person following her would be scary, so I try to let go of what I want to do. I want to be the perfect ally, but she's saying, "No."

This is what no looks like. I work at WAVAW (Women Against Violence Against Women) a rape crisis centre. We work really hard to hear no and listen to no. So I'm thinking, "Vikki, you've got to hear no too."

So I know this is going to be imperfect, she's probably OK-enough, and she's probably lived with this her whole life.

I turn around. There are three other women at the bus stop and we are a real multiplicity of women. And one of them looks at me, looks at everyone else, and says, "This is nobody's stop, is it?"

And we say, "No."

"We're all going to wait for the next bus?"

We all chuckle and respond, "Yeah."

And that was my moment of the social divine (Lacey, 2005), that four different women would get off at the wrong stop to accompany this woman who didn't need us to walk her home, and didn't thank us. And the big First Nations guy and the young, possibly gender-variant person, and all the folks who "leaned in" on the bus are a part of the fabric of the social divine.

These are beautiful moments. When people do the right thing.

And there I was saying, "Oh man. What am I doing alone at night at an unfamiliar bus stop? This isn't the best scene for you, Vik."

But I have these other women in solidarity on this street, and I know there are accountable men and gender-variant folks on that bus. This changes things for me, it matters for me. I hold these moments of the social divine alongside the terror of the racism this Chinese woman experienced. That's the real story, and that's a heart-breaking story (Reynolds, 2012).

Introduction

In community work informed by justice-doing, we act in solidarity with shared purposes and shoulder each other up to resist structural violence and abuses of power and work to create a more just society (Reynolds, 2010a). This requires us to act as allies to each other across the differences of privilege and access to power that we hold. Allies belong to groups that have particular privileges, and work alongside people from groups that are subjected to power in relation to that privilege. The role of the ally is to respond to the abuses of power in the immediate situation, and to work for systemic social change (Bishop, 2002). Allies work collectively to contribute to the making of a space in which the person who is subjected to power gets to have their voice heard and listened to. Being heard is not enough — a person's words must matter and not be dismissed. This contributes to the creation of "spaces of justice" (Lacey, 2005).

Being an ally is not a badge of honor but a sign of privilege and it is risky to be romantic or sentimental about this. When we experience being the subject of power, abuses of power, oppression, or attacks on our dignity we accept allies because we need them, not because it is safe or because we have reasons for perfect trust. We invite good-enough allies, despite past acts that are not trustworthy as imperfect allies are required when the stakes are high and risk is near. The need for allies speaks to structures of social injustice. Our greater purpose is to deliver a just society, not to show up as allies, because our access to power makes that possible. Ally work requires humility and a resistance to righteousness, alongside the skill and moral courage required to name abuses of power from people within the same groups allies belong to.

Power relations are complex and, in order to resist simplification, I will speak of subjection as well as oppression. Oppression does exist, but it is not the only way in which power is used to subject people. All abuses of power are not oppression. As well, power is not always oppressive, and can be generative. I borrow this teaching from critical Trans theorist/activist Dean Spade (2011):

> I use the term "subjection" to talk about the workings of systems of meaning and control such as racism, ableism, sexism, homophobia, transphobia and xenophobia. I use "subjection" because it indicates that power relations impact how we know ourselves as subjects through these systems of meaning and control... "oppression" brings to mind the notion that one set of people are dominating another set of people, that one set of people "have power" and another set are denied it...The operations of power are more complicated than that...our strategies need to be careful not to oversimplify how power operates. Thinking about power as top/down, oppressed/oppressor, dominator/dominated can cause us to miss opportunities for intervention and to pick targets for change that are not the most strategic. The term "subjection" captures how systems of meaning and control that concern us permeate our lives, our ways of knowing about the world, and our ways of imagining transformation. (p. 25)

For example, this racist attack on the Chinese elder on the bus is not the only way all of the folks on the bus are subjected to power. It is not only a case of one individual white man attacking an individual woman with verbal racism. What happens is made possible by the existence of a background discourse that structures what happens on the bus. Racist immigration laws in Canada, which prohibited Chinese immigration, disrupted family unification and refused citizenship, and the Chinese Head Tax and Exclusion legislation, which impoverished Chinese families, are particular policies that have fostered this racist attack[54]. Corporate media coverage of "boat people" as threatening and not worthy of refuge is another part of the operating context.

On the other hand, the elder Chinese woman's multiple acts of resistance are responses to her subjection to power. Looking down, being hunched over, and not engaging anyone, are acts of resistance that make up an intelligent and prudent resistance strategy. She has probably had success staying safe-enough by taking less space. Her acts of resistance are responses to her subjection to power, as there is always resistance to oppression and attacks on people's dignity (Scott, 1985, 1990; Wade, 1996, 1997; Reynolds, 2010b).

Simultaneously, the cultural stories the white guy is immersed in are also part of the context. They continually promote a notion of white men as a vulnerable population at the hands of multiculturalism and feminism. He is on a bus, and guys should drive cars. He is by no means the perfect oppressor, and is subjected by the lies of the particular culture of masculinity held up by capitalism and patriarchy which demand that men should be in charge (drive) and be rich (own a car). Perhaps he is responding to the ways in which the dominant discourse positions him as a failure. This event is thus more than a singular act of oppression of a Chinese person by a white person. It happens at the point of intersection of "lines of force" (Deleuze, 1995, p. 85) about gender, immigration status, age, class and

---

[54]   In 2006 the Canadian Prime Minister apologized for the Chinese Head Tax as part of a spate of 'non-apologies' (Coates & Wade, 2009) to various communities. The Conservative government decided to compensate only surviving Head Tax payers and their spouses. This settlement has only been available to 500 Head Tax families and represents only about one half of one percent of all affected Head Tax families. The Chinese Head Tax and Exclusion laws impoverished families and halted all Chinese immigration from 1923 to 1947. Each Chinese worker was required to pay a fee equivalent to the price of a house. Many families were separated for decades, some never reunited. See the Head Tax Families Society of Canada website for background (http://www.headtaxfamilies.ca/).

race, which are all part of the particular context. It is not accidental, for example, that this racist attack is not targeted at a Chinese young man who is in the company of six large friends.

While I find Spade's analysis of power useful, it is problematic that the above passage appears agentless: there are no offenders or agents that write, print, circulate, gossip, lie, belittle, and invent the "systems of meaning and control." But these meaning systems that appear disembodied are linked to systems of oppression, violence, relations of physical and material and social power, and arguably inseparable from them. Agentless constructions, such as "systems of meaning" cannot by themselves do injustice: they must be produced, warranted, justified, replicated, used, sanctioned and so on — by social agents (A. Wade, personal communication, 2012). But neither can individual agents act oppressively without the background systems of meaning (J. Winslade, personal communication, 2012). The main problem with Spade's view of subjection is that it does not begin to explain the actions of the people on the bus, not even the drunk white guy shouting racism.

Fluidity and Groundless Solidarity

Like the folks on the 20 bus, we are never perfect allies, but may become imperfect allies, momentary allies, creating moment-to-moment alliances which are flawed, not necessarily safe, but required and of use. Being an ally is not a static identity that requires perfection and always getting it right. It is a tactic informed by strategies, a performance (Butler, 1990). Ally work is comprised of actions potential allies take together across the differences of privilege that divide them to address abuses of power. Queer theory has brought exciting ideas to ally work (Jagose, 1996; Butler, 1997) inviting fluidity, which is movement from the fixed and certain to the confused and unstable (Queen & Schimel, 1997).

Embracing fluidity in ally work means that being an ally is not a fixed position. Fluidity is useful for ally work because it acknowledges that in particular situations we all need allies, and in different contexts we can all

9

serve as allies (Reynolds, 2010c). For example, the First Nations guy on the bus is called on to act as an ally to the Chinese elder, and to all of the women and gender-variant people on the bus, because of his access to gender privilege. Simultaneously, all of the settler people are required to have his back, as the police might attend and he could easily become the victim of police officers enacting colonization and racism by reading him as the perpetrator of violence and dragging him off of the bus. Fluid ally positioning is responsive to the multiple different domains that construct our identities and the access to power we hold in relation to these domains.

Categories, like domains of identity, are useful at times, but also problematic. American critical race theorist Kimberlé Crenshaw writes about how her identity as a Black woman is constantly subject to erasure (Namaste, 2000) and disappearance by categories (Namaste, 1995). When the category being attended to is race, she is left behind as a Black woman. When the category is gender she is seen as a woman, but being Black is invisibilized. Her work illuminating the intersections of domains of identity has been useful in contributing to a more complex understanding of the intersectionality that comprises identity (Robinson, 2005). Ally positioning must always attend to this fluid intersectionality of sites of access to power, and being the subject of others' power, within the same moments and within the same conversations.

Canadian anarchist/academic Richard Day writes about "groundless solidarity" (2005, p. 18), meaning that our activism need not always be tied to one location of power. No location is seen as the organizing principle in all situations; rather, the intersections and the gaps between our multiple locations in relation to privilege and oppression are tended to in a complex analysis. Sometimes we need to address sexism, sometimes it is more important to attend to racism, and, in another interaction, class privilege requires our attention. Of course, we can and must often attend to more than one domain of power at a time. We do not need to move our attention from one mutually exclusive category to another, but can engage in a dance that simultaneously addresses the complexities that comprise power relations.

In Canada, where I live and work, this intersectional approach always exists on colonized territories. In order to resist replicating colonization, we enact a decolonizing practice, which means acting in ways that simultaneously attend to the abuse of power that is happening, and holding ourselves to account in resisting ongoing colonization (Walia, 2012; Richardson & Reynolds, 2012; Lawrence & Dua, 2005). This might sound like inconsistency, but as anarchists say, "We can walk and chew gum."

In the situation on the 20 bus, we could address men's violence and attend to colonization at the same time. To do so requires that we always situate ourselves on the land in an accountable way and from that stance we respond to abuses of power. For example, the network of activists resisting the poverty, gentrification and homelessness that resulted from the 2010 Olympics in Vancouver began all organizing from the decolonizing position, 'No Olympics on stolen Native land'. From that place, we then addressed the devastating social impact of the Olympics facing most folks, not just Indigenous people. We structure decolonizing practice and accountability into all of our organizing, whatever the specific context of power abuses.

"Leaning in" and Collective Accountability

Individual accountability is a limiting idea that does not require us to be responsible for more than our own actions, but social injustice requires enormous, collaborative, and resourced social responses from all members of society, reflecting our "relational responsibilities" (McNamee & Gergen, 1999). Whether we intend to or not, many of us benefit from the oppression of others. We need not feel guilty about this, but we are required to respond to the unearned privileges we hold with accountability. I did not personally take anyone's land as a settler person in Canada, but I certainly benefit from citizenship in the nation state of Canada, which exists on these Indigenous territories. Activism teaches us to analyze structures of power, not just attend to our individual acts. Collective accountability (Reynolds, 2009) requires that we take actions together to change these underlying structures that create the conditions for abuses of power.

For example, as a heterosexual person, I hope to respond to another heterosexual person who is performing homophobia by embracing collective accountability, and acknowledging the relationship that connects them to me through our shared site of privilege. I want to locate myself as collectively responsible for the performance of homophobia, and for the fact that it advantages me. I do not have to perform homophobia or racism or transphobia in order for my status to be elevated on the backs of others. I have to be accountable for more than just my personal actions. The seduction of identifying individually and separating myself off from any participation in collective responsibility at these times can be intense — I want to identify myself as, "not that kind of straight person." As an ally, I identify collectively as a heterosexual person in the presence of homophobia, and act to help my fellow straight person move towards accountability as well. I want to "lean in" with humility and resist being righteous and attacking the dignity of this heterosexual person. I do not think of people as homophobic, but I know we swim in a culture that hates homosexuals and that, if we do not resist homophobia, we will replicate it. I remind myself in "leaning in" that this person did not invent homophobia and it is now my job to help them understand this and resist this, as others taught me. "Leaning in" towards the other allows us to move toward solidarity, and act in ways that make space for that person and for us to be walking alongside each other.

Collective responsibility also contests the limits of human rights talk and legislation as the only measure of justice-doing. Legal protections would probably not allow for the prosecution of the white guy on the bus who was attacking the elder Chinese woman with racism. As one direct action activist told a white supremacist who asserted he was not acting illegally by trying to disrupt an anti-racism march, "There are a lot of things that are not illegal that you ought not to be doing."

Some laws are inherently racist, and the law is part of the mechanism that subjects people, so it is more than the application of law that is the issue (Spade, 2011). Collective accountability speaks to a social justice perspective, which may include legal rights, but is much more expansive. It requires us to show up and take imperfect actions immediately in the face of the white guy's attack, and to try to hold what the Chinese woman needs at the centre. Collective accountability invited all of the actions allies took on the bus, and more. It suggests that we all work to address racism and men's abuses of power, and to transform contexts that make such attacks possible.

Walking the Talk: Engaging a Hopeful Skepticism

Kvale's hermeneutics of suspicion (Kvale, 1996; White, 1991), invites a healthy and hopeful skepticism toward our own practice as to whether we are enacting our ethics and acting as allies in any moment-to-moment interaction. Holding an anti-oppression decolonizing framework is fabulous, but theorizing is of limited value in itself (Tuhiwai Smith, 1999). Despite the promises of critical theory we have not delivered a just society. Allies engage with the reflexive question activists ask, "Am I walking the talk?" They also embrace "infinite responsibility" or to always attempt to be "open to another other" (Day, 2005, p. 18.) and to the multiplicity of ways we are not acting as allies, despite our intentions.

Would-be allies can inadvertently replicate power-over, lecture righteously, take center-stage, and make situations worse and possibly violent. Any information a person from an oppressed position gives potential allies in any interaction about our abuses of power or less egregious ally-fails are gifts to us. These teachings benefit allies at the cost of the person needing an ally (Tamasese, 2001). Allies work to accept critique with open hearts, and collectively withstand the spiritual pain we experience when we transgress (Reynolds, 2011). The following example speaks to the generous "leaning in" that I experienced in response to my ally-fail with a dear fellow activist.

As part of a Free Tibet rally I gave a speech critiquing the human rights record of the People's Republic of China. After the rally, my longtime activist ally, Sid Chow Tan, approached me, thanked me for my work and my speech, and then let me know that when I was speaking of the human rights violations of the People's Republic of China I only used the words

13

'China' and 'Chinese'. For Sid that meant that he was implicated in these human rights violations because of his ethnicity. I had denigrated every Chinese person, including the Chinese allies who had been present to protest actions of the Chinese government. I felt a wave of shame, as, of course, this had not been my intention. I thanked Sid for this, and let him know that I would be accountable and attend to differentiating the Chinese government from Chinese people in my future activist work. I apologized for the pain I had caused him, and named what I had enacted as racism. (Racism against Chinese people is something I get caught up in, living where I do in Vancouver, where it passes easily in polite white Canadian society). Sid immediately put aside our conversation, as it was time to go back to work.

He said, not unkindly, but pragmatically, "We just need to be able to work together; we need you in this movement. I just wanted you to know."

This event was over a decade ago, and Sid and I continue to work in a less-than-perfect and mutually respectful spirited solidarity. I hold onto this learning as a gift from my fellow activist who has been racialized and minoritized[55]. I welcome this enabling shame (Jenkins, 2005; 2006) as it reminds me of my failure as an ally, and my need to stay critical and to make repair when I transgress. The relationship of solidarity Sid and I have in social justice work across decades allowed my transgression to be seen in context, not as the only story of me as an ally. Sid's willingness to "lean in" towards me, to teach me and not to sever relations with me allowed me to exhale, embrace being imperfect, and invited me to responsibility to act more accountably.

Trusting allies is risky, because, as allies, we can always choose to be accountable for our access to power, or not. As allies we can decide to back

---

[55]   The terms 'minoritized' and 'racialized' are used for the purpose of naming the power and intention required in the racist and colonial project of re-constructing the majority of the world's people as a collection of minorities (Reynolds, 2012d).

down, not notice, be silent, minimize, accommodate, or smooth things over. As allies, we need to hold our actions and words accountable to the person who is the subject of another person's power. The ally works to make space and then gets out of the way. For example, a feminist with white skin privilege talking on behalf of women who are racialized risks further marginalizing the women she seeks to be an ally to. The ally may need to make space and not speak, because allies are not qualified to speak. I do not know colonization outside of an academic understanding and teachings from witnessing people's suffering. For example, I did not suffer colonization and have not paid the price of this knowledge and so I am unqualified to speak about it.

An anti-oppression stance requires awareness of our locations in relation to power, and that we act with accountability for that access to power (Razack, 2002). As allies we make our privilege public as an accountability practice. For example, when I work in the impoverished community of Vancouver's Downtown Eastside, I find ways to be public[56] about the fact that I have never lived on the street or struggled with substance abuse. I do this, because I am sometimes read as someone who has had these experiences, and these misunderstandings invite a trust and sister-feeling from workers and clients that is neither earned nor real. People may feel more affinity and safety with me than my privileges warrant. Later, they may feel that they have been lied to or that some truth has been withheld from them. When we act as allies and make our privilege public, it can serve as a beginning place for trust to grow.

---

[56]   American collaborative therapist Harlene Anderson offers the language and practice of 'being public' in response to her useful critique of the term transparency. Transparency makes a claim that our work is see-through and this is not possible. The onus is on me to make my work public. It is my obligation to show, not the client's obligation to see (2008, p. 18). When we make our work public we invite a richer critique, which invites accountability.

Limitations of Allies: Embracing Imperfection

Ally work is complicated and messy. As allies we can engage in tactics that are direct actions to resist and respond to abuses of power in the moment. We do not often have the luxury of time to step out, call a meeting and discuss strategies and develop perfect responses, as we need to respond in the moment. That is why it is useful not to hold ourselves to a perfect standard of ally acts, but to reflect after such events to critique our actions, strategize how to take on the broader social issues, and make repair, if that is required. For these reasons it is useful to engage with ally work as an imperfection project.

For example, the gender-variant and possibly queer young person on the bus acted immediately to put their body between the Chinese elder woman and the angry white guy. The First Nations guy invited everyone who was willing to participate to converse with him about their "boats" in an effort to complicate the situation, move attention off of the elder Chinese woman, and create some safety for her, while simultaneously responding to the white guy in a collective way that required that he address another man. The collection of folks on the bus did not need instruction on the purposefulness of the First Nation guy's actions, and possibly some folks did not read the invitation, or chose for their own reasons to pretend nothing was going on, but the folks who "leaned in" responded spontaneously and collectively to structure some safety and invite some accountability.

At times it is more useful to survive events, and help people who are experiencing abuses of power get through them than to publicly challenge hate. Would-be allies often share their shaming silences with me; times they did not step up or speak out. Other times potential allies fail because of ignorance, not reading the situation, fear of being wrong, political correctness, the "politics of politeness" past harms, self-interest, indifference, being tired, or being busy. While I invite accountability for times we side with neutrality or fear, I distinguish these times from events in which it is not safe-enough to speak out. In risky situations, allies are often compelled to attend to the person who is abusing power, and this centers the perpetrator, as well as further isolating the victim[57]. I invite allies to centre their responses in relation to the victim. What do they need? How will my actions serve the victim? This may require being silent, not making a scene, and accompanying the victim to safer ground. In the absence of the First Nations guy on the bus, I would not have confronted the angry white guy, but would have stuck close to the Chinese elder women and prioritized her safety. In situations where there is the potential for physical violence, allies need to be aware they could easily make situations worse.

Imperfect Solidarity: Resisting Unity and Division

Solidarity is not synonymous with unity. As community workers, we look for common ground on particular issues, rather than a unified position. While holding a common ground on particular issues and declining unity, workers simultaneously decline invitations for division (Bracho, 2000). Such imperfect solidarity requires discernment between division and difference. The point is not to achieve unity by smoothing the edges of all differences, but to find points of connection in relationships that bring forward an "intimacy that does not annihilate difference" (Palmer, 2003, p. 49).

As community workers, we often experience our work as very individual, which brings with it continual invitations to division. We are separated from each other as workers and organizations competing for scarce resources in the midst of overwhelming need in a political climate of greed and privileged individualism. Invitations to division abound in community work, and we can be seduced into judging other workers, their positions, and

---

[57] The terms 'perpetrator' and 'victim' are used here purposefully to put words to deeds in a particular interaction, as Canadian response-based practitioner Allan Wade would say, and to identify who did what to whom in this event. I am not using perpetrator and victim as identity categories, or to reify any person as a perpetrator or as a victim. Critically engaging with language is required because language can often be used to obscure violence and abuses of power (Coates & Wade, 2007; 2004).

their professions. In contexts of adversity, the point is not to figure out which workers and organizations to blame, but to think of ways to change social contexts. Our greatest resources for doing that are each other. The First Nations guy invited me in as an ally without invisibilizing our important differences; in fact, he used our different locations in relation to colonization to invite me to perform some accountability to both him and to the elder Chinese woman by acknowledging that my people also came to Canada on boats, that I am a settler. This created a point of connection, but did not require us to be in unity. Imperfect solidarity invites workers to be alongside each other, because we need each other, and because it doesn't serve our communities for us to be divided off (Reynolds, 2010c; 2011).

Creating a Culture of Critique

Being allies and working in solidarity does not mean that we are ever hoping to achieve total agreement in collective community work. Creating a culture of critique in which we can challenge each other and hold our practices and theories up to generative and creative scrutiny in order to serve our families and communities better is a useful practice. Being allies to each other in community work invites us to hold each other to account, but we are not acting as allies when judgment and attack are used to silence other workers and discredit them. Discerning critique from attack is part of our work as allies.

Creating a culture of critique begins with "leaning in" and seeing the collective ethics (Reynolds, 2009) we share as our first point of connection; from there we can disagree and critique theory and practice. There are always some collective ethics we share or we would not be meeting together. These collective ethics are the values at the heart of our work, the points of connection that weave us together as workers. They are the basis for the solidarity that brought us together and can hold us together. Our practices of solidarity are emergent from our collective ethics. When collective ethics are hard to trust, I always remind myself that no one is in this movement by accident, and that no one came to community work to hurt people.

Conclusion

Becoming an ally is not a developmental process toward an achievable state or goal, as we are always "becoming" allies (Bishop, 2002), and continually being awoken to our locations of privilege. I did not know I had gender privilege, because I saw the world in the binary of men and women, and only read myself as a potential and actual victim of men's power. And yet all transgender and gender-variant people know that in the domain of gender I hold the privilege of being cisgendered, meaning that my biology, my identity and how I am read are all congruent, all read as woman. They know that I am safer going to a public bathroom, that I will not be questioned by other women, or followed in by security guards. This unfolding awareness has invited me to respond with new ways of being an ally and to unveil more of my privilege.

Ally work is not innocent, as we learn it on the backs of others. We work to stay ever mindful that the potential fall-out or backlash for our actions will fall on the people who are the subjects of power, the victims of perpetrators, not on us. This requires us to stay humble, willing to learn and open to critique. Our acts of being allies are not enough, nor are they the end of our responsibility. Acting as allies does not end oppression; it is a small piece of a larger response that is useful, but, on its own, never enough. Allies do not act out of charity for the betterment of "under-privileged" folks, but in order to enact our own ethics and our desires to live in a society free of hate. Our collective goal is not to be good allies, but to co-create a society in which everyone experiences justice.

Despite the absence of any prior relationships, many folks on that 20 bus immediately recognized and acted upon our pre-existing points of unity in imperfect solidarity. We did not discuss our willingness to perform as allies who embodied some collective ethics. In that moment we knew enough about each other to "lean in," respond immediately, and act collectively and imperfectly.

Dedication

For Sid Chow Tan, for his great-hearted solidarity and creative activism, for staying teachable and being of use across a lifespan, for tenacity and moral courage, and for many teachings given with humility, generosity of spirit and revolutionary love.

Appendix: Two Exercises

An Inquiry into Ally Work: Imperfect & Fluid Allies

Ally Work: Experiences of Needing Allies

Find a person you have a safe-enough experience of to engage with in this exercise.

Consider a particular time when you were experiencing an attack on your dignity, or when you were the subject of another person's power. Choose an experience that is particular and that you remember details of, not a general feeling. Choose something that is real, but that you can contain yourself in sharing — meaning stay present, not necessarily meaning experience without pain.

Thinking back on this experience in the relative safety of this conversation, offer your witness a thumbnail sketch of this event, with your experience of oppression at the centre:

- Did you have any allies in this experience?
- What actions did allies take, individually or collectively, that were supportive?
- What difference did these ally actions make?
- How did you communicate to allies what you needed? Appreciated?

- Was there anything that your ally did that you would have liked your allies not to have done? (replicate power-over, be righteous or shaming, take centre-stage, or take actions that make the situation worse)

- Thinking back on this experience in the relative safety of this conversation, what ally actions would you have appreciated that didn't happen?

- What did allies or would-be allies do or say that invited your trust or got in the way of your trusting? What past experiences promoted or harmed your trust of would-be allies?

- Was there any way you could have welcomed in some/more allies?

- What have these allies taught you about being an ally?

Ally Work: Acting as an Ally

- Consider a particular experience when you were an ally to another person who was experiencing or an attack on their dignity or oppression, while you were in a location of power and/or privilege:

- What was required of you in terms of being an ally in this context?

- How did you get your experiences of oppression out of the centre in order to be an ally?

- How did you get your own access to power and/or privilege out of the centre in order to be an ally?

- What actions did you take as an ally?

- What differences might your ally actions make for the people involved? Perpetrator, victim, ally, others present?

- What response did you get from the person you were trying to be an ally to about your actions or intentions? How could you invite responses about if or how you were being an accountable ally in this situation?

- How did you stay open to hearing if you were not acting in line with your ethics and intentions for being an ally?

- Thinking back on this experience from the relative safety and community of this conversation, what different actions might you have taken? (If you had more access to power/less access to power?)
- How can you plan to respond with the discomfort and possible pain that may come from being in an ally position?
- What differences has being an ally made in your life? Community work?

Stepping Up: Reflecting on our Fluid Positions as Imperfect Allies

- What people or communities have I made myself available to as an ally? What multiple ally positions do I hold?
- What qualifies me as an ally? What ways of being and qualities do I hold that are useful to me in being an ally?
- Who am I comfortable/experienced being an ally to?
- What trainings/knowings from my life have taught me how to be an ally in this context?
- What ally positions have I not taken? Why?
- What trainings experiences in my life have made me less capable/able to be an ally in this context?
- What qualities and ways of being about me get in the way of me being an ally?
- What barriers get in the way of me acting as an ally in these other contexts? (for example: ignorance, not reading the situation, fear of being wrong, political correctness, the "politics of politeness", past harms, self-interest, indifference, being tired, being busy...)
- What will it take for me/us/our staff team/this organization to act as an ally in less comfortable/less familiar contexts?
- What would it look like?

The Big Questions (To Hold Reflexively, Not Solve, but Always respond to...)

- How would you describe the anti-oppression stance you hold for your work?
- What understandings of the intersections of your access to power and being subjected to another person's power do you hold?
- How do you/can you center your work in decolonizing practices while holding this anti-oppression stance?

References

Anderson, H. (2008, September). *Collaborative practices in organization, therapy, education and research contexts.* Paper presented at the Social Construction Relational Theory and Transformative Practices Conference, Sarasota, FL.

Bishop, A. (2002). *Becoming an ally: Breaking the cycle of oppression in people* (2nd Ed.). Halifax, Nova Scotia, Canada: Fernwood Publishing.

Bracho, A. (2000). An institute of community participation. *Dulwich Centre Journal, 2000* (3).

Butler, J. (1990). *Gender trouble: Feminism and the subversion of identity.* New York, NY: Routledge.

Butler, J. (1997). *Excitable speech: A politics of the performative.* New York, NY: Routledge.

Coates, L., & Wade, A. (2004). Telling it like it isn't: Obscuring perpetrator responsibility for violence. *Discourse and Society, 15,* 499-526.

Coates, L., & Wade, A. (2007). Language and violence: Analysis of four discursive operations. *Journal of Family Violence, 22,* 511-522.

Coates, L. & Wade, A. (2009). "For this we are sorry:" A brief review of Canada's most recent non-apology to Aboriginal peoples. In *Under the volcano festival of art and social change program.* Vancouver, Canada: Under The Volcano.

Crenshaw, K. (1995). Mapping the margins: Intersectionality, identity politics, and violence against women of colour. In K. Crenshaw, G. Gotanda, G. Peller, & K. Thomas (Eds.), *Critical race theory: The key writings that formed the movement* (pp. 357-383). New York, NY: The New Press.

Day, R. (2005). *Gramsci is dead: Anarchist currents in the newest social movements*. London, UK: Pluto Press.

Deleuze, G. (1995). *Negotiations*. New York, NY: Columbia University Press.

Fassinger, R., & Arsenau, J. (2007). "I'd rather get wet than be under the umbrella:" Differentiating the experiences and identities of lesbian, gay, bisexual, and transgendered people. In K. Bieschke, R. Perez, & K. Debord (Eds.), *Handbook of counselling and psychology with lesbian, gay, bisexual and transgendered clients* (2nd Ed., pp. 19-50). Washington, DC: American Psychological Association.

Jagose, A. (1996). *Queer theory: An introduction*. Melbourne, Australia: Melbourne University Press.

Jenkins, A. (2005). Knocking on shame's door: Facing shame without shaming disadvantaged young people who have abused. In M. Calder (Ed.), *Children and young people who sexually abuse: New theory, research and practice developments*. London, UK: Russell House.

Jenkins, A. (2006). Shame, realisation and restitution: The ethics of restorative practice. *Australia and New Zealand Journal of Family Therapy, 27*(3), 153-162.

Kvale, S. (1996). *Inter-views: An introduction to qualitative research interviewing*. London, UK: Sage Publications.

Lacey, A. (2005). Spaces of justice: The social divine of global anti-capital activists' sites of resistance. *CRSA/RCSA, 42*(4), 407.

Lawrence, B., & Dua, E. (2005). Decolonizing antiracism. *Social Justice, 32*, (4), 120-143.

McNamee, S. & Gergen, K. (1999). *Relational responsibility: Resources for sustainable dialogue*. London, UK: Sage Publications.

Namaste, V. (2000). *Invisible lives: The erasure of trans-sexual and transgendered people*. Chicago, IL: University of Chicago Press.

Nataf, Z. (1996). *Lesbians talk transgender*. London, UK: Scarlet Press.

Queen, C., & Schimel, L. (1997). *Pomosexuals: Challenging assumptions about gender and sexuality*. San Francisco, CA: Cleis Press.

Razack, N. (2002). *Transforming the field: Critical antiracist and anti-oppressive perspectives for the human service practicum*. Halifax, Canada: Fernwood Publishing.

Reynolds, V. (2009). Collective ethics as a path to resisting burnout. *Insights: The Clinical Counsellor's Magazine & News*. December, 6-7.

Reynolds, V. (2010a). A supervision of solidarity. *Canadian Journal of Counselling, 44*(3), 246-257.

Reynolds, V. (2010b). Doing justice: A witnessing stance in therapeutic work alongside survivors of torture and political violence. In J. Raskin, S. Bridges, & R. Neimeyer (Eds.), *Studies in meaning 4: Constructivist perspectives on theory, practice, and social justice*. New York, NY: Pace University Press.

Reynolds, V. (2010c). Fluid and imperfect ally positioning: Some gifts of queer theory. *Context,* (October)*,* 13-17.

Reynolds, V. (2010d). *Doing justice as a path to sustainability in community work.* Retrieved from http://www.taosinstitute.net/

Reynolds,V. (2011). Resisting burnout with justice-doing. *The International Journal of Narrative Therapy and Community Work, 2011*(4), 27-45.

Reynolds, V. (2012). A story from the 20 bus. *WAVAW (Women Against Violence Against Women) Newsletter 2012*(1), 3-4.

Richardson, C., & Reynolds, V. (2012). "Here we are amazingly alive:" Holding ourselves together with an ethic of social justice in community work. *International Journal of Child, Youth and Family Studies, 1*, 1-19.

Robinson, T. (2005). *The convergence of race, ethnicity, and gender: Multiple identities in counseling* (2nd Ed.). Boston, MA: Pearson Education.

Scott, J. (1985). *Weapons of the week: Everyday forms of peasant resistance.* New Haven, CT: Yale University Press.

Scott, J. (1990). *Domination and the arts of resistance.* New Haven, CT: Yale University Press.

Spade, D. (2011). *Normal life: Administrative violence, critical trans politics, and the limits of law.* Brooklyn, NY: South End Press.

Tamasese, K. (2001). Talking about culture and gender. In C. White (Ed.), *Working with the stories of women's lives* (pp. 15-22). Adelaide, Australia: Dulwich Centre Publications.

Tuhiwai Smith, L. (1999). *Decolonizing methodologies: Research and indigenous peoples.* London: Zed Books.

Wade, A. (1996). Resistance knowledges: Therapy with aboriginal persons who have experienced violence. In P.H. Stephenson, S.J. Elliott, L.T. Foster, & J. Harris (Eds.), *A persistent spirit: Towards understanding aboriginal health in British Columbia.* (Canadian Western Geographical Series, 31), (pp. 167-206). Vancouver, B.C.: University of British Columbia Press.

Wade, A. (1997). Small acts of living: Everyday resistance to violence and other forms of oppression. *Journal of Contemporary Family Therapy, 19*(I), 23-40.

Walia, H. (2012). Decolonizing together: Moving beyond a politics of solidarity toward a practice of decolonization. Retrieved from http://briarpatchmagazine.com

White, E. (1991). Between suspicion and hope: Paul Ricoeur's vital hermeneutic. *Journal of Literature and Theology*, 5, 311-321.

TWO

Fluid and Imperfect Ally Positioning: Some Gifts of Queer Theory

You can hear a pin drop in the conference room where we are engaged in a queer, transgender and two-spirit workshop for community workers. A participant has just stolen our breath saying, "We've heard a lot about heterosexism, trans-phobia, and homophobia. When are we going to talk about heterophobia and the way that they hate us?" Although this is a common-enough experience, and the comment is not unexpected, our transgender presenter is visibly shaken. He gestures towards our gay presenter who looks pissed off. He turns towards me, stares me straight in the eye, inviting me to say what either of them could have said.

Following their lead, as an ally, I respond. "We're actually not going to talk about the way that you and I are oppressed as straight people. That's like talking about men being raped by women in a workshop addressing men's violence. It's uncomfortable looking at our power and privilege and the ways we participate in the oppression of queer, transgender and two-spirit people. I'm open to talk with you later, as this is our work as heterosexual people to do together. For now we're going to return to the agenda everyone has agreed on, understanding the different and often hidden ways that people who are queer, transgender and two-spirit are oppressed."

The presenters exhale, the room of people visibly relaxes. Despite the firm clarity of my voice, I am awash with shame. I have a sick-in-the-belly response to being listened to as an ally because of my heterosexual, white, cisgendered privilege. At the same time, people who are transgender, queer and racialised, who taught me what I know about this, are silenced.

In activist cultures, an ally is a person who belongs to a group which has particular privileges, and who works alongside people from groups that are oppressed in relation to that privilege. The hope is to create change and increase social justice in relation to this oppression. I will describe my understandings of ally work alongside queer, two-spirit and transgender communities, and particularly the gifts of queer theory in terms of attending to the fluidity of ally positions. I will outline the analysis of power that invites collective accountability for allies and the possibilities and hope that being imperfect allies offers. Finally, I will describe some of the limitations of ally work, and practices for holding onto hope when we fail to be in line with our commitments to being allies, and our responsibilities to each other to stay alive in our collective ally work.

Queer theory has brought many gifts to ally work, especially the idea that being an ally is a performance, something we do together across the differences of privilege that divide us. Queer theory frees us from taking on being an ally as a static identity, which could require being perfect and always getting it right. Queer theory invites fluidity, movement from the fixed and certain to the confused and unstable. This is exciting for ally work because it acknowledges that we can all be allies to each other in a constant flow depending on our contexts and relationships of power.

I am often situated as an ally in my work alongside queer, transgender and two-spirit people because I am heterosexual and hold cisgendered privilege. At other times, in response to class privilege or the privilege of growing up with money or gender privilege, or holding more power in the organisations we work in, queer, transgender and two-spirit persons may need to serve as allies to me. Categories are useful at times, but problematic, as I am never just a heterosexual person. I am always a white, Canadian-born, able-bodied, Irish Catholic, working class woman, indivisible from the intersecting domains of privilege and oppression that I carry. Ally positioning must always attend to this fluid intersectionality within the same moments within the same conversations.

Activism has informed me to of look for 'groundless solidarity', meaning that our ethics are not always tied to one location of oppression. No location is seen as the organising principle of all oppression in all situations; rather, the intersections and the gaps between our multiple locations in relation to privilege and oppression are tended to in a complex analysis. Sometimes we need to address sexism, sometimes it is more important to attend to racism, and in another interaction money privilege requires our attention. Of course, we can and must attend to more than one domain of power at a time. 'Infinite responsibility' invites us to always attempt to be 'open to another other', to the multiplicity of ways that I might not be in accord in relation to my ethics; ways that I am not acting as an ally.

When serving in the role of ally it is important that I locate myself in my privilege. I have been respectfully referred to as a "queer-passing straight girl" by members of queer and transgender communities. Early on, I find ways to publicly position myself in these privileged aspects of my identity. I do this by making reference to my male partner. It is important that I do not pass for a member of queer and transgender communities, as people may experience more affinity and safety than my privileges warrant. Later, people may feel that they have been lied to or that some truth has been withheld.

The role of the ally is to address power, and try to contribute to the making of a space in which the person who is oppressed gets to have their voice heard and listened to. It is not just a matter of being heard; a person's words must matter and not be dismissed. Paulo Freire names this authentic dialogue, which he describes as an act of revolutionary love. If we are replicating oppression we are not in dialogue with each other. Lacey eloquently calls these spaces of justice, which allies contribute to, "the social divine".

Responding to backlash

In the presence of backlash, creating room for people to speak authentically becomes problematic. As with all anti-oppression work, we anticipate the backlash, which is the cost of speaking truth to power. Backlash refers to responses that support and reinforce the positions of power being questioned. Backlash takes the focus off of the oppression. Anticipating and planning a useful response to backlash, which may or may not show up, is important in terms of having a safe-enough structure and some confidence that paralysis, anger or fear will not silence our responses. Negotiations of who will respond to backlash need to be accountable to the people who are oppressed by it.

Often, a good person to reply to backlash is an ally, as they are most likely to be heard and least likely to be personally oppressed in the moment. Deciding to give voice to allies in addressing backlash is a strategic decision that aims to create more change, but it comes at a cost. A shaming memory I hold close is being listened to as an ally of privilege when marginalised people were silenced.

In instances where I have responded to backlash as an ally, I work to differentiate the person from what is spoken. The person who has brought the backlash position forward is a member of the same group as I am. Here I want to move in solidarity towards this person, and not shame them, while being clear about naming and resisting oppression.

Collective accountability

We live in a world where many of us, whether we intend to or not, benefit from the oppression of others. Activism teaches us to analyse structures of oppression. Collective accountability requires that we take actions together to change these underlying structures that create the conditions for abuses of power. Feeling personal guilt about that is not the same as accountability.

As a heterosexual person, I hope to respond to another heterosexual person who is performing homophobia by seeing them as my brother, by locating myself as collectively responsible for the performance of homophobia, and for the fact that it benefits me. In relation to my privilege, I don't have to perform homophobia or racism or transphobia in order for my status to be elevated on the backs of others. This means that I have to be accountable for more than just my personal actions. The seduction of identifying individually at these times is extreme – I want to identify myself as, "not that kind of straight person". As an ally I identify collectively as a heterosexual person in the presence of homophobia, and act to help my straight brother move towards accountability as well. Collective accountability invites us to see another other as a part of us, belonging with us, and declines the invitation of locating ourselves as not that other. Collectively addressing any form of oppression is not a heroic act, but a performance of our collective, ordinary respect and dignity.

Individual accountability is a limiting idea, as it constructs the responsibility for social contexts of injustice on the backs of individual allies, and doesn't require us to be responsible for more than our own actions. Injustice requires enormous, collaborative, and resourced social responses from all members of society, reflecting our relational responsibilities. Collective accountability promotes our sustainability by contesting the individuation of responsibility, and offers hope for finding ways forward together.

The true privilege of being an ally is the fact that we get to choose those moments when we are going to be an ally. When you are the queer, two-spirit or transgender person experiencing oppression you don't get to choose to not be in those locations. An ally position is a voluntary thing I can sign up for and I always have the privilege of walking away. This makes it risky to trust allies.

Kiwi Tamasese, a Samoan leader with the Just Therapy Centre in New Zealand, profoundly influenced my stance for being an ally alongside racialised, minoritised and colonised women. Kiwi needs to know how long allies are going to be in the struggle and the nature of their commitment. She wants to know if I am a tourist, putting my toe in the water to see if I am going to jump in, or if I am in for the long haul. This is important, because an ally position is not static or fixed. As a straight white woman of privilege from the global north, I can choose to act as an ally alongside marginalised women and then choose to leave the struggle. Accountability requires that I make public the particularities of my commitment. When there is trust that I am a committed ally over the long haul, my unavoidable (yet not innocent) mistakes can be held alongside my acts of solidarity. Kiwi might say, "Vikki has been with me before, she is going to be with me and with my communities into the future. It is worth teaching her about this. Her intentions were probably not to replicate this oppression with me". Committed relationships that are made public and open to invitations to accountability contribute to ally partnerships across differences.

A hopeful scepticism

I invite a healthy and hopeful suspicion about whether or not I am acting as an ally in any moment-to-moment interaction. This is informed by Kvale's hermeneutics of suspicion, where we look to our practice to see if we are enacting our ethics. Activists ask, "Am I walking the talk?". Holding an anti-oppression framework is fabulous, but theorising is limited, and despite the promises of critical theory we have not delivered on a just society. What matters is that we enact our ethics. I make claims to being an ally and to acting accountably for my access to privilege, but whether or not I actually perform as an ally is best judged by the person I am trying to be an ally to. If a queer person says, "You helped make space for my voice to be heard, then you got out of the way, and I experienced that as accountable" then I know that I am in line with my ethics and hope for being an ally in that moment.

Any information a person from an oppressed position gives me in any interaction about my abuses of power or the way that I haven't been an ally are a gift to me. I want to accept this critique with an open heart. I need to be able to withstand the spiritual pain I experience when I transgress against my ethics for being an ally. I don't try to smooth these transgressions over, but hold them close to remind myself to be with care and accountability.

Becoming an ally is not a developmental process. I am always becoming an ally. I am continually being woken up to my locations of privilege. I didn't know I had gender privilege because I saw the world in the binary of men and women, and only read myself as a potential and actual victim of men's power. And yet all transgender people know that in the domain of gender

I hold the privilege of being cisgendered. They know that I am safe going to a public bathroom, that I won't be questioned by other women, or followed in by security guards, that I won't be at risk for being seen as a person who has trespassed.

This unfolding awareness has required me to respond with new ways of being an ally. I am required to unveil more of my privilege and acknowledge that as a person who holds cisgendered privilege I never have to risk coming out to my family or my loved ones. I don't need to tell them, "I am not a woman, I'm a man". Butler speaks about the limits of acceptable speech, meaning the parameters of what can be said before there are repercussions for transgressing across lines backed up by power. With this speaking I would risk potentially losing my relationships of belonging in the world.

Imperfect allies

In trainings or supervision, people sometimes reflect that what I am proposing in terms of infinite responsibility and groundless solidarity sounds exhausting. Becoming an ally can certainly be painful, uncomfortable and confusing. I try to remember that ally relationships are always more risky for the oppressed person. When we experience oppression we accept allies because we need them, not because it's safe or we have good reasons to trust each other. We invite good-enough allies despite past acts that were not trustworthy, as imperfect allies are required when the stakes are high and risk is near. This fluidity makes more room for imperfect allies, momentary allies, and moment-to-moment alliances, which are flawed and not safe, yet required and of use. Challenging the binary of ally/oppressor, these imperfect alliances bring some trust for some solidarity and for more accountable ally relationships to begin to grow.

If I am not in an ally position I am going to risk replicating oppression. I was trained up in a racist and homophobic society. If I don't take an overt, intentional, active position against racism and against homophobia I will replicate them. The hard work of trying to be an ally, trying to "do the right thing" as Spike Lee would say, is worth the effort. The risk of transgressing and enacting racism, homophobia, and other oppressions is ever near. I hold close a useful humility that when I have replicated oppression and abused power marginalised people have needed allies against me.

Limitations of allies

The limitations of allies are enormous and important to hold alongside our willingness to act. As allies, we're not the ones who shoulder the burden. Allies need to stay ever mindful that the potential fall out or backlash for our actions as allies will fall on the oppressed people, not us. This invites a caution to take actions when asked.

Allies who are harmed in this difficult work can begin to identify as the oppressed, which is both seductive and disastrous. Some heterosexual people who hold cisgendered privilege respond to the discomfort of having homophobia and transphobia discussed by claiming that they are being oppressed or attacked for even having to hear these oppressions named. Dealing with this pain and hurt is the work of the ally, to move in and not leave this situation to queer, two-spirit and transgender people. This is difficult and often unsafe work. However, the hardships of the positions of the ally aren't the same as the consequences and real harms to queer, two-spirit and transgender people experiencing this backlash. I hold close this unsettling and discomforting knowing.

Allies are often accused of being too political by people holding privileges they do not want to be responsible for or accountable to. I am often identified as political, a political therapist, or a political activist. Of course, all helping professionals are political, dealing in relationships of power. All positions are political, and neutrality often goes uncontested while being a profoundly political position.

Potential allies often share their shaming silences with me: times they did not step up or speak out. While I invite accountability for times we side with neutrality or fear, I discern these times from events in which it is not safe enough to speak out. Being an ally requires strategising, and at times it is more useful to survive events, and help oppressed people get through than to publicly challenge hate. For example, challenging a drunk and angry man on a bus shouting homophobic words may not be the most useful act of the ally. Accompanying the persons attacked, and inviting solidarity from other riders may be a more prudent response. Often members of oppressed groups speak of these moments in which they remained silent as evidence of internalised homophobia. I invite a wider reading of power. Defending against attack is not siding with hate, and the responsibility again is more easily and safely taken up by allies in these events.

Allies risk siding with oppression and disrespect when fear of being homophobic, transphobic or racist silences them from inviting queer, two-spirit and transgender people to accountability. I have invited transgender men, gay men and two-spirit men to account for negative judgments of women. This is always hard to do and requires skill and moral courage, but more importantly being in relationships. As allies alongside each other we need to resist oppression on all fronts, even when we are performing it.

As allies, we learn on the backs of others: there is no innocent position. I acknowledge I will never "get it" – never know fully despite queer, transgender and two-spirit people's many efforts to educate me on the realities of their lives. I work to stay humble, willing to learn and open to critique.

Conclusion

While I have attempted to offer an understanding of my ethical stance for being an ally it is important for me to acknowledge that this positioning is still and will always be in motion. Naming the fluidity of this position and its incompleteness means more than just being open to critique. My ethical stance cannot be complete because of my limited knowledge and the ever-changing contexts of social justice that inform it. I think of this ethical stance for being an ally as an 'imperfection project'.

I work hard at being an ally, and cannot do my work without this orientation, but I simultaneously work towards a just society. I don't equate our acts of being allies as enough or as the end of our responsibilities. Acting as an ally doesn't end oppression; it's a small piece of a larger response that's required, important, but never enough. Our collective goal is not to be good allies, but to help everyone experience justice, co-creating a society in which allies would not be required. This is ambitious and possibly unlikely but, as Freire says, unapologetically, our project really is to liberate the world!

Despite our failures and our pain as imperfect allies to each other, we continue to lend our privilege to the social project of doing justice, because everyone will benefit from a more socially just world. We take on the hard work of making repair when we transgress as allies because, as Leonard Peltier says, "We are not supposed to be perfect. We're supposed to be useful".

My straight partner and I are out of town visiting our family of choice. We have stayed connected across borders, and decades, connected by familial love, art, and justice-doing. When I met Jake, he was a self-identified "bull dyke". I stood up as Jake's family when she married the love of her life, a lesbian woman named Carmen. A decade later, Jake has transitioned to his preferred identity as a man. During our present visit, there is much excitement as the happy couple tells us that they have decided to become parents. My heart expands, I'm thrilled for them, and say, "Which one of you is going to have the baby?"

There is a profound silence that Jake speaks into saying, "Well, Vikki, I'm a man. So I won't be having a baby". Transgender men can and do have babies, but Jake does not identify as transgender, and that makes my response different and oppressive. This is bigger than the times I didn't get Jake's new name right, or used the wrong gender pronouns. Despite being one of Jake's firmest allies across time, heterosexual normativity has captured me, and I'm the voice of power, obliterating Jake's autonomy in naming and creating his own gender identity.

Jake saves us all by accepting my apology and commitment to accountability. He hugs me close, saying he needs me and my partner "to be there for our kids when other folks like you pull this stuff in the future".

Thanks to the many people, named and unnamed (due to access to power), who informed this writing, especially Heather Charlton, Nikki Gravelle, Lorraine Greives, Devon MacFarlane, Aaron Munroe, Ema Oropeza, Evin Taylor, Al Zwiers, and all the folks I "supervise" at Prism. And AIDS activists from San Francisco days with Act Up and Queer Nation who dared, broke down doors, and then were disappeared.

This article is dedicated to the memory and lifework of Catherine White Holman, whose ally work alongside transgender communities holds people on this planet.

Exercise: Reflecting on our fluid positions as imperfect allies

- What multiple ally positions do I hold?
- What multiple ally positions have I not taken? Why?

Consider a particular ally position, for example, being an ally to transgender people, to two-spirit people, to queer people:

- What is required of me in terms of being an ally in this context?
- How will I get my locations of oppression out of the centre in order to be an ally?
- What expectations of me and other allies are held by transgender, two-spirit and queer people?
- What practices of accountability will I enact? How can I engage with accountability instead of guilt?
- How can I plan to deal with the discomfort and possible pain that comes from being in this ally position?
- How will I know when I am being an accountable ally?
- How will I be open to knowing when I am not being in line with my

ethics and intentions of being an ally?

- What differences has being an ally made in my life? My work?

Consider the fluid ways you have experienced the solidarity of having allies, and the differences having allies has made in your life:

- Who have been my allies in spaces where I am oppressed or subject to structural power?
- What differences have allies made in my life?
- How have I let allies know what I expect?
- What I appreciate? What is not useful?

References

Bishop, A. (1994) Becoming an Ally: Breaking the Cycle of Oppression. Halifax, Nova Scotia, Canada: Fernwood Publishing.

Bornstein, K. (1994) Gender Outlaw: On Men, Women and the Rest of Us. New York: Routledge.

Butler, J. (1990) Gender Trouble: Feminism and the Subversion of Identity. New York: Routledge.

Butler, J. (1997) ExcitableSpeech: A Politics of the Performative. New York: Routledge.

Crenshaw, K. (1995) Mapping the margins: Intersectionality, identity politics, and violence against women of colour. In K. Crenshaw, G. Gotanda, G. Peller & K. Thomas (Eds), Critical Race Theory: The Key Writings that Formed the Movement, 357-383. New York: The New Press.

Day, R. (2005) Gramsci is Dead: Anarchist Currents in the Newest Social Movements. London: Pluto Press.

Fassinger, R., & Arsenau, J. (2007) I'd rather get wet than be under the umbrella: Differentiating the experiences and identities of lesbian, gay, bisexual, and transgender people. In K. Bieschke, R. Perez, & K. Debord (Eds), Handbook of Counseling and Psychology with Lesbian, Gay, Bisexual and Transgender Clients (2nd Ed.), 19- 50. Washington, DC: American Psychological Association.

Freire, P. (1978) Pedagogy in Process: The Letters to Guinea Bissau. New York: Seabury Press.

Freire, P. (2001) Pedagogy of Freedom: Ethics, Democracy and Civic Courage. Lanham, MD: Rowman and Littlefield.

Jagose, A. (1996) Queer Theory: An Introduction. Melbourne, Australia: Melbourne University Press.

Kvale, S. (1996) Inter-views: An Introduction to Qualitative Research Interviewing. London: Sage Publications.

Lacey, A. (2005) Spaces of justice: The social divine of global anti-capital activists' sites of resistance. CRSA/RCSA, 42 (4), 407.

Lee, S. (Producer/Writer/Director) (1989) Do the Right Thing [Motion Picture]. United States: 40 Acres & A Mule Filmworks.

McNamee, S. & Gergen, K. (1999) Relational Responsibility: Resources for Sustainable Dialogue. London: Sage Publications.

Nataf, Z. (1996) Lesbians Talk Transgender. London: Scarlet Press.

Peltier, L. (1999) Prison Writings: My Life is My Sundance. New York: St. Martins Griffin.

Queen, C. & Schimel, L. (1997) Pomosexuals: Challenging Assumptions about Gender and Sexuality. San Francisco, CA: Cleis Press.

Reynolds, V. (2009) Collective ethics as a path to resisting burnout. Insights: The Clinical Counsellor's Magazine & News, December, 6-7.

Reynolds, V. (2010) Doing justice: A witnessing stance in therapeutic work alongside survivors of torture and political violence. In J. Raskin, S. Bridges, & R. Neimeyer (Eds), Studies in Meaning 4: Constuctivist Perspectives on Theory, Practice, and Social Justice. New York: Pace University Press.

Robinson, T. (2005) The Convergence of Race, Ethnicity and Gender: Multiple Identities in Counseling (2nd Ed). Boston, MA: Pearson Education.

Tamasese, K. (2001) Talking about culture and gender. In C. White (Ed), Working with the Stories of Women's Lives, 15-22. Adelaide, Australia: Dulwich Centre Publications.

Tuhiwai Smith, L. (1999) Decolonizing Methodologies: Research and Indigenous Peoples. London: Zed Books Ltd.

Wade, A. (1996) Resistance knowledges: Therapy with aboriginal persons who have experienced violence. In P.H. Stephenson, S.J. Elliott, L.T. Fos-ter, & J. Harris (Eds), A Persistent Spirit: Towards Understanding Aboriginal Health in British Columbia. Canadian Western Geographical Series, 31, 167-206.

Wade, A. (1997) Small acts of living: Everyday resistance to violence and other forms of oppression. Journal of Contemporary Family Therapy, 19(l), 23-40.

White, E. (1991) Between suspicion and hope: Paul Ricoeur's vital hermeneutic. Journal of Literature and Theology, 5, 311-321.

THREE

Beyond Trans Tolerance and Trans Inclusion

Contributing to Transformative Spaces in an all-genders youth, live-in, substance misuse program

Vikki Reynolds in dialogue with James Kelly

James Kelly has been working in the social services sector in Vancouver for close to two decades, in both front line and management capacities. Currently, he is the Executive Director at Peak House, a provincial, alcohol and drug, live in program for youth. James, a white settler, is Trans identified, lives in East Van, and is passionate about social justice, and providing anti oppressive and inclusive services in his community. He has worked with several organizations and individuals providing consultation, workshops, mentorship and leadership training.

After over a decade of front line experience working primarily with street involved, exploited and vulnerable youth in Vancouver, James took his passion for social justice, and commitment to providing anti oppressive and inclusive services for young people into his leadership work with community.

For the past nine years James has been the Executive Director of Peak House, a provincial alcohol and drug treatment centre for youth. The former longstanding Co-Chair of the Catherine While Holman Wellness Centre, a volunteer run health clinic for Trans and non-conforming people and an active advocate and community educator working toward reducing barriers for youth, those struggling with poverty and enhancing accessibility and inclusion for Trans and those living outside of the gender binary.

James identifies as a Trans man. As a white Trans person in a leadership role, James understands the importance of his privilege and works to use his opportunity to give back to his community. The acknowledgement of privilege, personal experience and the wisdom shared by the youth and families he has worked with over the years has helped shape his lens on service delivery, giving back and the power of staying true to his leadership values and vision.

Vikki Reynolds PhD RCC is an activist/therapist who works to bridge the worlds of social justice activism with community work & therapy. In all of her paid and unpaid work Vikki's intention is to be un-settled as a settler, and work to decolonize herself, her communities and families; to work in ways that do not replicate oppression and abuses of power, and to actually *do justice* in action and participate in transformative and liberatory practice (Reynolds & polanco, 2012). Vikki is a white settler of Irish, Newfoundland and English folks, and a heterosexual woman with cisgender privilege. Her experience includes supervision and therapy with refugees and survivors of torture, sexualized violence counsellors, mental health and substance misuse counsellors, housing and shelter workers, activists and working alongside gender and sexually diverse communities.

Vikki is an Adjunct Professor and teaches with VCC, UBC, Adler University and with City University of Seattle, Vancouver. She has written and presented internationally on the subjects of resistance to 'trauma', ally work, justice-doing, a supervision of solidarity, ethics, and innovative group work. Vikki's book *Doing Justice as a Path to Sustainability in Community Work*, is available free on her website along with articles and addresses (www.vikkireynolds.ca).

Vikki is the Therapeutic Supervisor at Peak House, where she served as a Family Therapist for ten years, and has been the Supervisor for the past fourteen years.

VIKKI: When I got the invitation from the good people at Context to write something about work with gender diverse youth, I was very humbled and honoured to be invited in to act as an ally (Reynolds, 2013) with cis-privilege. I'm involved in a lot of exciting work in Trans communities. I've been involved in a transgender free clinic here in Vancouver. I was the volunteer Clinical Supervisor for six years, and you were a founding board members for five years. I also work with Trans Care BC. I'm helping supervise folks who are doing educational work to transform the way health authorities serve gender diverse communities throughout the province. I also work with Aaron Munro, a Trans man and a Director at RainCity, on a Queer/Trans youth project for housing. My role is trying to articulate our collective ethics (Reynolds, 2009) for this work and how we can honour youth wisdom and resist the temptation to try to tell Trans youth how to live (Munro, Reynolds & Townsend, 2017).

But when Context invited me to talk about transformational work I immediately thought of Peak House and your role as Executive Director there. Peak House is such a small, important gem of a program that's really been transformative in so many young people's lives. We did so much work with First Nations and Indigenous communities, and with Queer communities to be educated by them and to be useful, safe-r (Bird, 2004) and worthy of trust. But I think the most exciting thing for me in the last decade has been Peak House trying to transform itself to be more open and useful to youth who are gender diverse. Something is happening there that's really inspiring. And when I was thinking about things that made a difference, I thought of you and your leadership as the Executive Director, and your own path—specifically, your own identity and transitioning as part of it in your role as Executive Director. Also the things you have transformed structurally, taking on a whole organization. Structurally some things have really exploded. I train around the province and everywhere I go, especially isolated communities, people really are desperate to get youth that are gender diverse or gender questioning into Peak House. It's not so much about their substance misuse- problems. It's about where to refer youth that is safe-enough and where they're going to be honoured.

JAMES: It's honouring you would think that. One thing that I want to preface our conversation with ahead of time is that this work is not new work. It's a continuation of work that's been happening long before I came to Peak House. You're talking about community reputation, and I think Peak House has a reputation for many years of being innovative and being on the forefront of meeting the needs of young people and their families, or trying to better meet the needs. Some of the work that I feel like I've been able to step into has been as a result of work that started long before me. Lorraine Grieves—who is now at Trans Care BC—did a ton of work that helped pave the road, when she served as Co-Director with Wendy Wittmack. That innovative risk-taking and resistance that happened before perfectly positioned me to take on some of the things that we're doing as a collective now.

VIKKI: In particular, what do you think are some of the historical pieces that were put in place there that helped to make more space for you to bring a fuller experience of your gender identity and this transformational work?

JAMES: The first thing that comes to mind is Wendy, and I will speak about this because Wendy has spoken about this publicly. About 20 years ago Wendy came out as a lesbian when it was very risky to do that in live-in or 'residential' care.

VIKKI: She had worked at Peak House and was in the closet for over five years there. It was super painful. She was not even safe-enough to be out with all of the staff. And of course we're not imposing the need to come out on marginalized workers, that's a pretty white and moneyed imperative (Hammoud-Beckett 2007a; 2007b), but Wendy wanted to be able to be safe-enough to be out at work.

JAMES: Yeah. Which, today telling that story seems inconceivable and like, "Why not?" But at the time, it was a huge risk, especially as she was also a sole-parent and didn't have access to structural power in the organization as she worked as a Youth Counsellor.

VIKKI: Wendy had been at Peak House for five years when I was hired as a Therapist. And she had been not out with the youth or most of the staff in the program. At that time, we used the language of it being a residential program. Meaning, a live-in program. We don't use that language now because of the legacy of residential schools in Canada. But it was a live-in program, and it was very risky to be Queer, or Gay, or Lesbian and work in a house where children slept and had bedrooms, right? So, Wendy did all the hard work that was required to come out at Peak House and absolutely transformed the place. And then, of course, we started to be—on her back, I think, as a lesbian single mom—we started to make more room for Queer and questioning youth to see Peak House as a place where we might be safe-r, there might be enough-space for them. And that became our reputation.

JAMES: Absolutely. And it's still our reputation based on some of the work that Wendy did so many years ago—and that was also supported by other people, like yourself. You were a solid ally to Wendy to make space for that. One person can't make that kind of change. From an organizational perspective, other people need to get onboard with that. But I think if you were to ask around today, people would still say Peak House is the place where you can send your Queer youth, it's safe. Or safe-r. And now we're just continuing that with gender diversity.

VIKKI: When I think about Wendy coming out—I know that my acting as her ally was important. And we published an article about that, *Weaving Threads of Belonging* (Reynolds, 2002), about Cultural Witnessing Groups. But when Wendy came out, although it took a lot of people acting as allies to do it, the vulnerability and risk was on her shoulders. Some things move forward on the back of vulnerable folks, right?

JAMES: Absolutely.

VIKKI: And, of course, youth changed the programs dramatically, so we don't want to underplay the role of youth and what they brought. I want to acknowledge it's a group that foments change, but we also have to realize that while lots of people are in play, in terms of making structural change, the risks are not equal.

JAMES: And it could have gone either way for Wendy—it could have gone very badly for her - regardless of your support.

VIKKI: Exactly. And I would have been fine—and she would have been out—in the cold.

JAMES: That's right.

VIKKI: Yeah. And, for me, the fact that you transitioned while you were in the position of Executive Director of Peak House, is one of the things I talk about when I talk about the work at Peak House, both as a metaphor and as a very real, practical thing. People are absolutely blown away to hear that, and inspired, and I think they feel as I did, that it takes so much courage and vision. There's a lot to that. And, of course, you must have a structure. You're not a foolish person. You know, this wouldn't be safe-enough for me to do, or I could tolerate the risk, or something, but you taking that position and being out in various ways, I think that just created so much more space. And not just for Peak House. The ramifications, I think, are bigger than we know, because the program has a huge reputation. We do a lot of teaching from Peak House. A lot of people read our stuff and are onto our work, and then when they hear about your very public transformation it can be astounding to folks.

JAMES: That's cool for me to just hear you say that now, because I didn't really know that those conversations are happening.

VIKKI: Yeah. What's it like to think about being a part of those conversations?

JAMES: It's great. In some ways, transitioning on the job was calculated and thought through and on the other side I knew it was something I needed to do for myself. I thought about the ramifications on the program, both positive and potentially negative. I did think about cultural shift, and I thought, probably as Wendy did many years ago, "What kind of difference is this going to make in the lives of young people and their families?" I also thought about my own professional safety and what kind of impact this may have on my career and my continued employment in the sector. I put a lot of intention into trying to create the most positive, experience for everyone. When I hear that those conversations are happening for other people, I wonder what kind of difference that makes for other people that find themselves in a similar situation. I was having a similar conversation with a Trans identified young person at Peak House the other day. I think it's important for all the young people in the program to have access to people in power.

If they want to meet with me, I will make time for them within 24 hours. But, in particular, with Trans youth, if they want to have a session or sit down, I like to have that conversation with them, because I think it's important for them to see someone they might identify with in a leadership role. There are not a lot of out Trans people in program leadership so I want to make sure that youth have access to seeing positive role models that are doing well, living positive lives. There are a lot of stories in the media and elsewhere about our suicide rates, about unemployment, negative outcomes for Trans people. It is important for youth to see another Trans person living a good and happy life. Anyways, on this day I had a meeting with a youth that had just entered our program. And the thing that this Trans-identified youth said was, "I came here because all my counsellors said someone in the higher-ups was Trans and I'd be safer here." And that right there, though, is a lot to live up to, because I really hope that we're achieving that as an organization. But that is the reason we take personal and professional risks when it is safe enough to do so, so that we can help to create this kind of visibility and more inclusive spaces.

I was reflecting back on conversations that happen that we're not aware of much in the way I did not knowing you were talking about my on the job transition or that referring counsellors had this as part of the narrative as to why we are a safer space for marginalized youth. It is humbling when you step back and think about it.

VIKKI: Absolutely. And that's how we structure safety, isn't it? It really matters what kind of stories are told about Peak House— and who we are as people. People have descriptions of the program and stuff, that's one thing, but a real referral is being able to tell you, "There's a person there that I have respect for who I can trust—to send you to". You said that you had to track a bunch of different things, in terms of you transitioning on the job. One was ramifications for the program, can you say more about that?

JAMES: Well, much in the way that you just described Wendy's process so many years ago, I run a program where parents and caregivers send their children to come live with me, and I'm responsible for them during that time. I would say there's been a lot of educational advancements in media and such in the last five years. A significant amount, actually. And there's still a long way to go. In the last five years, in particular, a lot more understanding, which is not to say that those are all positive, but I think people have the word trans/transgender on their radar.

One of my main concerns five years ago was, "Would me being out as a Trans man prevent young people from reaching our services?" "Would there be discrimination for people sending their young people to us?" "What would those preconceived notions be? Could I be seen as a possible threat or a risk in caring for young people?" That definitely played on my mind, "Would there be media attention that could be negative? If there was an incident that happened at Peak House, could that be translated back, in some way, to me being out?" So, from a program perspective, I was primarily concerned with what youth would be losing out on Peak House. And it would probably be the young people that really needed to be there the most.

VIKKI: When you say, "the young people that really needed to be there," say a bit more about that. Because you have a really complex analysis and understanding of the different kinds of risks that gender non-conforming youth are faced with.

JAMES: Yeah. So, my concern was that young people that really needed to be at Peak House, young people that were non-binary, maybe young people that were in a questioning period, Trans young people, Queer young people, marginalized folks in general. That somehow parents or caregivers that were not open minded could get in the way of young people sourcing out our program, and coming for the very reason that they needed to be.

VIKKI: But also transphobic Drug and Alcohol counsellors.

JAMES: Totally.

VIKKI: To get into Peak House, youth 13 to 18, you have to be referred by a

Drug and Alcohol Counsellor. If those folks are taken with transphobic ideas, it's not going to be a possibility for youth, right?

JAMES: Exactly. I don't think I really thought about that. I like to think that the professionals in our communities are professionals in our communities. That being said it is possible for sure.

VIKKI: Yeah.

JAMES: While that very much could be true, it was more about thinking about caregivers that might block youth accessing Peak House. That was more my though process. There's lots of layers. From that perspective, if we got any media attention, could that be positive or could that be negative? Would my board be supportive? How would this impact me and my funder? How would this impact me as a professional in the community? Could I be at risk of losing my job, or under scrutiny of my job? How would the staff team receive it? Would they be supportive? Yeah, there was a lot of thought that went into it, and at the same time, not a lot of decision making around it.

VIKKI: And so you said before that you felt there was a part of the decision process that was about what you needed to do personally, something you just needed to do for self.

JAMES: Yeah, I was going to come out (as Transgender, James was out as Queer at that time, a community and politic he continues to identify with), and I was going to transition, and I was hoping I would do both while still being employed. But it was happening either way. The pieces I spent more time—and was quite intentional about trying to have it be the most positive outcome for not only myself, but on the program, as well—I think I went about it in an intentional way—I consulted. I talked to you— and I talked to other people about wanting to set the program up for a success, but also create enough generosity of spirit that folks could come alongside in a way that could feel good for everyone. I think we all did a good job of moving through those spaces in beautiful and imperfect ways.

VIKKI: Yeah. When you look back at it now what difference do you think all that preparation work made in terms of how it went and the kind of changes you were able to make for yourself, and for Peak House, and for Trans youth and questioning youth.

JAMES: Yeah, I don't know. Because you can't know, right?

VIKKI: Yeah.

JAMES: You don't know after the fact what was useful and what was not useful. I think for the time—and again, we're only talking five years ago—I think for the time, it was highly necessary. I don't know if that much preparation in our current location in the city of Vancouver, in this time and space, would be as required. I think it helped me, as an individual though, as well, prepare.

VIKKI: For sure.

JAMES: And I think it provided—I was talking about generosity of spirit—I think it's really important to help bring people alongside in a way that is not shaming, but encouraging, that gives people—we talk about gender identity and we talk about name changes and pronoun changes, and there's an expectation in this moment that as soon as you declare something other than how people have known you, that we should all get onboard immediately. And that's an awesome thing to do, and it's also a hard thing for some people to do. I think in the Queer community or in the Trans community, we've got a lot of practice. I have lots of friends who have changed names and pronouns, and I'm pretty good at it. Imperfect, but pretty good at it. But, you know, for a lot of people this isn't part of their regular vocabulary, it takes some time. And so I think the preparation helped people ease in, and my part of that was being generous, and patient, and reminding in gentle ways.

VIKKI: Yeah. Who were your allies? What did you need, in terms of allies, to do this whole thing for yourself personally, but also in that program and structurally?

JAMES: Yeah. I needed Wendy, first off. Wendy has been a really strong ally. And I say this with a smile on my face, because she's also the person who really struggled with pronouns, and names and all of those pieces.

VIKKI: Yeah, because Queer is not Trans right? She's a lesbian.

JAMES: Yeah, and she still, sometimes in conversation, she gets the languaging wrong, but she gets the heart right every time. And she immediately was supportive, and that was such a reassurance. I had your support as the Therapeutic Supervisor. I think at the time you were off, and we had someone filling in, Christine Dennstedt. She was amazing. I tell this story, and at the time—I sometimes get embarrassed easily, and this was one of those moments. But I look back and I'm like, "Wow! How amazing." I decided to tell my team at a staff meeting, because I wanted everyone to have the information at once, which was a fairly terrifying thing to do. It was not a comfortable thing to do, in terms of putting myself in a vulnerable position to everybody at once, which is funny because I do tons of public speaking engagements and workshops. The response from Christine, who was the Clinical Supervisor in those few months when you weren't present, was that she brought a cake. Who gets a cake? I got a cake!

And I think, in that way, I'm so privileged, honoured, and lucky that all of you really helped me to shape the best way to move forward with the team, and with the Board, and with caregivers. So, I think that act of vulnerability of talking to you all individually and having that allyship, and then using that consultative process really helped support that.

VIKKI: Yeah, yeah. I'm also thinking about—when you talk about this as something you needed to do for yourself, at one point you called it selfish. For me, the word doesn't fit—would it be selfish if an Indigenous person said that they needed to do something to open space? How would that be selfish?

JAMES: Right.

VIKKI: We would think that was just absolutely required.

JAMES: Yeah.

VIKKI: And in response we could easily link that back to white supremacy and colonization right? Meaning invasion, occupation, genocide, and assimilation, right? (Hill, 2010). So, I'm just wondering if you think about it as something different than selfish.

JAMES: Yeah. And that probably was one of those instances where the wrong word creeps out, but it's rooted in some historical pieces.

VIKKI: Yeah, it's not just a language problem. It's not just using sloppy language.

JAMES: Yeah. I'll tell you though, because you've highlighted it, if anyone else had done that I wouldn't think it was a selfish act.

VIKKI: Right. To transition.

JAMES: Of course not, of course not. When I think of my own experience, I also came out and transitioned at 38. So, there are some layers of things behind why did it take me so long, which is another conversation for another time. I was out as Queer since I was 18, but I wasn't out as a Trans man publicly until I was 38. So, perhaps there's some underlying pieces of work there that snuck out in the word "selfish". Yeah, I think what I was trying to get at was I factored in all of the professional things. I factored in the program, and the wellness of the program, and the young people, and the staff, and all of those things, and also it was something that I needed to do for self.

VIKKI: Yeah. I'm not locating it in you needing to do more self-care. It's a sign of where we're at in terms of that whole idea of trans-inclusion. Because we're not—you know what I mean? A lot of programs and people are talking about being trans-inclusive, and you and I had a conversation that there's all kinds of places that are merely or possibly trans-tolerant now.

JAMES: Yeah.

VIKKI: Because a bunch of us have banged on the doors and dragged all kinds of stuff in through the backdoors, so people realize they have to be trans-tolerant in Vancouver.

JAMES: Or they have to say that they are.

VIKKI: Yeah, they have to at least make a claim to that because that's where we're moving in terms of a social justice movement. But the difference between trans-inclusion and trans-tolerance is massive, right?

JAMES: It's massive.

VIKKI: Yeah. And also, the limitations of talking about inclusivity, being included isn't what we're after for Trans youth. That's a pretty low bar. Justice isn't about inclusion, it's about justice. It's a different project, right?

JAMES: Yes. And I think you're absolutely right. I think organizations are realizing that this is something that they need to be saying that they are. And they do a workshop sometimes—

VIKKI: With you.

JAMES: - sometimes I do that workshop with them. And then they can check off a box and forward they move. And while all that is great, it's great that the languaging is on their radar, it's great that they're thinking about—I don't think anyone ever says we're trans-tolerant, although, the interpretation is that's what they are. But they say, "We're inclusive," and all these things, and maybe they even change the sign on their bathroom. All those things are super good.

VIKKI: Yeah.

JAMES: The problem that I see, as it relates to social service work is that the expectation that have clients and families coming to those services is that it actually is an inclusive, or a welcoming, or an environment where that's not going to be the same kind of issue as it may have been in other environments. And doing a workshop and changing the bathroom sign doesn't equate to an inclusive environment. It doesn't mean they will respond to oppression, to transphobia, it does not mean they will take action to make it a safer place.

VIKKI: It doesn't shift the culture. That cultural shift. That's the other thing I'm wondering about, is in terms of—because everything you've talked about, this is very much your own personal experience. But in terms of its relationship to Peak House, which is a program for youth, you've been framing this very much from a client-centered perspective. Like, you are the ethical center of your life, in terms of transition and risk. But in terms of work, this is about, "Is this going to hurt the program? Is this going to make it impossible for these young ones to access this program?"

JAMES: That's right.

VIKKI: So, in terms of that, I'm just wondering what kinds of shifts, or what kind of differences, or what kind of space do you think has been made for gender diverse youth connected to you publicly taking that space and that location and shifting the culture at Peak House?

JAMES: Right. You ask me the impossible questions, because you know me well enough to know I don't like to pin anything on—what has happened as a result of me transitioning and being out at work? I don't know. I can tell you where we are as a team, but I do think it's on multiple layers, right?

VIKKI: Yeah.

JAMES: It starts with the team. First off, it starts with education and training. So, as a result of coming out and transitioning at work, I organized a bunch of training. And all of that has trickled into the level of service that young people are receiving. So, I'd say that's one key piece.

VIKKI: And what I would say for my perspective as a Clinical Supervisor, is that it has had deeply rooted influences— in the way we do our "therapeutic work".

JAMES: It has. Yeah, there are so many things. I think right down from education, to signage, to visibility, to staff hiring practices that stem from who we bring onto the team. Like, what we're looking at in terms of diversity on the team now, right? To what our staff forms look like, to what our program forms look like. To advocacy that we've had to do with the pharmacy that works with the program, or the extended health benefits that our staff team access. So, there's all those kind of little layers, and they seem like they're not that important,

VIKKI: But they are.

JAMES: Because you change the intake form to be gender inclusive, it's not really a big deal until you have a young person for whom it is a big deal and they notice that it's inclusive, and that makes all the difference. We've changed the groups that we lead. We do something called Healthy Tuesday, which primarily focuses on health and wellbeing, but has a lot to do with sexual health and relationships.

VIKKI: And Harm Reduction.

JAMES: Harm Reduction, those pieces. We re-wrote all of that with gender inclusive language. And so we're doing sexual education in the house that's completely gender neutral in terms of languaging, which is a tricky thing to undertake, but so important. So, there's those pieces. We do Gender Groups weekly at Peak House—and you can speak to this as you co-created that innovation in our therapeutic practice. It is so important for us to speak with the young people in the program and really break down the ways that gender plays into their relationship with drug and alcohol use, and the stories that they're told in the media—and we've done a lot of work about being part of the culture of honourable young men (Reynolds, 2014a), and sexism, and misogyny. We do all of this work, and that is so important. And finding ways to maintain the importance of that work, and also have space for people outside of the binary and for Trans folks. So, I think, as you ask me about it, there's been some radical shifts within the program. One of my favourite stories is last summer, the youth were making friendship bracelets, and I came in and they were like, "James, do you want a friendship bracelet?" "Sure, that'd be great. Awesome." And they're all sitting on the floor. It was a beautiful little arts and crafts moment.

VIKKI: Yeah.

JAMES: And they said, "Which one do you want?" They brought out a bag and they were all gender identity flags.

VIKKI: Wow.

JAMES: And they probably had 25, which is significantly more identity categories than I was aware existed. And the youth started saying, "Hey, I'm wearing these three because…." and "I'm not choosing just one." It was a really beautiful thing. And I took my bracelet and we had a nice little chat, and it was just a regular kind of day, but it was so impactful. And so we had a variety of different young people from different locations, from different places, some of whom have never heard this terminology. We had a Trans young person in the program, we had someone who was in a questioning place who was just kind of looking at their gender identity and their sexual orientation, and we had a young person who came from a really homophobic religious background, and they were all engaged in this work together. So, when you ask me what kind of influence have I had on the program, it's what kind of influence do those youth now have when they leave the program, that is really the exciting piece.

VIKKI: Absolutely. That's a beautiful story. I'm thinking, too, about—there's gender inclusion, but I think what you're talking about is gender expansion. Like, there's an expansiveness about it. When you say that Peak House changed the forms to be gender inclusive, it was more than inclusive because it's not a new category of Trans. It's this expansive space where actually everybody's not required to get boxed.

JAMES: Yeah.

VIKKI: Right? I'm just wondering, too, not only what kind of changes your personal transition, and also the transformation of the culture at Peak House, I'm thinking what kind of changes that makes for youth and for the program in ways that aren't actually about gender identity.

JAMES: Well, that's just it, right? And so I think these young people wearing multiple bracelets was a beautiful representation of that. And it's one of those things that's not tangible. You can't always see what that looks like.

VIKKI: I'm thinking about interlocking sites of oppressions. And when you make things better for gender diverse youth, you make more space for youth struggling with other oppressions, right? Like racism, colonization, poverty. And all the other stuff we line up there, right?

JAMES: Yeah.

VIKKI: You take it on on any front, and as soon as we start to shift—Dean Spade talks about social justice trickling up (2011).

JAMES: right

VIKKI: And so when we move towards the folks who are marginalized and make space for them, what's required for them makes so much more liberatory space for other folks.

JAMES: Absolutely. You make space for someone, you make space for other people. Absolutely. I think the other thing that's really struck me is this—I feel very intentional about being out at work. So, if you go on the Peak House website and you look at my profile, I mention that I'm a Trans person there. And it's not a conversation I have every day. I don't constantly out myself. One of the things that's important is that I use the fact that I'm in a privileged position in a way that's useful. I have a lot of privilege. I'm white— I'm male identified, I live in Canada I came out at work, I kept my job, I was celebrated in it, I was able to create some real shifts within my work environment that were not only meaningful to me, but meaningful to my values and the values of Peak House. I could go on and on. I also have points of marginalization and oppression. It's really important for me to recognize the ways I benefit from my privilege and try to use it in a way that's useful. One of those ways is to be out and visible at work. I think it is important, and helps to shape the cultural shift that we're talking about. Those kinds of points of visibility make it easier for youth to sit around making bracelets, knowing that that's something that will be celebrated by the program. There's been more than a handful of young people I've met with at Peak House who have said, "You're the only Trans person I have ever met."

VIKKI: Yeah.

JAMES: And what an honour that they feel safe-enough to share that with us.

VIKKI: I think you're a person who's got a lot of vision. I've been at Peak House a long time and I've really appreciated the vision you have for Peak House.

JAMES: Thanks, Vikki.

VIKKI: Yeah. Something more than even what we can envision. We're envisioning something expansive that's very exciting. What I'm wondering is, where do you think things might actually go—your own personal path, but also Peak House. The work that we're all doing in community in different spaces—where do you think we're going? What do you think might also be possible at Peak House? For me, directly related to you, having an out Queer Trans man Executive Director, and Wendy a Lesbian Program Co-ordinator.

JAMES: You make it sound so cool.

VIKKI: Well, when I talk about it people get pretty excited, because a lot of workers who are really trying to hold Queer and gender diverse youth at the centre. When they hear that—I tell them that because it gives them so much hope, James, because they're in some organizations that they describe as broken and that are so homophobic and hateful they can't imagine the possibilities of places like Peak House. It's not imagining now, it's something that's actually happened somewhere, and it makes it possible. Makes it more possible than it has been for them to imagine transformation in their work sites and cultures. I'm just wondering what kind of things you might be—

JAMES: I'm just digesting that. That's really nice to hear, thank you. My hope is that in some way we can serve as a model to other organizations of what is possible, in terms of an all gender program. There's a lot of programs saying, "We're Trans-inclusive," or" Trans people welcome," or whatever the terminology is. And those programs are often binary programs. I know there's been some great work done around shelter access for Trans folks in Vancouver and so I think when we're looking at youth programs, especially a live-in program, having what we used to call a co-ed program, was risky, like, "Ooo, how do you do that?"

VIKKI: When we started doing a young men and young women program *that* was risky.

JAMES: That was risky, right? "How were you doing that?" And then we had openly Queer youth, and it was like, "Well, how are you doing that?" So, I'd like people to look at us as an imperfect model. But an opportunity on how you can remove the binary and still keep safety, make places safe-r for all young people, and successfully operate an all-gender program, an all-inclusive program, regardless of what points of marginalization(s) you're trying to help ease for people, is possible. That is my hope.

VIKKI: Yeah, that's a lovely thought.

JAMES: In terms of Peak House, in particular, I'd like to see us expand, and I'd like to see greater opportunity, especially for younger folks that we serve that maybe have more significant struggles than the structure of our program can support. So, a lower barrier service, and then something addressing transitional housing for youth that maybe have come through our program. And, as you know, housing is a huge problem here in Vancouver. And especially for Trans and gender non-binary folks it's even harder. So, something that helps fill that gap in a safe and supportive way that helps meet their needs around their substance misuse. I've got lots of ideas, but in the short-term, I would love to see people look to us as a possibility for their own programs.

VIKKI: And then the other thing I'm thinking about in terms of possibility is how does this make more transformational and liberatory spaces of justice (Lacey, 2005)? Because I always feel, when you have marginalized folks like yourself—like you said, you have privilege, but you have points of oppression—when space is made for you, there's more space for folks. And I'm wondering about how the hard work everybody's done to shift the culture at Peak House, in terms of gender diversity, and sexual orientation, and diversity, how can we use that to make sure we get more space for Indigenous folks. To make sure we have more space to acknowledge white supremacy and racism. Just taking oppression on on all fronts. And this requires that we face the discomfort that is required to address privilege and actually do justice in practice (Kumashiro, 2004; Heron, 2005; Reynolds, 2014b). It just gets me excited, because you just start somewhere, you start to make more space, and then you're going to make more just-spaces, spaces of justice, right?

JAMES: Well, yeah. And I think, again, that is the history of Peak House long before I came. And I've been at Peak House a number of years. I did frontline work with street involved youth for many years. And I worked relief at Peak House not for the money, but for the hope. So, the youth I worked with in my regular job were in really tough and desperate places in their lives, many lost their lives during their struggles on the street. It was beautiful and painful work, and I would work at Peak House a couple times a month to see the other side.

VIKKI: Absolutely.

JAMES: It kept me alive in the work I was doing on the street. To be honest, it was a touchtone that supported my heart to keep doing front line street work for so long. I worked at Peak as a relief working then over time did other things, consulting and some contract work, and ended up in this position, with great appreciation to Lorraine Greives, and yourself, and other people who helped mentor me into this role. But in the same way that so many years ago Wendy took the risk, and others like yourself took the risk to support her, because there's also a risk in allyship.

VIKKI: Yeah, sure. That is true, and the differences in the risk are always paramount, but it is important that we are fluid allies to each other across time and different spaces, for sure (Reynolds, 2010).

JAMES: Absolutely. I think when I look at the history of Peak House, this piece of work is a perfect fit in the continuum of the work that Peak House has done and will continue to do. And when I look at what's next or what's coming, everything is next and everything is coming. As you know, we've been doing a significant amount of work right now around white privilege, in particular. And that's a piece that I think has been influenced by the space created for Trans and gender diverse folks. And you're absolutely right, creating the space there and the openness there is creating space and openness in other areas. And all of this is continual, so we don't do queer inclusion and then we're done, and then, oh, white privilege we've knocked that off. This is all continuing work and we're all continuing to learn. And, as you know, next month we've got some training coming for our team to look at body politics, and fat politics. I'm working with the team and young people around oppressive languages and ideas around bodies, body shaming, fat-phobia, and some other pieces.

VIKKI: And continually asking how much that's got to do with substance misuse?

JAMES: Of course, it's all connected. The team is constantly bringing new and exciting pieces for us to work on. But more than any of us, it's the young people that challenge and engage us in the work that needs doing.

VIKKI: Absolutely.

JAMES: All of this is informed by the young people.

VIKKI: Yeah. Well, thanks so much for this, being vulnerable, and bringing your own struggles to this interview. Is there anything swimming in your noodle you just want to add or anything we didn't talk about you wanted to touch on?

JAMES: No, I think the pieces that I really wanted to get across is if you have the opportunity to be in a privileged position, to please use it, especially if you're in position where young people are going to benefit, or you have the opportunity to mentor young people. And not everyone has that or is in a safe enough place to use it but when we do it's so important. We often take for granted that everyone is as informed or has access to the same information as us. It is not the case, I often chat with youth from rural communities for instance, and they inform me that they have never seen a Trans person, or had the opportunity to meet another person like themselves. Not everyone has internet access. That everyone is as informed and as connected as we are. I tell my team never underestimate the importance you have on someone's life. It can be a two second interaction that you think is nothing. You might have thought you had this fantastic check-in with something for two hours, but they might never remember, it didn't stick for them like it did for you. But that one minute interaction where you said something positive or negative can really stay with people. So, I think that is the piece. And the other piece is for folk to shake up their organizations. The way things have been done doesn't need to be the way that they are. They don't need to follow our model, but there's a lot of creative thinkers out there. There's a lot of ways to do thing differently that create more space for everybody.

VIKKI: I teach a lot internationally and write, and people get very excited when I speak about Peak House for really good reasons. But for me, the goal is not for everybody to come try to work at Peak House. We're all not just trying to serve folks right? Or accommodate youth to lives of oppression. We are actually committed to the project of transforming our societies (Kivel, 2007).The goal is for people to align with those collective ethics where they are, start where they are, because it's all interlocking oppressions. Take on whichever one you've got some access to power to shift and change—that transformative or organizational work, which is what I think you have really done at Peak House. So, it's great to talk to you about this.

JAMES: It's been an honour, thanks.

Acknowledgments

This work occurred on Indigenous territories of the Musqueam, Skxwu7mesh-ulh Uxwuhmixw (pronounced Squamish) & Tsleil-Waututh nations which were never surrendered.

Dedication

We dedicate this writing and on-going work to all of the gender non-conforming, questioning and Trans youth we work alongside who question, challenge, educate and transform us. We honour the strength and moral courage required to trust us enough to share their identities with us, and acknowledge the silencing pain we contribute to for all of the youth for whom we were and are not safe-enough to be out with.

References

Bird, J. (2004). *Talk that sings: Therapy in a new linguistic key*. Auckland, New Zealand: Edge Press.

Hammoud-Beckett, S. (2007a). Nurturing resistance and refusing to separate gender, culture and religion: Responding to gendered violence in Muslim Australian communities. In Eds. White, C & Yuen, A, (2007). *Conversations about gender, culture, violence and narrative practice*. 43-51. Adelaide: Dulwich Centre Publications

Hammoud-Beckett, S. (2007b). Azima ila Hayati-An invitation in to my life: Narrative conversations about sexual identity. *The International Journal of Narrative Therapy & Community Work*, 1, 29-39.

Heron, B. (2005*). Self-reflection in critical social work practice: Subjectivities and the possibilities of resistance*. Journal of Reflective Practice, 6(3), 341-351.

Hill, G. (2010). *500 Years of Indigenous Resistance*. Vancouver: Arsenal Pulp Press.

Kivel, P. (2007). Social Service or Social Change? In INCITE! Women of color against Violence, (Eds.). *The Revolution will not be funded: Beyond the Non-Profit industrial complex*. 129-150. Cambridge, MA: South End Press.

Kumashiro, K. (2004). *Against common-sense: Teaching and learning towards social justice*. New York, NY: Routledge.

Lacey, A. (2005). *Spaces of justice: The social divine of global anti-capital activists' sites of resistance*. CRSA/RCSA, 42(4), 407.

(Munro, Reynolds & Townsend, 2017).

Reynolds, V. (2014a) Resisting and transforming rape culture: An activist stance for therapeutic work with men who have used violence. *The No To Violence Journal*. Spring, 29-49.

Reynolds, V. (2014b) Centering ethics in therapeutic supervision: Fostering cultures of critique and structuring safety. *The International Journal of Narrative Therapy and Community Work*. No. 1, 1-13.

Reynolds, V. (2013). "Leaning in" as imperfect allies in community work. *Narrative and Conflict: Explorations in theory and practice*, 1(1), 53-75.

Reynolds, V. (2010). Fluid and Imperfect Ally Positioning: Some Gifts of Queer Theory. *Context*. October 2010, Association for Family and Systemic Therapy, UK, 13-17.

Reynolds, V. (2009). Collective ethics as a path to resisting burnout. *Insights: The Clinical Counsellor's Magazine & News.*, December 2009, 6-7.

Reynolds, V. (2002).Weaving threads of belonging: Cultural Witnessing Groups. *Journal of Child and Youth Care*, 15(3), 89-105.

Reynolds, V. & polanco, m. (2012). An ethical stance for justice-doing in community work and therapy. *Journal of Systemic Therapies.* 31(4) 18-33.

Spade, D. (2011). Normal life: Administrative violence, critical trans politics, and the limits of law. Brooklyn, NY: *South End Press.*

FOUR

The Role of Allies in Anti-Violence Work

In anti-violence work we act in solidarity with shared purposes and shoulder each other up to resist patriarchy and misogyny and create a society that is safer for everyone. Accountable men, including transgender men, work as allies alongside women anti-violence workers to address men's power and to transform a rape culture. But as "women" we are also required to act as allies to each other as we are not all in equal positions of power or risk in relation to this work. In activist cultures an ally is a person who belongs to a group which has particular privileges, and who works alongside people from groups that are oppressed in relation to that privilege. The hope is to create change and increase social justice in relation to this oppression (Bishop, 1994).

Being an ally is not a fixed position, it is fluid, and based on the different domains of our identity and the access to power we hold in relation to that domain This means that at times, I will be an ally to a person around one domain of power, but they may be an ally to me around a different part of our identities (Crenshaw, 1995). For example, I am required to act as an ally to a woman who identifies as queer because of my access to heterosexual privilege. In another moment, the same woman may be required to be an ally to me around issues of class background, or organizational position. Ally work is fluid, meaning that we need to attend to the power that is present, back each other up and be in solidarity with each other across the differences that divide us (Reynolds, 2010a).

When serving in the role of ally it is important that I locate myself in my privilege. When I work with anti-violence workers and women in the impoverished community of Vancouver's Downtown Eastside, I find ways to be public about the fact that I have never lived on the street or struggled with substance abuse. I do this because I am sometimes read as someone who has had these experiences, and these misunderstandings invite a trust and sister-feeling that is neither earned nor present. It is important that I do not pass for a woman who has had these experiences, as women may feel more affinity and safety than my privileges warrant. Later, a woman may feel that they have been lied to or that some truth has been withheld from them. I make my privilege known as an act of accountability for my access to power and as a beginning place for trust to grow.

Allies choose to be accountable for their power. Our access to power makes us hard to trust, as we can decide to back down, not notice, be silent, minimize, accommodate, or smooth things over. The role of the ally is to make space for the person who is oppressed to be able to step into and be heard, and have their words matter and hold power. As an ally I hold myself, my actions and words, accountable to the person who is oppressed. The ally makes space and then works to get out of the way. A feminist with white skin privilege talking on behalf of women who are racialized risks further marginalizing the woman she seeks to be an ally to. The ally may need to make space and not speak because allies are not qualified to speak. As an ally to a colonized woman I am unqualified to speak because I do not know colonization outside of an academic understanding and teachings from witnessing people's suffering. I did not suffer colonization, I have not paid the price of this knowledge. Being an ally is hard work and not without risk, and especially hard to get "right". But I always remind myself the woman who needs me to be an ally in this moment is the person who is being oppressed by power, and that the risk to me is not the same. Allies do not carry the burden, and when our actions are unskilled or fail the oppressed person pays the largest consequences (Reynolds, 2010b).

Allies are invited in to speak when oppressed people cannot be heard. At times allies are the best people to speak as the risks of backlash are high and a woman may ask an ally to speak. This is, however, risky and imperfect and requires humility and accountability practices and relationships of enough-trust, as well as practices of not stealing knowledge or appropriating experiences.

As anti-violence workers we can experience our work as very individual, which brings with it continual invitations to division. We are separated from each other as workers and organizations competing for scarce resources in the midst of overwhelming need in a political climate of greed and privileged individualism. Invitations to division abound in our community work, and we can be seduced into judging other workers, their positions, and their professions. In contexts of adversity, the point is not to figure out which anti-violence workers and organizations to blame, but to think of ways to help women and families and change the social contexts that support violence in all its forms. Our greatest resources for doing that are each other. Doing solidarity invites anti-violence workers to be alongside each other because we need each other, and because it doesn't serve woman and families for us to be divided off.

I try to build solidarity in all of the work that I do, whether it be activist, community, counselling, or training work. I hold close my desire to be in solidarity with everyone who picks up anti-violence work. This invites a leaning in towards the other. It reminds me that acting in a way that harms the dignity of another person, especially publicly, is not in line with the ethics I hold. I remind myself in these moments that my aim is not to be right, correct, or seen as smart. My aim is always moving toward solidarity, and so I need to act in a way that makes space for that person and me to be walking alongside each other.

One teaching from anti-oppression work that I hold close is an understanding that there is always more solidarity than we know of.

In Ecofeminism, Indian feminist physicist, Vandana Shiva, and Maria Mies, a German feminist scholar, weave together feminism, activism and environmentalism. This positioning of environmentalism as activism has had an impact on me, as it helped me begin to draw connections between social movements and see the intersection and solidarity of multiple paths towards global justice. Prior to this learning I had been part of perpetrating the rifts between environmentalists and social justice activists, seeing them as separate, individual and competing projects. This separation ended for me when I worked alongside a survivor of torture from Nigeria, whose activism was environmentalism. After working alongside this activist/environmentalist I could never again entirely separate one from the other. It is fabulous that fifteen years later, this division needs to be explained. This has me wondering in our collective anti-violence work what other divisions and barriers are keeping us from seeing who is in solidarity with us (Reynolds, 2010c).

I remind myself that there are some collective ethics we share or we would not be meeting in this space together. Working to address and resist violence and holding a feminist-informed anti-oppression stance is hard work that requires skill, moral courage, and commitments to justice. I remind myself that no person is in this movement by accident. Our collective ethics have brought us together, however imperfectly.

The collective ethics that I am talking about are those important points of connection that weave us together as anti-violence workers. We do not have to create perfect collective ethics, as points of departure and distinctions in our ethical positioning can offer the gifts of diversity and broader possibilities. In most of our work these collective ethics go unnamed, but they are the basis for the solidarity that brought us together and can hold us together.

Solidarity is not synonymous with unity. America Bracho is a medical doctor who works with Latino Health Access, and describes it as an Institute of Community Participation. Bracho says, "Unity in a community is never going to be generalized. It will occur only around certain issues. We do not seek to unify the community in any general way. We *do* however seek to find and build a sense of common ground on particular issues." She speaks about the inability even for people in a small village in Mexico to be united on any issue, and the basically racist assumption that Latinos in the United States should be united on most issues. While holding onto a common ground on particular issues and declining unity, workers at Latino Health Access also work purposefully to decline invitations for division. Doing solidarity requires discernment between division and difference. The point is not to achieve unity by smoothing off the edges of all differences, but to find points of connection in relationships that bring forward an "intimacy that does not annihilate difference" (Palmer, 2003, in hooks).

Being allies and working in solidarity does not mean that we are ever hoping to achieve total agreement or that shouldering each other up means always agreeing in our collective anti-violence work. We are required to create a culture of critique in which we can challenge each other and hold our practices and theories up to scrutiny in order to serve our families and communities better. Being allies to each other in anti-violence work requires that we hold each other to account, but we are not acting as allies when judgment and attack are used to silence other anti-violence workers and discredit them. Discerning critique from attack is part of our work as allies. All activists working in anti-oppression frameworks are familiar with the heart wrenching spiritual pain that comes when we replicate oppression.

Our hope in being allies to each other and working in solidarity in anti-violence work is to change the social context of patriarchy, violence, and oppression and not to replicate it with each other.

References

Bishop, A. (1994). *Becoming an ally: Breaking the cycle of oppression.* Halifax, Nova Scotia, Canada: Fernwood Publishing.

Bracho, A. (2000). An Institute of Community Participation. *Dulwich Centre Journal*, No.3. Adelaide, Australia: Dulwich Publications.

Crenshaw, K. (1995). Mapping the margins: Intersectionality, identity politics, and violence against women of colour. In K. Crenshaw, G. Gotanda, G. Peller, & K. Thomas (Eds.), *Critical race theory: The key writings that formed the movement* (pp. 357-383). New York: The New Press.

Palmer (2003) in hooks, b. *Teaching community: Pedagogy of Hope.* New York: Routledge.

Reynolds, V. (2010a) Fluid and Imperfect Ally Positioning: Some Gifts of Queer Theory. *Context*. October 2010. Assoc Family and Systemic Therapy, UK, 13-17.

Reynolds, V. (2010b). *Doing Justice as a Path to Sustainability in Community Work.* Taos Institute. Unpublished thesis.

Reynolds, V. (2010c). A Supervision of Solidarity. *Canadian Journal of Counselling*, 44(3), 246-257.

Shiva, V., & Miles, M. (1993). *Ecofeminism*. Halifax, Nova Scotia: Fernwood Publications.

FIVE

A Solidarity Approach: The Rhizome & Messy Inquiry

Introduction

A Solidarity Approach aims to hold all of the inquiry process to the ethics and practices of activist solidarity and in line with an ethic of justice- doing (Reynolds, 2010a, 2011a). This writing illuminates this inquiry process which was created for my PhD dissertation. The approach calls on Deleuze and Guattari's concept of the rhizome (2008) to describe the networked communities (Lacey, 2005a) in which my activism and paid work occur. This writing begins with describing my work supervising and training community workers and therapists who work within contexts of social injustice alongside people who are marginalized and oppressed. Next, a description of the interconnectedness of these communities and the usefulness of the concept of the rhizome in activism, community work and a Solidarity Approach to inquiry is offered. A hopeful scepticism around inquiry and writing is made public, and I will show how these concerns were addressed. Some of the work from Clarke (2005), Lather (1993, 2010), and Law (2004) that supports this engagement with a messy inquiry, an ethic of justice-doing and a Solidarity Approach will be discussed. Some strategies for the Solidarity Approach are outlined and I illuminate an Expansive Inquiry in which my work and ethical stance are placed at the centre of the inquiry in order to resist replicating appropriation or exploitation of oppressed people and workers. This work is then re-situated back into the rhizome, where there are possibilities of expansiveness and de-centering my work which, while useful, is only a connected filament that is profoundly co-created, inter-dependent and may be the stuff that foments other useful work.

The context: Supervising community workers struggling in the margins

The context of this inquiry is centered in my work as a clinical supervisor and consultant with community workers and therapists working in the margins of society with oppressed people, many of whom are exploited, racialized[1] and colonized. We are responding to human suffering, which is loosely talked about in medicalized ways as trauma or addiction. The context of our work is the realm of human suffering, which exists because people's human rights are not respected and because we have constructed an unjust society. I have supervised a center for survivors of torture (Reynolds, 2010b) and supervise a rape crisis center, addictions teams and housing and shelter workers in Vancouver's Downtown Eastside, which is the poorest off reserve area in Canada. This work occurred alongside queer, Two Spirit, gender variant and transgender workers[2], and direct action activists addressing a multiplicity of oppressions. All of these workers, activists and clients have profoundly contributed to this work.

A Supervision of Solidarity (2010c), which is how I describe my work, encompasses an ethical stance for justice-doing which is a response to the suffering, indignity, and violations of social justice that is the context of much of this community work.

Dire need compelled me to create practices that can be of use to the workers I supervise. Teachings from activist cultures have informed me on this path alongside community workers and clients, and my engagement with these ideas has proven useful on the ground. At times I have felt an affinity with Irish playwright Samuel Beckett's character who states, "I can't go on: I'll go on" (1958, p. 178). The absurdities faced by workers and clients within contexts of poverty and dislocation amidst great affluence and political apathy are often reminiscent of Beckett's austere and surreal landscapes. Despite not knowing what I was going on to, I found that something I dare to call a faith in solidarity helped me to go on.

Being of use has required immediate responses. This could not wait for better training, the arrival of the right teacher, or finding the right book.

Taking what I have learned from activist cultures, from progressive therapeutics trainings (Waldegrave & Tamasese 1993; Anderson 1997; Sanders 1997; Bird 2000; White 2007; Madigan 2011) and from my family and culture, I responded to need with action. A teaching from American anarchist theorist Noam Chomsky informs this work:

"Social action cannot await a firmly established theory of man [sic] and society, nor can the validity of the latter be determined by our hopes and moral judgments. The two — speculation and action — must progress as best they can, looking forward to the day when theoretical inquiry will provide a firm guide to the unending, often grim, but never hopeless struggle for freedom and social justice" (2005, p. 116).

Counsellors, shelter workers, and other community workers who had participated in a Supervision of Solidarity (Reynolds, 2010b, 2011b) let me know that they found the solidarity practices useful and in line with fostering sustainability and addressing the spiritual pain they experience when they are forced to work in ways that are not in line with their ethics (Reynolds 2009).

A hopeful scepticism

Norwegian qualitative researcher Steinar Kvale's "hermeneutics of suspicion"[3] has proven a useful practice for me in articulating and making public my ethical concerns with research, inquiry and publishing. Hermeneutics is the art of interpretation which resists authoritative truths, and engages with multiple meanings from different voices. This hopeful scepticism requires that theorists' claims are held in abeyance until the practice can be shown to reveal the theory. With this phrase Kvale invites us to take a critical distance from the claims we make, and invites a hopeful yet sceptical position, open to the possibility that our practices may reveal something other than our intentions.

Histories of appropriation have made me sceptical about researching or writing anything informed by activism. I do not want to exploit clients or workers by writing exotic tales of torture and dramatic pain. I am also cautious about claiming knowledge that has been created by unnamed collectives of activists and putting my name to it. Work with survivors of torture and political violence taught me that engaging in research and publishing is not a neutral activity. Research on therapeutic work with survivors of torture has been studied at places such as the School of the Americas, where torturers are trained (School of the Americas Watch, 2009) [4]. I have been careful in selecting what will be revealed and what might be risky in all of my writing, trainings and teachings. I remain aware I am not the one at risk.

Maori researcher, Linda Tuhiwai Smith, offers this caution on the legacy of research for colonized people:

> "'research' is probably one of the dirtiest words in the indigenous world's vocabulary...It stirs up silence, it conjures up bad memories, it raises a smile that is knowing and distrustful...The ways in which scientific research is implicated in the worst excesses of colonialism remains a powerful remembered history for many of the world's colonized peoples. It is a history that still offends the deepest sense of our humanity" (1999, p. 1).

American Black critical pedagogy educator bell hooks writes about the risk of activists' work and knowledge being appropriated and subsumed by people working from academic frameworks, particularly in relation to early writings from feminist communities (2000). Publishing was a useful tactic to get feminist perspectives legitimized specifically in academic discourses. However, this knowledge became the property of academics and was distanced from the activist communities which developed it. According to hooks, feminist activists became less relevant and were not seen as qualified to speak of feminism when these feminist discourses were finally legitimized by academic institutions.

When I began my PhD I recognized and was attuned to these risks. At the same time, I was encouraged by many practitioner and trainer colleagues to make public the ethical positioning I had relied on as I developed some useful practices. As an activist I am always striving to change the social context in just directions. Making an offering to knowledge in an academic context is part of a diversity of tactics that aims to promote just social changes. I felt compelled and in some small and humble way collectively accountable to bring this work to a wider audience.

bell hooks evokes a spirited solidarity when she writes:

> "I came to theory because I was hurting— the pain within me was so intense that I could not go on living. I came to theory desperate, wanting to comprehend — to grasp what was happening around and within me. Most importantly, I wanted to make the hurt go away. I saw in theory then, a location for healing" (1994, p. 59).

Imelda McCarthy (2001) from Ireland's Fifth Province team writes of the necessity to make public the privatized pain of clients that individualized practices, such as individual therapy, can contribute to. McCarthy describes how "public problems become private and privatized issues" in therapeutic practice:

> "It is crucial that the private issues of clients need to be entered into the public arena if social change is to occur. This publication does not refer to the specific details of confidential material but of the themes and trends... The private and the public cannot be separated when one works with the poor; otherwise we are in danger of creating yet another arena for their silencing and further oppression" (2001, pp. 271-272).

hooks and McCarthy's invitation to make public the privatization of suffering has accompanied me and encouraged me to engage with making my work more public, with an aim to contribute in some way to the social change McCarthy envisions.

Bridging the worlds of activism and academia is at the heart of my work. Theorizing is not a neutral practice. I believe that theorizing holds the promise of justice-doing and that liberatory theorizing can engender liberatory practices. I have approached theory with an intention of excavating histories of both acts of resistance, and of acts of justice.

Theorizing has been useful in my activist work by drawing links across differences, and making public acts of power that are often obscured in the mystification of media, and what passes for normal: the way things are. Theorizing informed by liberatory intentions can open up possibility: the way things might be. In this work I borrow on the hope of bell hooks, who believes in the possibility that theory can be liberatory in social justice work (1984).

The rhizome

Activists' understandings of the rhizome are informed by the work of Deleuze and Guattari (1987). They use the rhizome to describe horizontally linked, non-hierarchical forms of social organization, thought, and communication. In botany, a rhizome is a horizontal plant stem, which exists underground, and from which the shoots and roots of new plants can be produced. Growing horizontally underground, rhizomes are able to survive extreme weather. The rhizome has been picked up in activists' cultures for its usefulness in dismantling hierarchy and power structures, while inviting a form that is more organic, responsive, co-creative and alive (Smith 2010, 2011). New Zealand/ Aotearoa narrative therapist John Winslade has investigated the usefulness of Deleuze's work in narrative therapy and conflict resolution (2009). Activist/scholar Anita Lacey illuminates the work of networked communities (2005a) and offers rich accounts of the multiple ways that the rhizome has informed activist networks and movements, including the riot girrrl network and the Anarchist Teapot Collective in London. The spirit of the rhizome is illustrated beautifully by Canadian anarchist and liberatory educator Scott Uzelman:

"Running bamboo often gives rise to unwitting bamboo gardeners. A single innocent shoot can stand alone for several years and then suddenly an entire field of bamboo begins to sprout. This leaves the unsuspecting gardener with a new bamboo garden that stubbornly resists attempts to get rid of it. While on the surface each shoot appears to be an individual, related but separate from its neighbors, underground all are connected through a complex network of root- like stems and filaments called a rhizome. During the years the gardener watched a single bamboo shoot grow tall, underground the bamboo rhizome grew horizontally, spreading throughout the yard, storing nutrients in anticipation of a coming spring. Like the bamboo garden, social movements are often rhizomic organisms growing horizontally into new terrains, establishing connections just below the surface of every day life, eventually bursting forth in unpredictable ways" (Uzelman, 2005, p. 17).

A Solidarity Approach

As an activist working and living in the rhizome of interconnected communities striving towards social justice I wanted to approach inquiry in line with my ethics of solidarity and justice-doing. Solidarity speaks to our hopes and practices that move us towards our collective liberation, and the belief that our paths towards something just, are woven together.

The ethics of solidarity require that I do not replicate exploitation or abuses of power in my work or the inquiry of it. Solidarity requires that I begin all of my work from a decolonizing place, trying to hold myself accountable to my settler privilege on the unceded indigenous territories in which I live and work. I hold a decolonizing and anti- oppression frame for all of my activism and my paid and unpaid work (Dua & Lawerence 2005; Reynolds 2010a; Walia, 2012). This requires an intersectional analysis (Crenshaw 1995) that takes on oppression on all fronts attending to lines of power and disadvantage. My relationship to solidarity is imperfect, and I embrace an imperfect solidarity as an anti- perfection project (Reynolds, 2010d, 2011c). And this makes it possible for me to go on without needing to be perfect, but knowing I can respond to oppression with action and engage accountability to repair imperfect actions.

Metis Response-Based therapist Cathy Richardson created a Metis Methodology for her PhD dissertation (2004), which held her entire process accountable to the cultural practices, traditions and ethics of her Metis culture. After consulting about my fears and concerns, Cathy inspired me when she suggested that what I needed was to create a Solidarity Approach that would help me hold all of my PhD process accountable to the ethics and practices of solidarity from my activist culture.

The engagement with solidarity is recursive, messy, and non-linear in this work. In fact, the same ethics that were the subject of this inquiry informed the inquiry process, the practice and the writing recursively. A Solidarity Approach became my response to the question of how I could hold all of my inquiry accountable to understandings and practices of solidarity that are at the heart of my work and activism.

An Expansive Inquiry

Alongside other academic/activists I believe that "Social researchers should always be the most vulnerable — not those being studied or 'left' behind once the research is complete" (Fine, 2006, p. 88). Writing myself into the work, and examining my own theory and practice invited enough-accountability for me to engage in line with this ethic. I put the development of my own practice, and my ethical stance for my work forward as the subject of this inquiry. I was encouraged in this direction by my dissertation instructors, Sally St. George and Dan Wulff who speak of research as daily practice, where they encourage practitioners to "examine data from our own clinical work to more richly understand our practices and societal discourses" (2012).

This Solidarity Approach led to an engagement with inquiry rather than research. This is important as inquiry allows for the messy, fluid, emergent dialogues that I thought would be more generative and useful than categories, evidence or truth. Ken Gergen, an American Social Constructionist, describes collaborative inquiry as a process in which the interests of participants inform the direction of the inquiry (2005).

For this project I could have researched the work of other practitioners and evaluated and categorized the results to judge if they were in fact engaging ethics. Instead of researching the work of others and distilling it down to results (or truth), I invited people into my practice. I was not looking to deliver a perfect model of practice, or any manualized tools. What I was interested in articulating was my ethical stance from which generative practices emerged. I did not want to reify any of my practices, such as the Solidarity Group — I used it mainly to invite other workers to explore and co-investigate my ethical stance. My hope was that practitioners would respond by creating their own practices in line with some of our collective ethics for doing justice, expanding possibilities outwards from this experience. In consultation, my dissertation advisor Ken Gergen described my process as an Expansive Inquiry, and sketched a picture:

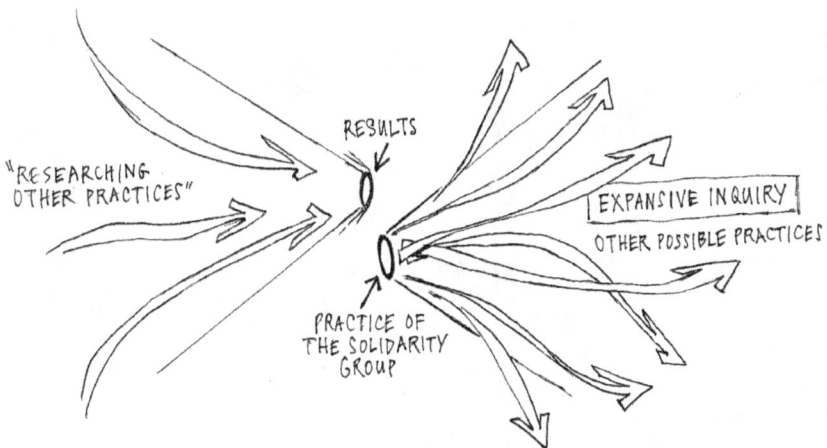

Solidarity Practices describe the practices I have developed as they all follow from a commitment to an ethical stance for justice-doing. The rhizome drawings illustrate that the Solidarity Practices emerge organically from the ethical stance, which is comprised of the Guiding Intentions:

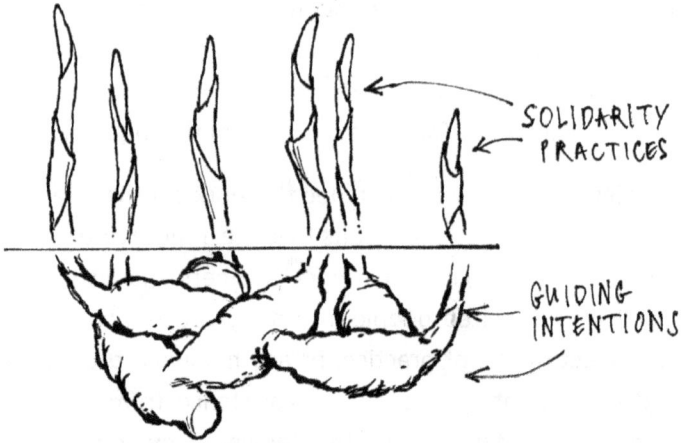

The Solidarity Practices that arise from the Guiding Intentions include Solidarity Groups 5, Solidarity Teams, the Witnessing Supervision Interview, and people-ing the room, among others (Reynolds, 2011b). The Solidarity Group practice was chosen for use in this inquiry because of the energy, interest and usefulness which the group inspired in the community workers who participated in it.

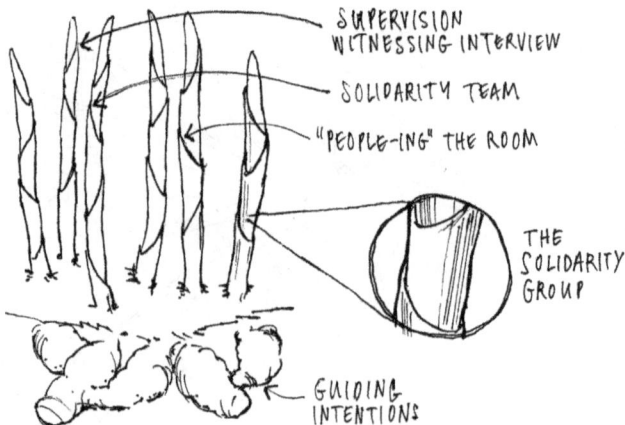

The reflections and critiques offered by workers participating in Solidarity Groups became the stuff that contributed to articulating and describing the particular Guiding Intentions from which the practices grow.

Messy and fluid inquiry

The pragmatic approach to inquiry of Patti Lather, an American feminist poststructuralist social science researcher prioritizes action/ activism. Lather speaks of catalytic validity, and asserts that the value of research should be based on how it can be used, not how it can be measured (1993). As anarchists say, 'talk-action=zero'. My work and activism is informed by anti-colonial struggle, feminist and queer theory and anarchist theory. The threads of this collective and possibly inconsistent theorizing (Newbury, 2011) name power, address structural abuses of power and contest the construction of normal. It also requires a complex understanding of power, and acknowledges people's acts of both resistance and solidarity as acts of power (Reynolds, 2010b; Wade, 1997). I aim to respond to oppression and resistance to make social change in line with a decolonizing and anti-oppressive stance and direct action. I wanted my inquiry to attempt to do the same.

Queer theory has been inspiring for me in this process as it invites fluidity, which is movement from the fixed and certain to the confused and unstable, a privileging of flow and mutability, a refusal to be stable or static, and an ability to morph (Butler, 1990; Jagose, 1996). Engaging with fluidity helps us to resist constructing dialogues that are sedimented, reified, static, and immutable (McNamee, 2008). Fluidity also offers a resistance to definition or explanation.

Working to discern the differences between description, under- standing and explanation has been liberatory. Austrian philosopher Ludwig Wittgenstein writes that, "We must do away with all explanation, and description alone must take its place" (in Shotter, 2008, p. 13). Explanation is a finite process that claims to state what something truly means. Description, on the other hand, brings people closer to the experience and creates a space for the reader's own perspective. Norwegian therapist, Tom Andersen, critiqued his earlier claims to explanation in an epilogue saying, "If I had written the book today the words explain and explanation would have been replaced by understand and understanding" (Shotter and Katz, 1998, p. 81; Andersen, 1991, p. 158). I was not after a rigid stable explanation of my work, but a fluid and useful engagement with it.

Janice DeFehr, a Canadian social construction informed therapist, introduced me to compelling practices of dialogical approaches to inquiry that invite a messy and generative process to emerge (DeFehr 2008, 2007; Lather 2010; Law 2004). This excited me as I wanted to find a way to attend to outliers in my inquiry, reflections that were in the margins not the centre, as that is where activists are, as well as many people I know as workers and clients. Imelda McCarthy captured my interest speaking of her Irish informed understanding that "the illumination is in the margins" (personal communication, 1996). McCarthy credits her culture-informed reading of the Book of Kells with this teaching (Kearney et al. 1989). The Book of Kells is a precious copy of the gospels in which the text is surrounded by beautifully painted borders containing elaborate celtic knots. I wanted to amplify teachings from the margins that were evoked in my inquiry.

Outliers can be silenced in research, and I engaged a spirit of solidarity to resist producing normalizing, heteronormative research. I didn't want to 'prove' anything. As Leonard Peltier, a political prisoner and American Indian Movement leader says, "We're not supposed to be perfect, we're supposed to be useful" (1999, p. 10). I wanted to engage queer and anarchist space, "spaces of justice" (Lacey, 2005b), and deliberately forged "spaces of inclusion" (Lacey, 2010a). This required resisting the disappearances that result from using mutually exclusive categories. African-American critical race theorist Kimberly Crenshaw's work on intersectionality problematizes categories as a taken for granted useful way to make meanings of information. Crenshaw contests the creation of separate identity categories such as race and gender, "The categories we consider natural or merely representational are actually socially constructed in a linguistic economy of difference" (1995, p. 375).

Categories are always influenced by power and always exclude. They can obscure more than they reveal as they silence outliers and dissenting voices, which I was finely attuned to as an activist in the current political climate of the criminalization of dissent.

In response to these concerns and intentions for the inquiry process I engaged with Adele Clark's postmodern response to Grounded Theory, which she calls Situational Analysis (2005). Clark resists analysis that delivers the truth of situations, and employs messy mapping to make space for outliers, complexity and divergent voices. Messy Mapping invites the person doing the inquiry to show up, not disappear, in the decision making process of deciding what will be attended to, what resonates and what is of use. From this lovely mess of responses a more ordered or understandable story of the experience can be told.

Messy inquiry allows for attending to what is of interest and what resonates. Over eighty practitioners who participated with me offered reflections and critiques of their experience from within the practice of Solidarity Groups. These groups were not homogeneous, and varied in the number of workers involved and the context of the work. Some occurred as part of paid supervision work, others were hosted at conferences, trainings and team days. Questions were offered to evoke responses, but these questions changed in the process as better questions were offered to me, and as some workers responded by writing emails, or phoning, or catching up afterwards for dialogue in person. As well my interest and focus was transported by some of the experiences of the group, and I inquired about different aspects of the work. Engaging with a messy process allowed for continually redirecting the inquiry based on what participants found interesting and what they were paying attention to. I also attended to my own interests, reading, resonating thoughts, and emergent practices. These generative responses informed both the doing of the Solidarity Group and the attempts to describe the Guiding Intentions that grounded it.

The diagram above is a skeletal retelling of the messy map created from practitioners' responses to what they thought were the ethical underpinnings of my practice and our collective experiences in the Solidarity Groups. Using this messy map, I discerned six Guiding Intentions. Committing these Guiding Intentions to writing required that I order them in some way. Despite using letters instead of numbers I couldn't get outside of rank ordering in the writing. To destabilize the notion that these Guiding Intentions exist in a hierarchy I used Deleuze and Guattari's rhizome to illustrate them, allowing for more fluidity and mess.

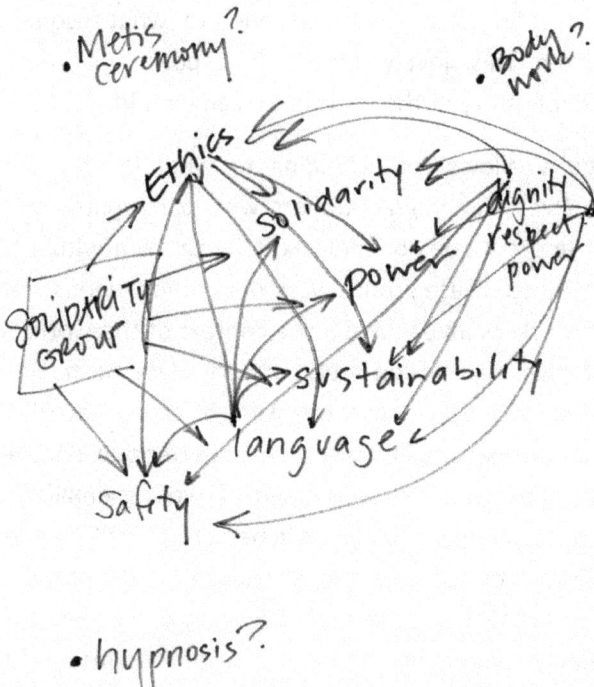

Like a rhizome, the Guiding Intentions were rough around the edges, disorderly, not of equal size, and resisted mathematical precision. They defied mutually exclusive categories, and grew into and out of each other, The Guiding Intentions that emerged in the inquiry were: centering ethics, doing solidarity, fostering collective sustainability, addressing power, critically engaging with language, and structuring safety. (See Appendix 1 for a description of the Guiding Intentions. For a rich description there is a chapter on each Guiding Intention in the dissertation [Reynolds, 2010a] Doing justice as a path to sustainability in community work).

Guiding Intentions coexist in relationship with each other, much as the filaments of a rhizome. They are linked, overlapping, living, and fluid. For example, all of the Guiding Intentions are inextricably linked with Structuring Safety, and yet Structuring Safety is itself considered a Guiding Intention. Taking one Guiding Intention out of the rhizome for investigation is required, but artificial, as they exist relationally, and need to be re-connected in the rhizome, with the other Guiding Intentions in order to be useful, much as an ethical stance requires intersectionality, solidarity, and is immensely inter-dependent.

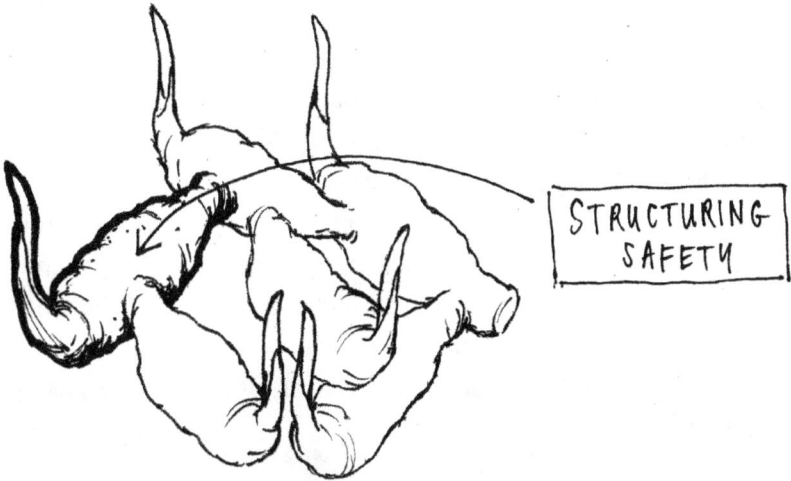

STRUCTURING SAFETY

The writing of this ethical stance and the six chapters which offered rich descriptions of the Guiding Intentions which comprised it can be read in any order. They could have been organized in different ways, as the rhizome can be entered onto at any point and defies a static order. The Guiding Intentions are differentiated under six headings to provide clearer understandings, but there could have been ten headings, or four. These six Guiding Intentions identify the main threads of my ethical stance, and they also flow well into the themes that I follow in practice. For the purposes of clarifying the Guiding Intentions I differentiated them from each other. In practice and in action, however, it is not possible, nor required, to completely separate one Guiding Intention from another.

These Guiding Intentions differed from principles in that they had fluid boundaries and were not mutually exclusive. Guiding Intentions were more slippery to operationalize than a set of principles. Practice is messy, and people do not actually engage with linear principles. The Guiding Intentions were offered as an heuristic, which is a possible way of moving towards a goal (Moustakas, 1990). This differs from principles which may comprise an algorithm which is a set of specific steps that will lead to a predetermined and known end.

This ethical stance is not finite or fixed, but always in flux, expanding in width and depth with changes in texture and tone as experience, community workers, and clients inform and transform me, and as we counter influence each other, our communities and our environment. This reflexive process of examining and re-creating my ethical stance follows critical educator Paulo Freire's teachings of praxis (1970). Action is followed by reflection, which informs actions which are more just, which rolls into further reflection, and so it continues. Popular Education teaches that acting without theorizing can be unsafe and ineffective (Fanon, 1961; Freire, 1970). Without this understanding of theorizing as a reflexive exercise I could replicate oppressive practices, or more simply, use power in unethical ways.

In consultation John Winslade offered this insightful critique of my use of the term 'theory' in the Solidarity Approach, particularly as it denotes a "level of abstraction" when my inquiry is alive and practice- based. He suggests Deleuze's understandings of 'concepts' as a more useful description:

"Deleuze talks in one place about the task of the philosopher as being to generate 'concepts' that people can use (the rhizome is an example) and it seemed to me that this is in part what you are doing. Working to identify from the discourse at the local level expressions that can be treated as useful for doing meaning-making around and doing justice with" (personal communication, 2012).

Strategies for a Solidarity Approach

Many strategies were engaged to promote the spirit of solidarity through-out this inquiry. Some of the most useful ones are outlined here. (They are not rank ordered.)

1. Not researching people who are exploited

The centre of this inquiry was my work, which I invited workers I supervised to critique and reflect upon as an accountability practice.

2. Resist contributing to dead knowledge

It was important that this work matter, that it could possibly make a contribution to social change and that I did not engage with inquiry primarily to earn a higher degree. As Lather says, this work tries to do something, not say something.

3. Frontline worker consultant and reader

An intention of the work was to welcome all workers, including those unfamiliar with social justice language and therapeutic language into the work. To serve this purpose a new community worker, Jaime Wittmack, served as an outside reader and a cultural consultant (Waldegrave & Tamasese 1993). Jaime read all of the drafts and offered a critique to encourage clear-enough writing, accessibility, and promote the purpose of the writing, which was to engage and invite, not marginalize. This consultation was generative in multiple ways. For example, Jaime encouraged the use of footnotes not merely as references, but to expand the text while keeping it uncluttered. She reflected that extensive references inside the writing distracted her from the ideas, and left her feeling 'stupid'. Jaime suggested that the people being referenced be introduced, and I took the opportunity to identify their profession and culture to give newer readers some context and possible connection to the knowledge. Jaime taught me to write in ways that honoured and welcomed the workers I was most trying to be of use to.

4. Networked communities of cultural consultants

Cultural consultants from anarchist and activist communities, queer and transgendered communities, as well as refugees and survivors of political violence and torture played an important role in this inquiry. These cultural consultants offered critiques of this writing and my work and analysis with an aim towards more accountability and resisting the appropriation of ideas. The qualification for these consultants was not their academic certification but rather their life experiences and positionings. These generative critiques freed me from being paralyzed by guilt, and helped me resist a false humility that could have silenced what I do know and have done. This inspiring and committed collection of folks served as my Solidarity Team (Reynolds 2011b) for this inquiry.

5. Referencing widely

References are a gift to the reader and, to invite more accountability, I identified my references in terms of their multiple cultural locations. Referencing widely, and attributing cultural knowledges to more than published works, helped historicize the knowledges of communities that could otherwise be disappeared. The history of the ideas and practices is as important to hold in collective memory as the more accessible published accounts of the ideas. This use of extensive referencing invited more history-making from the communities which have informed this work.

6. Resisting appropriation

While my ethical stance was fully my own and I held myself accountable to its claims, I acknowledge that it was co-created in important and meaningful ways. The teachings of the people I worked alongside who are refugees, activists, and survivors of torture and political violence are central to this stance. It is important to acknowledge the differential price extracted from people from the global south and racialized and minoritized people from the global north. I recognized the generosity which has enabled them to teach me and for me to benefit from their lived experiences. Part of this writing was a testament and witnessing of these ideas, offering an invitation into the rich histories of these ideas and practices in activist cultures and social movements. This stance of accountability, which is a teaching from activism, embodied my resistance to appropriation, which is always a risk for persons and groups holding non-academic and alternative knowledges.

7. Co-writing

This inquiry, like all of my work, was profoundly collaborative, so I worked to make the collaboration public by referencing widely, inviting reflections and co-authors, and weaving my relationships with real people into the scholarship, honourings and acknowledgments. Co- writing some of these stories helped bring the ideas from the academic realm into practice. Negotiating permission for this storytelling required slowing down the process and extensive back-and-forth dialogue. As part of this co-writing I engaged with real-time storytelling in hopes of offering a retelling that was close to the experience. This also allowed a person's own voice to carry their wisdom, as opposed to me interpreting and possibly appropriating their knowledge. I was invited into real-time storytelling by Arden Henley (1994, 1992), who credited the idea to the work of David Epston (1989) and most particularly David's inspiring story of Dory the Cat.

8. Public domain and free access

Because this inquiry was so profoundly collaborative the book is available for free download. Other writers have registered their work as Copyleft. Anyone can use it, morph it, and copy it, as long as they don't capitalize on it — sell it. In this sense it, like much activist collective wisdom, becomes part of the commons we hold collectively.

9. Engaging inconsistently with anonymity

In order to fully credit and name people's contributions and not subsume their ideas into my voice I resisted ideas of total confidentiality. The mixed approach to confidentiality was not smooth, and I reluctantly participated in the marginalizing of some communities by perpetrating the use of pseudonyms. The aim in doing this was to avoid putting workers at risk for sharing their knowledges. For example, in relating the story of Tina, who identified herself as an Aboriginal transgendered woman, I had the choice to steal her voice, silence it, or participate in making her knowledge sharing safe-enough by using a pseudonym. I have not resolved my ethical struggle and discomfort in relation to Tina, and my response to this is to work towards justice alongside other allies so that in a possible future she may use her own name and experience that as a safe-enough thing to do. A consistent use of confidentiality would smooth over this discomfort, but would also mask important differences in access to power that were made public by this messy and inconsistent use of pseudonyms and names.

10. Liberatory language practices

An important solidarity strategy was to commit to using language in ways that resisted the social construction of pathologizing and marginalizing identities. The possibilities created by language practices that assist people in being seen in ways they experience as liberatory inspired me. With this in mind I invited people participating in this inquiry to self- identify their gender, culture and orientations.

American queer theorist Judith Butler problematizes the binary of gender, man/woman, especially as it denies queer identities and alternative possible spaces (1990). I used androgynous language constructions such as 'them', 'they', 'our', and 'this person'. My purpose was for people to self-identify, or choose not to identify their gender. Some participants who self-identify as differently gendered people struggle to live and be seen outside of the binary of man/woman. The point is not to use inclusive and space-making language only when speaking of people who exist outside of the gender binary, but to use it everywhere to expand possibility for everyone's preferred and liberatory identities.[6]

11. Making discomfort and fear public

The ethical tensions experienced in the inquiry process were not smoothed over, but made public. This was of course flawed because my awareness and analysis is imperfect. Part of the aim was to invite more critique and generative engagement with the ethical struggles the inquiry engendered.

Emerging transformations: Holding onto a fish that is morphing into an octopus.

The reflexivity of this inquiry process has greatly informed my approach to the work and changed the practice itself. The participants engaged in the Solidarity Group served as witnesses for my work and for the Guiding Intentions that inform my practice. Several practitioners have caught me up on the value of participating in the process, an ethic that Tuhiwai Smith speaks of in Decolonizing Methodologies (1999).

Engaging in this process has contributed to the emergent creation of new practices in my work with community workers. This inquiry has invited generative conversations with colleagues which are unlikely to have occurred without this project. The critiques made by the cultural consultants, and the dialogues these consultations fostered, have been expansive and illuminating. I experience all of these unexpected developments as nourishing support for my own sustainability. My experiences in this inquiry have transformed me in terms of holding a more enriched and useful critical analysis. The experiences of activism and community work recursively transform and counter-inform each other as we bring learnings across domains of practice.

The collective dialogue from inside the practice is breathing new life into the doing of the Solidarity Group. In response to this still-continuing collaborative transformation, I experience writing up this work as akin to holding onto a fish that is morphing into an octopus.

Unsettled fears and discomforts

Inquiry does not exist without risk despite our just intentions. In a Solidarity Approach, like all anti-oppression activism, we strategize to hold our work accountable to our collective ethics. As American activist/ musician Ani DiFranco says, "Any tool is a weapon if you hold it right" (1993). I believe that the Solidarity Group can be used in harmful ways if it is picked up in a mechanistic or formulaic way divorced from the ethics for justice-doing on which it is rooted. If the ethical stance is read or presented as finished, fixed, correct and righteous it can also be used oppressively.

A lesser fear is that the work could be de-contextualized and de- politicized. Activists have seen this happen to many of our tactics and practices. For example, Adbusters magazine was initially a fresh voice of deconstructing capitalism's hegemonic advertising system (Adbusters: Journal of the Mental Environment). Over time, however, anti-ads became trendy and Adbusters finally became an unofficial textbook for advertisers, ultimately becoming a tool of selling (Heath & Potter 2004). The potential for liberatory tactics to be de-politicized or co-opted (Hayden, 2008) is not paralyzing for me. As activists we know that our tactics of resistance are anticipated and their effectiveness over time will be purposefully minimized. In a spirit of solidarity we respond to this with creative ways of being that bring forth our ever emergent resistance and the next liberatory tactic.

In contrast, the fear of my participation in the appropriation of activist culture is paralyzing. To this end, I have referenced widely, invited, pursued and sought out critique from diverse people who have the moral courage to confront me as a practice of solidarity. This is not based on righteousness, but on my experiences of being the person who has transgressed, and who others have needed allies against (Reynolds, 2010d).

This inquiry has occurred at the cost of my engagement with more direct forms of activism in terms of time and resources. I will probably not be able to smooth over my discomfort regarding the elevation of my status and the undeniable privilege that comes with academic qualification. This discomfort is not the same as guilt, as Chomsky invites us to not posture with false modesty, but acknowledge that in a diversity of tactics there are roles some of us accomplish easier and more usefully, and that we are less suited to other pieces of the work. Like many social justice oriented activist/academics I plan to be accountable for this academic privilege.

Re-situating the work back into the rhizome

Part of a Solidarity Approach requires that the work that is held up for consideration be re-situated within the rhizome, returning to the networked communities who fostered it. From here it might decompose and possibly nourish other work, or it could be morphed, changed, or reused.

Here the work settles as a re-connected piece of something far greater, something Lacey describes as contributing to spaces of justice (2005b). It becomes part of, another node of social justice activism and liberatory theorizing: No more and no less.

The value of the ethical stance described in the Guiding Intentions and of the practice of the Solidarity Group lie in how they are used. In bridging decolonizing anti-oppression activism and inquiry my hope is that practitioners will take up this invitation to join in a collaborative inquiry, and contribute multiple and generative responses to the Guiding Intentions and develop new practices. It has been increasingly sustaining for me to hear back from community workers who have taken up this invitation and furthered the diversity of possible practices that share a spirit of solidarity. Like "rhizomic organisms growing horizontally into new terrains, establishing connections just below the surface of every day life, eventually bursting forth in unpredictable ways" (Uzelman 2005, p. 17).

Dedication

For Arden Henley, Cathy Richardson and Allan Wade, who encouraged me back to the academy, and continue to feed my hungry hope for liberatory pedagogy that does more than make room for direct action activists, but meets us in the rhizome.

This writing took place on Indigenous land which has never been surrendered.

Acknowledgments

This work is profoundly collaborative, and co-created by diverse fellowships of activists, workers, clients, teachers, colleagues and family who have inspired, critiqued and taught me across time. Thanks to Gail Simon for finding value in my solidarity inquiry, affinity in the rhizome with her 'underground writing', and fostering our lovely and imperfect solidarity. My advisors at the TAOS Institute, Ken Gergen and Sallyann Roth allowed room for a Solidarity Approach, without which I could not have completed my academic writing. Other faculty, Sheila McNamee, Sally St. George, Dan Wulff and Imelda McCarthy, were generous with their expertise, time and critique. Fellow students, Christine Dennstedt, Aileen Tierney, Ottar Ness, Janet Newbury and Janice De Fehr continue to shoulder me up in the work, offering excellent and generative critique. Jeff Smith, John Winslade, Sheila McNamee, Mr. Peaslee, and Ken Gergen served as my Solidarity Team for this project. Their solidarity has been more important to me than they can know. Thanks to Marie Hoskins, who invited me to lecture her graduate students at the University of Victoria. The expansive critique which followed contributed to this writing. Finally, my appreciation for the creativity and talent of Kent Peaslee for the diagrams, and Yvonne Hii for layout.

Appendix 1. An ethical stance for justice-doing

My ethical stance for justice-doing is comprised of six Guiding Intentions:

A. Centering Ethics

The centre of my supervision is our relational ethics and ethical positioning as we respond to clients' varying needs from within contexts of power. When practitioners cannot act in accord with our ethics we experience spiritual pain. Spiritual pain speaks to the discrepancy between what feels respectful, humane, and generative, and contexts which call on us as community workers to violate the very beliefs that brought us to this field. I centre my inquiry on the ethical stance of the practitioner, our collective ethics, and how these ethics are revealed in practice.

B. Doing Solidarity

My understandings of solidarity are derived from time honoured activist traditions of looking for points of connection and weaving people together. I attend to both practices of resisting oppression and promoting social justice. This spirit of doing solidarity acknowledges that our struggles to promote social justice are interconnected.

C. Addressing Power

Addressing Power speaks to witnessing both resistance and acts of justice-doing. It also invites cultural and collective accountability. Accountability requires a complex analysis, in which the multiplicity of sites of both power and oppression are acknowledged and addressed.

D. *Fostering Collective Sustainability*

Sustainability refers to aliveness, a spirited presence, and a genuine connectedness with others. It requires more than resisting burnout, more than keeping a desperate hold on hope; and yet it encompasses both of these capacities. We are sustained in the work when we are able to be fully and relationally engaged, stay connected with hope, and experience ourselves as being of use to clients across time. Sustainability is inextricably linked with an alive engagement with a spirit of social justice, and openness to our transformations as practitioners across time.

E. *Critically Engaging with Language*

Language can be used to serve or resist abuses of power. I hold an overt intention of utilizing language in liberatory ways. Critically engaging with language also acknowledges the dialogue that exists outside of words, and invites languaging the body.

F. *Structuring Safety*

Co-creating relationships of enough-safety outside of the binary of safe and unsafe helps to structure safety (Bird 2000). All conversations across difference are risky, and are of greater risk to some than to others. The possibility of doing harm by replicating some kind of oppression is one potential risk. I am also aware of the limitations of accountability. Social justice is better served by creating contexts in which the transgression is less likely to occur. This requires Structuring Safety (Reynolds, 2010c).

Notes

1   The terms minoritized and racialized are used for the purpose of naming the power and intention required in the racist and colonial project of re-constructing the majority of the world's people as a collection of minorities.

2   "Queer" has been adopted by groups of people I work with, both workers and clients, who do not identify as strictly heterosexual. Using queer as an umbrella term to include folks who self-identify as lesbian, gay, bisexual, Two Spirit, questioning and queer, is problematic for many reasons (Fassinger & Arsenau,

2007). Primarily people who self identify as lesbian, for example, may not resonate with queer theory or politics at all, and be subsumed by that term. As well, some folks who do identify as queer mean specific things by it, such as resonating with queer theory in ways that do not align them with gay or lesbian identities, and find using the term queer as an umbrella term mystifies and erases the queer politics and ethics that are at the heart of their preferred ways of identifying (Aaron Munro, personal communication, 2012). People I work alongside who identify as queer may be in any of these groups, but primarily identify outside of heterosexual normativity, which refers to discourses which promote heterosexuality as normal. People who I work alongside who self-identify as Two Spirit refer to their cultural location as Indigenous people who do not identify as heterosexual: Two Spirit refers to rich cultural knowings as well. People who I work alongside who identify as transgender or trans do not identify strictly with the gender they were assigned to at birth, and may transition culturally, socially and/ or physically to a gender in which they feel more congruent, which could be something other than male or female (Nataf 1996; Devon McFarlane, personal communication, 2011). Many people do not identify their gender in any way, and others identify as gender variant, gender non-conforming or gender queer, meaning something different than trans and outside of the normative gender binary (Janelle Kelly, personal communication, 2011). All of these terms are problematic, contested and evolving. I am using these terms for clarity and because groups of folks I work alongside have settled on this imperfect phrasing for now (Reynolds, 2010b).

3   Kvale (1996, p. 203) borrows the term "hermeneutics of suspicion" from the work of French philosopher Paul Ricoeur (1970). "His hermeneutic is always informed by both a suspicion which makes him wary of any easy assimilation to past meanings and as hope that believes in complete appropriation of meanings while warning 'not here', 'not yet'. Via suspicion and hope, Ricoeur plots a hermeneutic course that avoids both credulity and skepticism" (White, 1991, p. 12).

4   "The School of the Americas... is a controversial U.S. military training facility for Latin American security personnel located at Fort Benning, Georgia, made headlines in 1996 when the Pentagon released training manuals used at the school that advocated torture, extortion and execution." Consult the School of the Americas Watch website for a critique of this military project (School of the Americas Watch, 2009).

97

5   The Solidarity Group is described extensively in my dissertation (2010a) and in an article entitled A Supervision of Solidarity (2010c). The Solidarity Group emphasizes our collective sustainability with a specific aim to build solidarity and an orientation for justice-doing. At the center of the conversation are themes connected to centering ethics, doing solidarity, addressing power, fostering collective sustainability, critically engaging with language, and structuring safety. This is different than organizing therapeutic supervision around specific problems and individual workers. The Solidarity Group is only one component of the necessary supervision of therapists,with an emphasis on collective sustainability of the therapeutic community and their relational ethics. In the Solidarity Group the supervisor is not the primary resource, this role is played by a community of workers. Although one person is interviewed, the centre is the whole group. In Solidarity Groups the therapeutic community is being supervised collectively. In many ways, it does not matter who is speaking as the entire group is at the center. As the supervisor I look for themes that resonate with the principles of a Supervision of Solidarity. I attend to emergent experiences which hold meaning for the therapeutic community, not necessarily the individual being interviewed. These experiences may be acts of justice, ethical struggles, startling successes, painful losses, or other occurrences which hold meaning collectively. As the supervisor it is my task to ensure that all participants are witnessed in the conversation, and that people are woven together.

6   An excellent example of binary busting language is the adoption of the term pomosexuality by some members of some queer communities. "Pomosexuality lives in the space in which all other non-binary forms of sexual and gender identity reside — a boundary-free zone in which fences are crossed for the fun of it, or simply because some of us can't be fenced in. It challenges either/ or categorizations in favour of largely un-mapped possibility and the intense charge that comes from transgression. It acknowledges the pleasure of that transgression, as well as the need to transgress limits that do not make room for all of us." (my emphasis) Queen & Schimel (1997, p. 23.).

References

Adbusters: Journal of the Mental Environment. Vancouver, British Columbia: Adbusters Media Foundation.

Andersen, Tom (1991). The reflecting team: Dialogues and dialogues about the dialogues. New York: Norton.

Anderson, Harlene (1997). Conversation, language, and possibilities: A post-modern approach to therapy. New York: Basic Books.

Beckett, Samuel (1958). The Unnamable. New York: Grove Press.

Bird, Johnella (2000). The heart's narrative: Therapy and navigating life's contradictions. Auckland, New Zealand: Edge Press.

Butler, Judith (1990). Gender trouble: Feminism and the subversion of identity. New York: Routledge.

Chomsky, Noam (2005). Chomsky on anarchism. B. Pateman (Ed.). Edin: AK Press.

Clarke, Adele E. (2005). Situational Analysis: Grounded theory after the Postmodern Turn. London: Sage Publications.

Crenshaw, Kimberle (1995). Mapping the margins: Intersectionality, identity politics, and violence against women of colour. In K. Crenshaw, G. Gotanda,

DeFehr, Janice (2008). Transforming Encounters and Interactions: A Dialogical Inquiry Into the Influence of Collaborative Therapy In the Lives of Its Practitioner. Retrieved from http://www.taosinstitute.net/

DeFehr, Janice (2007). Dialogical methods of social inquiry. Unpublished paper.

Deleuze, Giles & Guattari, Félix. (1987). A thousand plateaus: Capitalism and schizophrenia. London: Athlone Press.

DiFranco, Ani (1993). My IQ. On Puddle dive [CD]. Righteous Babe Records.

Epston, David (1989). Collected Papers. Adelaide, Australia: Dulwich Centre Publications.

Fanon, Frantz (1961). The wretched of the earth. New York: Grove Weidenfeld Publishers.

Fassinger, Ruth & Arsenau, Julie (2007). "I'd rather get wet than be under the umbrella": Differentiating the experiences and identities of lesbian, gay, bisexual, and transgendered people. In K. Bieschke, R. Perez, & K. Debord (Eds.), Handbook of counselling and psychology with lesbian, gay, bisexual and transgendered clients (2nd ed., pp.19-50). Washington, DC: American Psychological Association.

Fine, Michelle (2006). Bearing witness: Methods for researching oppression and resistance-A textbook for critical research. Social Justice Review, 19(1), 83-108.

Freire, Paolo (1970). Pedagogy of the oppressed. New York: Continuum. Gergen, Kenneth (2005). An invitation to social construction. Thousand Oaks, CA: Sage Publications.

Hayden, Tom (2008). Writings for a democratic society: The Tom Hayden reader. San Francisco, CA: City Lights Books.

Heath, Joseph & Potter, Andrew (2004). The rebel sell: Why the culture can't be jammed. Toronto, Ontario, Canada: Harper Collins.

Henley, Arden (1992). Dory the cat runs away. Australia and New Zealand Journal of Family Therapy, 13(4).

Henley, Arden (1994). Stories that have heart: Narrative practices with children and their families. Journal of Child and Youth Care, 9(2).

hooks, bell (1984). Feminist theory: From margin to center. Cambridge: South End Press

hooks, bell (1994). Teaching to transgress: Education as the practice of freedom. New York: Routledge.

hooks, bell (2000). Feminism is for everybody: Passionate politics. Cambridge, England: South End Press.

Jagose, A. (1996). Queer theory: An introduction. Melbourne, Australia: Melbourne University Press.

Kearney, Phil; Byrne, Nollaig O'Reilly & McCarthy, Imelda Colgan (1989). Just metaphors: Marginal illuminations in a colonial retreat. Family Therapy Case Studies, 4(1), 17-31.

Kvale, Steinar. (1996). Inter-views: An introduction to qualitative research interviewing. London: Sage Publications.

Lacey, Anita (2005a). Networked communities: Social centres and activist spaces in contemporary Britain. Space and Culture: The Journal. 8(3), 286-299.

Lacey, Anita (2005b). Spaces of justice: The social divine of global anti-capital activists' sites of resistance. CRSA/RCSA, 42(4), 407.

Lather, Patti (1993). Fertile obsession: Validity after poststructuralism. The Sociological Quarterly, 34(4), 673-693.

Lather, Patti (2010) Engaging Science Policy: From the Side of the Messy. New York: Peter Lang.

Law, John (2004). After method: Mess in social science research. London: Routledge.

Lawrence, Bonita & Dua, Enakshi (2005). Decolonizing Anti-Racism. Social Justice: A journal of crime, conflict and world order. Vol. 32, No. 4. 120-143.

Madigan, Stephen (2011). Narrative Therapy. Washington: American Psychological Association.

McCarthy, Imelda (2001). Fifth province re-versings: The social construction of women lone Parents' inequality and poverty. Journal of Family Therapy, 23, 253-277.

McLaren, Peter & Leonard, Peter (1993). Paulo Freire: A critical encounter. London: Routledge.

McNamee, Sheila (2008). The Lindberg Lecture. Transforming dialogue: Coordinating conflicting moralities. Retrieved from http://pubpages.unh.edu/~smcnamee/dialogue_and_transformation/LindbergPub2008.pdf

Moustakas, Clark. (1990). Heuristic research. Newbury Park, CA: SAGE Publications.

Nataf, Zachary (1996). Lesbians talk Transgender. London: Scarlet Press.

Newbury, Janet (2011). A Place for Theoretical Inconsistency. International Journal of Qualitative Methods. 10 (4): 335-347.

Peller, A. & Thomas, K. (Eds.), Critical race theory: The key writings that formed the movement (pp.357-383). New York: The New Press.

Peltier, Leonard (1999). Prison writings: My life is my Sundance. New York: St. Martins Griffin.

Queen, Carol & Schimel, Lawrence (1997). Pomosexuals: Challenging assumptions about gender and sexuality. San Francisco, CA: Cleis Press.

Reynolds, Vikki (2009). Collective ethics as a path to resisting burnout. Insights: The Clinical Counsellor's Magazine & News., December 2009, 6-7.

Reynolds, Vikki (2010a). Doing justice as a path to sustainability in community work. PhD thesis. Taos Institute.

Reynolds, Vikki (2010b). Doing justice: A witnessing stance in therapeutic work alongside survivors of torture and political violence. In J. Raskin, S. Bridges, & R. Neimeyer (Eds.), Studies in meaning 4: Constructivist perspectives on theory, practice, and social justice. New York: Pace University Press.

Reynolds, Vikki (2010c). A Supervision of Solidarity. Canadian Journal of Counselling, 44(3), 246-257.

Reynolds, Vikki (2010d). Fluid and Imperfect Ally Positioning: Some Gifts of Queer Theory. Context. October 2010. Association for Family and Systemic Therapy, UK,

13-17.

Reynolds, Vikki (2011a). Resisting burnout with justice-doing. The International Journal of Narrative Therapy and Community Work. (4) 27-45.

Reynolds, Vikki (2011b). Supervision of solidarity practices: Solidarity teams and people-ing-the-room. Context. August 2011. Association for Family and Systemic Therapy, UK, 4-7.

Reynolds, Vikki (2011c). The role of allies in anti-violence work. Ending Violence Association of BC Newsletter. (2) 1-4

Richardson, Catthy (2004). Becoming Métis: The relationship between the sense of Métis self and cultural stories. Unpublished doctoral dissertation. University of Victoria School of Child and Youth Care.

Ricoeur, Paul (1970). Freud and philosophy: An essay on interpretation. New Haven, CT: Yale University Press.

Sanders, Colin (1997). Re-authoring problem identities: Small victories with young persons captured by substance misuse. In C. Smith, & D. Nylund (Eds.), Narrative therapies with children and adolescents (pp.400-422). New York: Guilford.

School of the Americas Watch (January 26, 2009). Human Rights Advocates Face Six Months in Federal Prison for Nonviolent Direct Action Opposing the School of the Americas (SOA/ WHINSEC). Retrieved January 28, 2009 from http://www.soaw.org/pressrelease.php?id=143

Shotter, J. (2008). Conversational realities revisited: Life, language, body and world. Chagrin Falls, OH: Taos Institute Publications.

Shotter, John & Katz, Arlene (1998). 'Living Moments' in dialogic exchanges. Human Systems: Journal of Systemic Consultation & Management. 9(2), 81-93.

Smith, Jeff (2010). Entering the Rhizome: A description of a music therapy street outreach program. The Drumbeat, 11(2), 10-12.

Smith. Jeff (2011). Just orientations: Analysis of membership categorization during Response-Based conversations about violence and resistance. Unpublished doctoral dissertation. University of Victoria School of Child and Youth Care.

St. George, Sally & Wulff, Dan (2012, 2, 12). Research as Daily Practice. SOWK 655, Edmonton, Alberta.

Tuhiwai Smith, Linda (1999). Decolonizing methodologies: Research and indigenous peoples. London: Zed Books Ltd.

Uzelman, Scott (2005). Hard at work in the bamboo garden: Media activists and social movements. In A. Langlois, & F. Dubois (Eds.), Autonomous media: Activating resistance and dissent, pp. 17-27. Montreal, Quebec: Cumulus Press.

Wade, Allan (1997). Small acts of living: Everyday resistance to violence and other forms of oppression. Journal of Contemporary Family Therapy, 19(I), 23-40.

Waldegrave, Charles & Tamasese, Kiwi (1993). Some central ideas in the 'Just Therapy' approach. Australian & New Zealand Journal of Family Therapy, 14, 1-8.

Walia, Harsha (2012). Decolonizing together: Moving beyond a politics of solidarity toward a practice of decolonization. Retrieved from http://briarpatchmagazine.com/articles/view/decolonizing-together

White, Erin (1991). Between suspicion and hope: Paul Ricoeur's vital hermeneutic. Journal of Literature and Theology, 5, 311-321.

White, Michael (2007). Maps of narrative practice. New York: Norton.

Winslade, John (2009). Tracing Lines of Flight: Implications of the Work of Giles Deleuze for Narrative Practice. Family Process, Vol. 48, No. 3, pp 332- 346.

SOLIDARITY IN ACTION

ADDRESSING COMPLEXITY AND HOLDING TENSIONS

Structuring Safety in Therapeutic Work Alongside Indigenous Survivors of Residential Schools

Introduction

This writing addresses the theory and practices of structuring safety in community work and therapy. Specifically, we track our efforts for structuring safety in work alongside Indigenous people preparing to speak publicly about their experiences of violence in Canadian residential schools. This includes giving accounts for the first time in a number of settings such as in therapy sessions, in community healing workshops, in conversations with lawyers or social workers, and in giving testimony in truth and reconciliation tribunals. The risky nature of participation in these processes for Indigenous people required that we structure enough safety into our work with the intention of not retraumatizing people, and of creating some space for a witnessing of their stories and testimonies.

In this writing Cathy, who is a Métis with Cree and Dene ancestry, will set the context of the work by briefly describing residential schools and the devastating consequences for Indigenous communities existing within a historical context of colonial violence and land theft. Her social work across Indigenous communities has been based on an understanding of the relevance of historical and political violence for Indigenous communities today. Vikki is an activist and ally from settler culture. She will describe her theorizing and practices for structuring safety in therapeutic work: contesting neutrality, negotiating permission, making potential risks apparent, anticipating backlash, holding space for hope, engaging in reflexive questioning, and not retraumatizing the person. Vikki will offer questions specifically oriented to residential school survivors to show the theory in practice. Cathy will then reflect from within the specific context of her work alongside survivors of residential schools. This writing is framed as a collaboration, and we will indicate who is speaking throughout the writing in order to locate ourselves culturally and to resist conflating our important differences.

Residential Schools, Truth and Reconciliation and Settlement Tribunals

Cathy: Residential school is a term used to refer to institutions of internment and resocialization for First Nations, Inuit and, in some cases my people, the Métis in Canada (Logan, 2001). Residential or mission schools were instituted under Canada's Indian Act (Department of Justice Canada, 2011), a piece of racialized legislation designed to assimilate Aboriginal people in Canada (Leslie, 2002). This act was a form of federal domination ensuring that virtually every aspect of daily life for First Nations people was regulated and controlled (Government of Canada, 1996, p. 255). Aboriginal people were stripped of their rights, both natural and legal, and their lands were taken illegally (Harris, 2002, 2004). Various religious organizations such as Roman Catholic, Protestant, Anglican and Baptist churches were given contracts to run the facilities that would house over 150,000 children who were separated from their families and communities. One hundred thirty-two schools were located across the country in every province and territory except Newfoundland, New Brunswick and Prince Edward Island. The goal of the program was to remove the Indian from the child (Campbell Scott, 1920, cited in Regan, 2010). Residential schools opened in Canada before confederation and the last one was closed in 1996 (Aboriginal Affairs and Northern Development Canada, 2010). However, lawyer and researcher Bruce Feldthusen (2007) documents that these institutions for Indigenous children have existed on this land since the 1600s.

A Critique of Residential Schools

The term residential school is a colonial euphemism for what might more accurately be described as a prison camp or internment centre. In fact, attendance was mandatory and the method of transporting children constituted kidnapping in many cases. Parents who refused to comply faced prison and the government withholding resources from families. Children were forced to engage in studies of Christianity as well as provide their labour for the functioning of the school (Miller, 1996). For those not familiar with the details of residential school violence, recent stories are documenting physical, emotional, psychological, spiritual, cultural and sexualized violence against children. This ranged from public humiliation, child rape, deprivation, to sticking pins through children's tongues when they spoke their Indigenous language. The violence was systemic, across schools to varying degrees, and perpetrators were granted a form of impunity and were seldom removed or punished for their heinous acts. Sources have shown that Indigenous children were deliberately exposed to tuberculosis and many died from the disease, sometimes two thirds of a school population.

In addition to the focus on creating a class of future menial labourers, the violence perpetuated against the children was rampant and largely ignored by those who knew about it. According to Feldthusen (2007) from the University of Ottawa, between 48% and 70% of the children were sexually abused. In some schools this figure was as high as 100%. He notes that the non-sexual physical abuse was often barbaric and indicates that the violence was systemic and deliberate, that those in charge were aware and that this was no well-intentioned mistake (2007). While colonial or standard accounts (Chrisjohn & Young, 1997) are used to conceal violence, many scholars have concluded that "residential schools have been the single most devastating event to affect First Nations peoples since contact" and many former internees continue to live out the horrors of this past internment (Thomas, 2005, p. 239).

Today, as part of a national Truth and Reconciliation process, former internees are invited to come forward and publically describe accounts of the violence perpetuated against them by priests, nuns, staff and other students in these religious institutions. These statements or testimonials are being recorded for the declared purpose of educating Canada about these historic and recent atrocities (Truth and Reconciliation Commission of Canada, 2011). The terms "truth" and "reconciliation" are problematic in that they imply that we are reconstituting a relationship that was once whole whereas European and Anglo-colonialism in Canada has inherently involved violence against Indigenous people in an attempt to remove their land, wealth, resources and children and place them into a class of servitude. Words such as "torture," "genocide," "racism," and "white supremacy" are omitted from the discourse used to describe this deliberate violence against Indigenous peoples in Canada.   What follows is a summation of Vikki's stance for structuring safety in therapeutic and community work, with connections and invitations to make the ideas applicable to work with residential school survivors.

A Stance for Structuring Safety

Vikki: Structuring safety describes the practices of negotiating or co-constructing conditions, structures and agreements that will make space for *safe-enough* work alongside survivors of residential schools. Therapeutic relationships that are experienced as safe are not capricious, natural, or random. They require intentional practices that create consistency, predictability, and set the space for *safe-enough* conversations (Reynolds 2010a, 2010b). Structuring safety is not something therapists do to get ready for the real work, it *is* the real work. Developing a capacity for structuring safety is a core competency for therapists working alongside residential school survivors, requiring skill, complex analysis of power, moral courage, compassion and critical supervision. Most of what I have learned about safety comes from my work with refugees who are survivors of torture and political violence, where the risks of transgressing safety are huge (Reynolds, 2010b).

There is no perfectly safe therapeutic relationship, as there are always risks of transgressing safety. We contest the binary of "safe or unsafe" when we co-create relationships of *enough-safety* with our clients (Bird, 2000, 2004). I work to create *some-safety*, *enough-safety*, or a *safe-r* conversation and relationship. All conversations across difference are risky because power is always at play. Doing harm by replicating oppression is always a potential risk. This is true despite our commitments to social justice and our collective ethics (Reynolds, 2009). As part of structuring safety I believe we are required to contest objectivity and neutrality and take an overt position for justice-doing. I take an overt stand of naming the political violence of residential schools. This is required in my work, especially as a response to and resistance against silencing popular discourses, such as the government's recent non-apology for residential schools (Coates & Wade, 2009).

Therapeutic and community work is not objective, neutral or innocent. I employ the metaphor of a bathtub to describe our work because once you get into that bathtub, like this work, there is no way to keep any part of the water pure or squeaky clean. We can't pretend that our positions in this work are innocent or neutral, or that there isn't a risk of us hurting a person.

In work with survivors of political violence, and here I include survivors of residential schools, it is imperative to hold understandings of the complexities of power and of the political world. Safety is not assured by being well intentioned but can be fostered by holding a critical analysis and an anti-oppression framework (Reynolds, 2010a). Many Indigenous clients are required to educate their therapists about colonization, the atrocities of residential schools and the structural oppressions faced by their communities.

Ideally residential school survivors will see therapists who share their culture and histories. Until that can be a reality allies will need to do this work (Reynolds, 2010c). Therapists who are not Indigenous must understand the history and impact of colonization and genocide as their responsibility in order to be qualified to work alongside Indigenous clients. Allies work to change the social contexts in which these atrocities occurred (and still occur) as our collective accountability as settler people for the violence of colonization.

Collaboration contributes to structuring safety by honouring the autonomy of the survivor of residential school in deciding what will be talked about and what will be of use. Survivor-centered work requires that I am de-centered as the therapist (Reynolds, 2010b; White, 2007) and resist taking a position of expertise on the life of the survivor. Collaboration invites the sharing of power and responsibility. As therapists, we do not save people and we are not responsible for people dying (Reynolds, 2010a). A collaborative stance requires the letting go of some power on the part of the therapist (Anderson, 1997; Anderson & Goolishan, 1992). This can be experienced as profoundly discomforting for us as helpers when the survivors we work with are in extreme situations and death is ever-near.

Structuring safety requires that we trust people with their own lives. It is patronizing for me to decide a survivor is not up to giving testimony or participating in a tribunal. I can collaborate with folks and ask questions to help them make informed choices, but I want to side with the ethical principal of autonomy and not replicate oppression by siding with paternalism. As a person from the dominant culture, that is settler culture, this is profoundly important in conversations with Indigenous people negotiating their engagement with the Canadian government given our past and present violence which is often backed up by paternalism.

Practices of Structuring Safety

There are many paths to structuring safety in terms of preparing the space to foster safety. What I think is most important is that the setting serves as a response to the questions:

- How does this space (office, counselling room) foster safety?
- How does my performance of myself, (my clothing, posture, tone of voice, attitude) foster safety?
- How do I locate my privilege and acknowledge my cultural locations in an attempt to foster safety?

I make my privilege and cultural connections known as part of structuring safety. I am Irish Catholic with ties to Newfoundland and England. It is important that I name my cultural locations because I am from settler cultures. Not locating myself is a threat to safety, as Indigenous survivors will probably assume I think that I'm just "normal" while they have a culture and need to be explained, or that I'm uninformed enough to think my locations of privilege do not matter.

Negotiating participation in the tribunals structures safety by slowing the retellings down so that survivors have agency about what is spoken or not spoken (Bird, 2006). This practice positions the conversation as something different than interrogation. These questions help the person consider their decision to participate in a residential school tribunal:

- What might be useful in your participation in this tribunal across time to you?
- What might be useful to your family, to your community?
- What might be the potential costs of participating in this tribunal?
- How might your participation in this tribunal get in the way of your participation with your family, with your community?

Continually negotiating permission can engender safety. This practice addresses the relational nature of permission, which is different than assuming permission is some*thing* that can be obtained through signing forms. It is important that people know that they can withdraw their participation in the tribunal process at any time, and that the therapist act in ways that would lend survivors confidence that there would be no consequences if they decide to withdraw. Foregrounded against a backdrop of political violence and state oppression, this permissioning of the survivor can be transformative.

Structuring safety in the context of residential school tribunals or any public retellings of the survivor's experiences requires planning useful responses to potential backlash. These questions help prepare responses to backlash:

- What are the possible risks of backlash for your speaking out?
- Given all of these risks, why might you still be willing to do this?

- What will it be like for you to have decided to do this painful thing if nothing happens from this but backlash? How are you going to respond to that?

- How might considering the risk of backlash now, before you agree to speak, invite you to think differently about participating in the tribunal?

- If you choose to speak, how can we strategize to respond to the backlash?

Safety is structured in conversations when therapists amplify their hearing of "no," and make space for the survivor to speak their "no":

- What ways of knowing yourself have you trusting that you will be able to say "no" to me if I ask something that is not okay?

- What will it take for you to be able to say "no" to me if I ask you a question that's not all right? (Reynolds, 2010b)

When we do recognize, make space for, and respond to the survivor's "no" we can inquire about what saying no says about the person's qualities and ways of being:

- What does your "no" say about our work together and about your ability to decide what's going to happen and not happen in our work together?

- Is there anything I'm doing, or anything I've done, that's got you saying "no"? Or is this you deciding where this work is going and how fast?

Negotiating telling and not-telling is collaboration in practice, and requires the therapist have a genuine desire to be informed and even directed in their work by the survivor. This practice and the following questions are informed by the supervisory work of narrative therapists Johnella Bird (2006) of New Zealand/Aotearoa and Michael White (2000) of Australia:

- As we're sitting here now and you are considering what you're going to tell me, I would like you to travel ahead in time until after this meeting and think about how you will be with the telling. How might you feel about the telling tomorrow? Might the telling of this get in the way of our counselling relationship? Might the not telling of this get in the way of our counselling relationship?

- As you're sitting here now, and considering what you're going to tell me, I'd like you to consider knowings you hold about yourself that let you trust that you can be the person to decide if there will be speaking or holding of your own counsel. What do you know about our relationship that might help you trust your right to tell or not tell? (Reynolds, 2010b)

As a practice of structuring safety I try to ensure that the therapeutic relationship can hold the person, can offer some containment for experiences of suffering, and not be experienced as retraumatizing for the survivor. This requires that we create relationships of dignity (Richardson & Wade, 2010) and respect, and that we can respond to suffering immediately and in useful ways.

Retelling details of torture, with no transformation or libratory negotiations of new meaning, can be retraumatizing for the survivor. For example, refugees who are torture survivors have to tell their whole torture story at hearings to gain refugee status in Canada. This allows torture's story of the person to be the only story required and witnessed. This is dangerous, not useful for the person to reexperience, but required for legal purposes. We need to resist these totalizing victim stories and ask for and participate in bringing forward and witnessing the person's resistance stories (Reynolds, 2010b; Wade, 1996). Whenever people are oppressed they resist, and giving voice, dignity, and respect to these stories of resistance are useful to the survivor in multiple ways. They offer an account of the person as intelligent, creative, and resourceful, and they contest seeing the person as an object of violence without autonomy or dignity (Richardson & Wade, 2008; Wade, 1997).

The government has an ethical obligation to provide on-going care for the people who come forward to participate in the tribunals. Therapists will need to know what other resources will be made available to participating survivors, including counselling and benefits, and have extensive knowledge of community oriented and culturally relevant resources.

As therapists, even after negotiating consent and after the person has agreed to the telling, we have an ethical obligation to plan for the actual and potential harms of these conversations, and have responses available:

- How can your body be useful to you in this telling? What do you feel, sense, that indicates that it is time to slow down, maybe stop, or take a break?

- What body experiences let you know you are okay-enough in the telling? That you can do this in a good-enough way?

- Would it be okay if I check in whenever my body's telling me to slow us down, maybe get out of our chairs and take a breath together?

Survivors require a safe-enough plan for every part of the process, in the conversation, the rest of the day, that night, tomorrow. These questions invite containment throughout the work:

- It is likely that these are going to be heartbreaking stories for you to tell. This will be difficult. We'll need a safe-enough plan for you, to hold you in the thinking and telling, and afterwards. I believe this, because other people who have participated in truth and reconciliation tribunals have taught me this.

- How will you care for yourself today and throughout our work together preparing for the tribunal?

- How can you invite collective care for you today, in the future and throughout the tribunal process?

- How are you going to be there for yourself in the days of the tribunal? I always anticipate the backlash, and it's not unlikely that, after speaking, there is going to be some thinking based on real actions of oppression you have suffered, that you are going to be punished for this. So how are we going to leave in an okay way and plan to be okay-enough for the rest of the day, after the tribunal?

Solidarity structures safety by contesting individualism, isolation and fear (Reynolds, 2010d). I invite survivors to think of who shoulders them up, who is alongside them in a good way in the work they're doing, who are their witnesses. I then invite survivors to people-the-room with these folks (Reynolds, 2011), and find creative and actual ways to invite people to be in solidarity with them as a practice of structuring safety.

The practice of peopling-the-room invites therapists and survivors to bring forward a spirit of solidarity by bringing these actual and imagined others to stand alongside us, for example in the tribunal proceedings. This practice aims to allow the person to be embraced with revolutionary love, reminded of their relationships of solidarity and dignity, and more able to be safe-enough in the retelling. These questions help residential school survivors people-the-room:

- Who do you want to be here alongside you physically throughout this work that you and I engage in? Who do you want at the tribunal? Why these people? How are these relationships useful to you in this difficult work?

- How are we going to people-the-room with your ancestors and your family, real people you would bring in, imagined others, to be your witnesses and shoulder you up?

- How can these allies serve to hold you up, remind you of who you are, and help keep you safe-enough in your telling?

- How are you going to hold on to those folks after the talk? How will their actual and imagined presence be useful to you?

- How might you negotiate their participation alongside you? How will you let them know what is expected and catch them up on their service to you?

Structuring safety requires that therapists resist getting caught up in compelling stories of pain and suffering. Questions informed by a naïve and intrusive curiosity pose great threats to safety. We can easily be seduced by the privileging idea that as therapists we have a right, and perhaps even a duty, to ask anything that captures our interest.

I aim to resist being seduced by oppression's story of the person, and instead engage with a helpful curiosity about the survivor's acts of resistance against the suffering and oppression. While I do not need all of the details of pain and abuse, I do need to know enough details so that the person's acts of resistance become apparent (Reynolds, 2010a; Wade, 1997). As Canadian response-based therapist Allan Wade (2008) says, much of the person's acts of resistance against oppression can be hidden by the ways in which therapists and other professionals talk. We ask questions that elicit accounts of the person's spontaneous, intelligent and prudent responses to the oppressions they are suffering.

I tell survivors that I need to know what they think I need to know, so that I can be of use. Sometimes the survivor wants a witnessing of all of their experiences, especially by a member of the dominant culture. I am willing to do this if it is useful to the person, but I also explore their sites of resistance. As therapists holding an ethic of justice-doing I believe we are required to enter any governmental process with a healthy suspicion alongside a believable hope. Some survivors may find the process meaningful and possibly healing. Again, it is patronizing, especially for settler therapists, to predict the outcomes of the tribunal, or its usefulness to survivors. These questions engender and amplify the survivor's relationship with hope:

- What is a possible believed-in-hope for what might come forward out of your participation in the tribunal?
- Who are the important witnesses you want your testimony to be heard by?
- Do you see any of this testimony work as acts of resistance against the political violence you experienced?

Survivors may choose to participate in the tribunal process for their own purposes, and may see this work as an act of resistance in itself. It is possible for survivors to experience respect, dignity, and being witnessed whether they participate in the tribunal, decline participation, or withdraw their testimony (Akinyela, 2004). If survivors decide to step out of the process they could say, "I was in it, and then I decided to have it stop." What does it mean for a survivor of political violence to be able to say, "I was in something not okay; I said 'no', and it stopped"? This gives a new map of the world that can be profoundly useful: survivors of torture have taught me this.

Structuring safety can guard against violations of peoples' dignity. Dignifying the people I serve is at the heart of my work. I might use these questions early on to structure safety and to build dignifying relationships:

- What do I need to understand in order to respect you, make space for you, and not transgress against you in our relationship?

- What do you hold sacred, close to your heart, that it would be useful and important for me to know?

Dignity can be afforded to people when they are given the power to define themselves (Bracho, 2000). As a practice of resisting replicating oppression in many forms, such as colonization, I ask people to self-identify how they wish to be located culturally. I ask everyone, including people I might read as from the dominant culture/white, what culture they belong to as a universal practice to resist the racism inherent in asking only non-white people about culture.

Structuring safety requires critical supervision which is ethically necessary in all therapeutic work and especially in the context of political violence. Therapists can also make use of reflexive questioning throughout their work, which can invite them to enact their ethics in therapeutic conversations. For example:

- How am I attending to power and accountability in this conversation with this person in this moment? How am I attending to the cultural differences between us in this work, and in this moment?

- How am I structuring safety and attending to negotiating permission in this moment-to-moment encounter?

In this work alongside residential school survivors it is imperative that therapists have cultural consultants who hold them to account (Waldegrave, 1990; Waldegrave & Tamasese, 1993) especially if the therapist is from settler culture, but also if the therapist is from a different Indigenous cultural group than the survivor. Practices of cultural accountability are required to address transgressions that replicate the oppressions of residential schools.

Therapists from the dominant settler culture must enter this work skeptically, critically, with great humility held alongside therapeutic competency, and with some welcome from Indigenous communities. They must hold solid competencies in structuring safety, and have access to excellent therapeutic supervision and structures in relation to cultural accountability. This cannot be overstated.

Reflections

Cathy: Through making space for naming violence and honouring the dignity of survivors in this consultation, I felt safety's presence. In our community work together, I have been moved by the tangibility of the safety you work to create. One example of this is when you create space for Indigenous people to talk, particularly when non-Indigenous people are taking time to tell others what life is like for Indigenous people or what we need. Vikki, what's the history of your engagement with structuring safety, and who are your teachers? Who influenced you to become mindful of being with respect and awareness as an ally?

Vikki: Survivors of torture and political violence are my real teachers, and I have learned about structuring safety off their backs. Teachings from my work in activist communities and new social movements over decades of fellowship are threaded throughout my work. I've also been informed by my extended family, my queer/refugee family-of-choice, Irish Catholic/English/Newfoundland culture, and most particularly my father's teachings on dignity.

These practices of structuring safety are centered within the context of work with survivors of the political violence of residential schools. However, risk is inherent in all of our therapy and community work across differences of power. My hope is that these particular learnings can be transferred into other contexts with an aim to promote structuring safety.

A Story of "People-ing-the-Room"

Cathy: I was invited to serve as a support person for a woman (a community leader) who agreed to participate in a residential school tribunal. It was to be held at a hotel in a B.C. city, far away from her home community. I felt honoured by the invitation and was mindful of the complexity of this event.

In beginning to choreograph some safety and ground of familiarity in this legalistic set up, I asked her the following questions:

- If you could make the space one where you felt comfortable, safe, supported
- and held by the ancestors, what would you do to the room?
- Who or what would you invite in?

She identified the people, both embodied and in spirit, that she would like to be there with her, sending her courage and love. We talked about the roles of her helpers and what each person would do. We talked about imagining the room the way she wanted it. This involved envisioning the particular kind of feeling, energy, colours and presence that would invite her to more safety. The day before, we both had lunch with her lawyer to get a picture of what the day would involve and to prepare ourselves and strategize for her optimum well-being.

On the day, we went to look at the room in advance. She brought a number of sacred objects to hold and to have in front of her during the strenuous interview process. She decided where she would sit and placed the little altar in front of her. We talked about the people who would be supporting her, before, during and after, and the particular roles they would have. This included laying the intention that particular people would be there in spirit to offer love and strength.

The hearing was difficult. Many of the questions were invasive and evoked hard memories, the kind of events people try to forget. She got a terrible headache. There was also a blanket in the room which at one point she used to cloak herself, for both protection and warmth. Uncomfortable feelings arose in response to the process. I wrapped the blanket around her shoulders. The inquiry lasted the whole day, with lawyers using their skill and diplomacy to elicit the kinds of answers that related in some way to the determination of compensation. Afterwards, we took a walk by the water, enjoyed the sunlight, the breeze and the trees in order to get some air and nurturance after sitting indoors all day in a sterile kind of surrounding. My companera saw an eagle fly overhead, which she received as a reminder from Creator that we are witnessed.

The following days were not easy as persistent and painful memories had been provoked in this hearing. She relied on the strength of prayer, family support and the knowledge of "what is right and good" to help her recover from the tribunal. The conviction that children should be treated with kindness can provoke many adults to such acts of bravery and courage.

Dedication

The survivors of torture and political violence we have worked alongside in various global communities and residential school survivors from the Indigenous territories of Canada are the heart of this work. This writing took place on Indigenous land which was never surrendered.

Acknowledgments

We raise our hands to Ann Maje-Raider, former chief of the Liard First Nation and Executive Director of the Liard Aboriginal Women's Society, and to the people who have "shouldered you up" over the years in the difficult work you have tackled so mightily. Spirited thanks to our heart colleagues Allan Wade and Linda Coates and to Johnella Bird for her moral courage and ever-unfolding teachings.

References

Aboriginal Affairs and Northern Development Canada. (2010). Backgrounder: Indian residential schools. Retrieved from http://www.ainc-inac.gc.ca/

Akinyela, M. (2004). Meeting the trickster at the crossroads: Oral cultures and the use of metaphor in therapeutic conversations. In S. Madigan (Ed.), *Therapeutic conversations 5: Therapy from the outside in* (pp. 111-122). Vancouver, BC: Yaletown Family Therapy.

Anderson, H. (1997). *Conversation, language, and possibilities: A postmodern approach to therapy*. New York: Basic Books.

Anderson, H., & Goolishan, H. (1992). The client is the expert: A not-knowing approach to therapy. In S. McNamee & K. Gergen (Eds.), *Therapy as social construction* (pp. 54-68). London: Sage.

Bird, J. (2000). *The heart's narrative: Therapy and navigating life's contradictions*. Auckland: Edge Press.

Bird, J. (2004). *Talk that sings: Therapy in a new linguistic key*. Auckland: Edge Press.

Bird, J. (2006). *Constructing the narrative in supervision*. Auckland: Edge Press.

Bracho, A. (2000). An institute of community participation. *Dulwich Centre Journal, 3*. Adelaide: Dulwich Publications.

Chrisjohn, R., & Young, S. 1997) *The circle game: Shadow and substance in the residential school experience in Canada*. Penticton, BC Theytus Books.

Coates, L., & Wade, A. (2009). "For this we are sorry": A brief review of Canada's most recent non apology to Aboriginal peoples. In *Under the Volcano Festival of Art and Social Change Program*. Vancouver, BC: Under The Volcano.

Department of Justice Canada. (2011). Indian Act (R.S.C., 1985, c. I-5). Retrieved from http://laws-lois.justice.gc.ca/eng/acts/I-5/

Feldthusen, B. (2007). Civil liability for sexual assault in Aboriginal residential schools: The baker did it. *Canadian Journal of Law and Society, 22*, 1, 61-91.

Harris, C. (2002). *Making native space: Colonialism, resistance, and reserves in British Columbia*. Vancouver: UBC Press.

Harris, C. (2004). How did colonialism dispossess? Comments from an edge of empire. *Annals of the Association of American Geographers, 94*(1), 165-192.

Leslie, J. (2002). Indian act: An historical perspective. *Canadian Parliamentary Review*.

Logan, T. (2001). *The lost generations: The silent Métis of the residential school system*. Winnipeg, MB: Southwest Region Manitoba Métis Federation.

Miller, J. R. (1996). *Shingwauk's vision: A history of Native residential schools*. Toronto: University of Toronto Press.

Regan, P. (2010). *Unsettling the settler within: Indian residential schools, truth telling, and reconciliation in Canada*. Vancouver: UBC Press.

Reynolds, V. (2009). Collective ethics as a path to resisting burnout. *Insights: The Clinical Counsellor's Magazine & News*. December, 6-7.

Reynolds, V. (2010a). *Doing justice as a path to sustainability in community work*. Retrieved from http://www.taosinstitute.net/

Reynolds, V. (2010b). Doing justice: A witnessing stance in therapeutic work alongside survivors of torture and political violence. In J. Raskin, S. Bridges, & R. Neimeyer (Eds.), *Studies in meaning 4: Constructivist perspectives on theory, practice, and social justice* (pp. 157-184). New York: Pace University Press.

Reynolds, V. (2010c). Fluid and imperfect ally positioning: Some gifts of queer theory. *Context: The magazine for family therapy and systems practice in the UK*, October, 13-17.

Reynolds, V. (2010d). A supervision of solidarity. *Canadian Journal of Counselling*, *44*(3), 246-257.

Reynolds, V. (2011). Supervision of solidarity practices: Solidarity teams and people-ing-the-room. *Context: The magazine for family therapy and systems practice in the UK*. August, 4-9.

Richardson, C., & Wade, A. (2008). Taking resistance seriously: A response-based approach to social work in cases of violence against Indigenous women. In S. Strega & J. Carriere (Eds.), *Walking this path together: Anti-racist and anti-oppressive child welfare practice*. Winnipeg, MB: Fernwood.

Richardson, C., & Wade, A. (2010). Islands of safety: Restoring dignity in violence-prevention work with Indigenous families. *First Peoples Child and Family Review*, *5*(1), 137-155.

Thomas, R. (2005). Honoring the oral traditions of my ancestors through storytelling. In L. Brown & S. Strega (Eds.), *Research as resistance: Critical, indigenous and anti- oppressive approaches*. Toronto: Canadian Scholars.237-254.

Truth and Reconciliation Commission of Canada. (2011). *The Truth and Reconciliation Commission of Canada: What will the TRC do?* Retrieved from http://www.trc.ca/

Wade, A. (1996). Resistance knowledges: Therapy with aboriginal persons who have experienced violence. In P.H. Stephenson, S.J. Elliott, L.T. Foster, & J. Harris (Eds.), *A persistent spirit: Towards understanding aboriginal health in British Columbia* (pp. 167-206). Canadian Western Geographical Series, 31.Victoria, BC: Western Geographical Press.

Wade, A. (1997). Small acts of living: Everyday resistance to violence and other forms of oppression. *Journal of Contemporary Family Therapy, 19*(I), 23-40.

Wade, A. (2000). Resistance to interpersonal violence: Implications for the practice of therapy. Unpublished doctoral dissertation, University of Victoria, British Columbia, Canada.

Wade, A. (2008). "Mind the Gap" Conference, Cowichan Bay, B.C.

Waldegrave, C. (1990). Just therapy. *Dulwich Centre Newsletter, 3,* 5-8.

Waldegrave, C., & Tamasese, K. (1993). Some central ideas in the "Just Therapy" approach. *Australian and New Zealand Journal of Family Therapy, 14*, 1-8.

White, M. (2000). Re-engaging with history: The absent but implicit. In M. White (Ed.), *Reflections on narrative practice: Essays and interviews.* Adelaide: Dulwich Centre Publications.

White, M. (2007). *Maps of narrative practice.* New York: Norton.

SEVEN

Hate Kills. A Social Justice Response to "Suicide"

This chapter originated as a keynote address delivered at the CASP (Canadian Association for Suicide Prevention) national conference. It comes from a social justice activist orientation that aims to respond to suicide from a broader context than psychology usually allows for. This work addresses resisting individualism, critically engaging with language, and relations of power. I consider political suicides and resistance in contexts of torture, armed and nonviolent struggle, and the resistance of political prisoners with an aim to problematize taken-for-granted ideas that any death named suicide happens in apolitical contexts. Responding to suicide from a social justice activist lens requires giving a wider context and making connections across different domains. I offer a practice example of how I respond to suicide with a supervision of solidarity and re-membering practices that aim to honour the person who has died and witness their resistance and teachings, as an alternative to supervision that aims primarily to guard practitioners against vicarious trauma. Finally I will reflect on some inspiring social responses to suicide from within networked activist communities.

An anti-oppression and decolonizing ethical stance and a social justice response to deaths languaged as suicide are the heart of this work (Reynolds, 2012). Engagement with social justice activism, and therapeutic and com- munity work, have taught me that hate kills (Richardson and Reynolds, 2012). Using the language of suicide masks the heart-rending suffering, daily indignities, and desolation many people struggle with. The language of suicide quiets our collective discomfort and provides a "cause" for these stolen lives, normalizing the social contexts of exclusion, stigma, and hate in which these horrid deaths occur. In this writing I aim to enact accountability for all the people I have lost to suicide, particularly gender and sexual di- verse and questioning youth who did not kill themselves but whose lives were stolen by hate. This is heartbreaking work. I respect that as activists and practitioners we can have broken hearts and continue to do this work. This orientation towards suicide is profoundly collaborative and informed by people and their families who have struggled and died by suicide. I have been informed by social justice movements, resistance against the death penalty, refugees and survivors of torture, rape crisis workers, and working alongside gender and sexual diverse people, and by all the therapists, com- munity workers, and teams that I "super"vise. All of my work and activism is grounded by my father's teachings on dignity and belonging, our extended and chosen family, and my Irish Catholic/Newfoundland/English culture. I am shouldered up by networked communities of social justice activism and hold an ethic of justice-doing in all of my paid and unpaid work (Reynolds, 2010a, 2010b).

Resisting Individualism and Attending to the Social Context

In *Suicide: Foucault, History, and Truth*, British scholar Ian Marsh provides a Foucauldian analysis that offers a groundbreaking framework for under-standing suicide on which my analysis is built. Marsh outlines the historical shift in understandings of suicide from issues of morality to issues of criminality through to the present construction of suicide as mental illness. Marsh argues that in our contemporary times, "an individualised, 'internalised,' pathologised, depoliticized and ultimately tragic form of suicide has come to be produced, with alternative interpretations of acts of self- accomplished death marginalised or foreclosed" (2010, p. 219).

A social justice perspective is in alignment with Marsh's invitation to resist the individualism of suicide. Suicide is not something that happens to one person, and it is not something that one person does. Nobody simply kills themselves. Events occur in context, and because we live in a society that has not delivered on the promises of social justice, which we are well qualified and able to deliver, we have to structure into our analysis of a person's death the context of social injustice in which they lived. I resist efforts to locate issues of social injustice inside the minds of clients, and I challenge dominant understandings that explain suicides as expressions of mental illness. While I do recognize the existence of mental illness and appreciate that not all suicides can be understood through the lens of social justice, at times we can replicate oppression by locating social justice issues inside the minds of people (Gergen, 1989). I believe that hate kills, and hate is not a metaphor (Richardson and Reynolds, 2012).

Canadian-born sociologist Erving Goffman (1963) connected stigma to oppressive practices that "other" people. Goffman argued that you have to attack to actively spoil identities. There is nothing wrong with a child until they find out they are not normal. Our children are born perfect: what is wrong is that we create structures of what is "normal." Categories are always organized by power (Crenshaw, 1995) and always exclude. Marginalized people are not "belonged," and are "othered" (Sampson, 1993). Remember when you went to school and found out you were different? I did not know that not everyone shared socks with their sisters – that everybody owned their own "stuff," and we were all supposed to be really invested in the idea of private possessions and ownership.

Critical Engagement with the Languaging of Suicide

When I talk about a critical engagement with language in relation to abuses of power, I am particularly informed by the work of Canadian response-based therapists Linda Coates and Allan Wade (2004, 2007). They have made unique theoretical contributions to understandings of people's responses to attacks on their dignity and safety that have important implications for work with people who have suffered violence. They outline these four operations of language:

1. obscuring violence,

2. hiding the victim's resistance to violence,

3. obscuring the perpetrator's responsibility, and

4. blaming the victim.

All four of these operations of language can also be seen in relation to survivors of torture and what gets called suicide:

1. When a survivor of torture dies by suicide, the violence of torture is obscured. What is revealed and investigated is the how depression, anxiety, or pills killed this person. The violence of torture is absent and disappeared. The language of suicide hides the victim's resistance to torture, which is politicalized violence. All of the people I work with survived torture, escaped from countries in which that occurred (unless they are survivors of Canadian residential schools), found me, and participated therapeutically with me. They fought full-on for their lives. Whenever people are oppressed, they resist, and the language of suicide lies about that (Reynolds, 2008, 2010a; Richardson and Wade, 2008). The fact that they lost that battle against torture speaks to the tyrannical power and inhumanity of their enemies; it does not reveal anything about them as the victims of torturers. The language of "committing suicide" hides the victims' resistance to violence and cannot fit within an anti-oppression stance.

2. The language of suicide also hides the perpetrators' responsibilities. When people who have survived torture lose their lives to what gets called suicide, they are held responsible for killing themselves. This exonerates the people who tortured them, the government that gave sanction to the torture and trained the torturers and ensured that they had political impunity – that they would not be held criminally responsible for murder. The corporations that funded governments to use political violence to make the country good for profit and for the neoliberal economics of exploitation are exonerated (Reynolds, 2010a). There are many people who are responsible for this killing, yet the language of suicide only blames this survivor of torture.

3. The language of suicide blames the victims of torture for their own murders. When someone "commits suicide," as in "committing a

crime," we can, as Goffman (1963) suggests, create a spoiled identity of a failed per- son. That conceptualization is dishonouring of the person. They did not kill themselves; I believe their lives were stolen. A social justice stance requires us to resist insidious practices of blaming the victims.

This understanding of the political operations of power is always part of my analysis of what gets called suicide. Here I am going to make visible the diverse but connected political contexts of the deaths that are called suicide in order to problematize how suicide passes for normal and masks social injustices and oppression.

Suicide and Resistance in Contexts of Political Violence

It is important to consider the specific contexts of political violence in which any suicide occurs. For example, when we look at Indigenous communities, where levels of what is called suicide are alarmingly high, we need to consider five hundred years of colonial occupation, that is, five hundred years of resistance, genocide, land theft, and residential schools – schools that had graveyards and provided very little education (Hill, 2010; Regan, 2010; Harris 2002, 2004; Miller, 1996). We must consider the ongoing apprehension of Indigenous children, a practice that persists because we have not committed to the social structures to keep families together – not because individual social workers are incompetent. We must consider Canada's hesitancy to sign the United Nations Declaration on the Rights of Indigenous Peoples.[1] When we use the language of suicide we construct not only Indigenous individuals as failed, but also their cultures and families (J. White, 2007). We must be critical about ideas and practices that keep us from looking at the wider contexts of injustice to understand things instead of inviting talk about the faulty interior of the minds of oppressed persons. Oppression does not happen to people in their minds, it happens in the world (Reynolds, 2010b).

What is discursively referred to as "political suicide" also needs to be problematized – for example, the death of Bobby Sands and the hunger strikes of Irish Catholic political prisoners against the British government in the 1980s. The purpose of those hunger strikes was to regain status as political prisoners, which the British government under Prime Minister Thatcher had rescinded, effectively criminalizing dissent. The hunger strike was used as a tactic because the political prisoners had no access to power. Thatcher refused to be influenced by the deaths of Sands and nine other political prisoners; even so, those deaths captured the world's attention, and Thatcher relented under international pressure. Constructing these deaths by hunger strike as suicide, issues of mental illness, and criminality misses entirely the mark of the prisoners' autonomy, courage, resistance, and intelligence. The language of suicide obscures the political situation in which these deaths occurred.

At the time of this writing, Attawapiskat Chief Theresa Spence is on day twenty-three of her hunger strike as part of the grassroots Indigenous movement "Idle No More" (Idle No More, n.d.). Her hunger strike is in resistance to Prime Minister Stephen Harper and the Canadian government's Bill C-45, which Idle No More activists say radically changes Indigenous rights and sovereignty and environmental protections for land and water, leaving Indigenous territories formerly protected by treaties open for destructive mining and capitalist exploitation. Spence's sole demand is that the prime minister meet with her, which he is refusing to do. On January 4, 2013, the *Vancouver Sun* (*Vancouver Sun,* 2013) ran an editorial titled "Attawapiskat Chief Is Wrong to Blackmail the PM." It began: "The threat of suicide is always ill advised or rooted in selfishness." Besides criminalizing protest as blackmail, the unnamed editor was declaring Spence's actions selfish, individualizing her while obscuring her participation with five hundred years of Indigenous resistance against colonization.

A heart-rending recent political development is the self-immolation of Tibetan activists. Almost one hundred monks and nuns "committed suicide" by setting themselves on fire in 2012. This is unprecedented historically and is a sign of how desperate people are in a country that has experienced genocide and widespread torture for over fifty years. The government of China is effectively wiping out the nation of Tibetans.

Desperate responses, such as political suicides, are escalating. Understanding these deaths as evidence of the mental illness of any of these people misses the political context in which their sacrifice occurs, obscures their activism, and effectively silences their dissent. A social justice stance requires us to resist understanding their deaths within the realm of psychology and mental illness, and instead situates these deaths in the political world in which genocide, occupation, and torture are happening.

An Eritrean refugee in Halifax killed himself after losing his case to stay in Canada (*Chronicle Herald*, 2010). Defining this person's death as suicide, depression, or anxiety totally obscures the context of his struggles. Other refugee claimants have died by suicide following the Canadian government's most recent repressive changes in refugee law and the massive increase in deportations of refugee claimants to countries where their lives are at risk (CBC, 2012). When questions about Canada's complicity in torture were asked of the federal government, the prime minister prorogued parliament in response, thereby suspending democracy (CBC, 2009). Saying that this refugee claimant committed suicide obscures the fact that he was at risk of being returned by Canada to a country where he would be tortured. Calling the death of any refugee at risk of return to torture a "suicide" mystifies the violence of the Canadian government and state, possibly obscuring a death that may be an act of resistance.

Rape culture (Buchwald, Fletcher, and Roth, 2004) describes a society that condones, promotes, and accepts sexual assault and a culture of violence (hooks, 2001). Canadians live in a rape culture in which one in three women is sexually assaulted in their lifetime and only 6 percent of these as- saults are reported (Johnson and Sacco, 1995). These statistics are not cur- rent because all of the funding for researching sexual violence for the National Action Committee on the Status of Women was cut following the publication of those findings and was never re-established. In the province of British Columbia, 100 percent of core funding for sexual assault centres was cut by the provincial government in 2002; a decade later, none of that funding has been returned. These examples of structural barriers that condone violence against women are alarming but not surprising to antiviolence workers. The UN estimates that globally, one in three women will be beaten, raped, or abused in their lifetime. Most often the perpetrator is a family member (UN Development Fund for Women, 2003). In naming misogyny, hate, and the murder of women, we need to consider the precarious lives of women with different access to power and safety. In Vancouver this means women in the Downtown Eastside (the poorest off-reserve part of Canada), women involved in survival sex work, and marginalized and racialized women. At WAVAW (Women Against Violence Against Women), a rape crisis centre where I serve as clinical supervisor, whenever a woman "commits suicide," we understand her death as connected to the violence of sexualized assault, heteropatriarchy, white supremacy, and poverty, and re- sist blaming her for either the rape she suffered or her death.

Resisting Medicalized Language

Much like the language of suicide, the languaging of "overdose" obscures violence, offering medicalized and sanitized reasons for death. I worked as an addictions supervisor in the Downtown Eastside, and I believe nobody simply dies of an overdose. Physiologically speaking, they do, but it is more complicated than that. Abuse and oppression happen to people in their lives, and when we use the language of overdose we obscure violence by invoking scientific, legal, and medical causes of death. Our question should be, "What is going on that people are dying here – that women's bodies are being found in dumpsters?" We cannot let words like suicide and overdose let us accept these as legitimate and normal causes of death.

"Natural causes" is also problematic from a social justice stance. Some doctors have told me about the spiritual pain they experience when they are required to use the language of natural causes to describe what I would call deaths by social injustice. When a thirty-eight-year-old woman doing survival sex work with no teeth, drug-addicted, HIV-positive, Hep C-positive, and homeless, dies of the common cold, it is not a natural death.

From the frame of social justice, this medicalized and bureaucratic language, while required for the structures we are in, obscures violence and ends our inquiry. Medicalized language also seduces us to abdicate our social and collective obligations to change the context in which these kinds of deaths occur – violence, poverty, and homelessness, none of which are natural. This can also direct all research and resources towards corporate medicalized responses to what are primarily social issues.

In the next section I show how this social justice–informed analysis of suicide informs my practice as a therapeutic supervisor responding to clients' deaths.

Responding to "Suicide" with Solidarity

As a therapeutic supervisor, I respond to suicide by engaging practices of social justice activism and solidarity, and bring practitioners together with an ethic of justice-doing. I never sit alone with suicide, torture, and terror. I am shouldered up by my Solidarity Team, the folks with whom I share collective ethics and whom I carry with me in a spirit of solidarity to help me do the hard things (Reynolds, 2011a, 2009). I envision the creation of networked communities (Lacey, 2005) that hold us together in nonhierarchical ways that defy individualism and are a step up against despair (Reynolds, 2011b). Social justice has brought an "ethic of belonging" (Richardson and Reynolds, 2012; Reynolds, 2002) to all of my work, paid and unpaid. I work towards a context of social justice in which everyone believes they are welcome on this planet. People who are "othered," whose identities get attached and spoiled, receive serious messages that they do not belong in this world. I have worked with men on the Downtown Eastside who have served twenty years in jail and survived it. They have hurt children and women. They come out of prison and are ostensibly seeing me about substance misuse, but mainly they are struggling with suicide. Many of these men feel they should enact the silent death sentence they believe society has put on them. My work resisting the death penalty has taught me that a person is so much more than the worst thing they have ever done (Reynolds, 2010a). We need to embrace an ethic of belonging that says everybody belongs in this world and in the human family: not just the good guys. We are required to create ways for men to be welcomed back into the culture of accountable men and to stop sectioning off who deserves to belong.

Activist communities' resistance to repressive governments that have murdered people in extrajudicial executions, and then have "disappeared" those victims, has inspired me. Activists and other organizers would disappear and there was no accountability for their murders. No bodies were returned to families, and there was no legal accountability for these killings. The purpose of political disappearance is to terrify and torture society as a whole so that people will not take acts for justice and overtly resist oppression. Political terror is a social project to paralyze communities and thwart active resistance (Martín-Baró, 1994). Activist communities resist these dis- appearances, remembering their dead loved ones openly, calling for political accountability. As activists we witness people who are disappeared to dignify that they were here, that they matter. Activist traditions of remembering the disappeared and not letting people who are killed by hate and political violence be silenced have had a profound influence in my work, particularly with regard to re-membering practices. I am inspired by teachings from narrative therapists (M. White, 2011, 2007; Madigan, 1997; Hedtke and Winslade, 2004[2]) informed by American anthropologist Barbara Myerhoff (1978, 1982), who wrote about the idea of people re-membering who they were in their lives, who they had been, and who they preferred to be, in what she called identity projects. I will offer an example of what this re-membering work can look like in practice.

Re-membering Practices and a "Supervision of Solidarity"

I supervise counsellors who work with sexual and gender diverse people. While people who are sexual and gender diverse differ in particular ways from people who are subjected to political violence, such as political prisoners, Indigenous people, and survivors of torture, there are important connections as well. People who are sexual and gender diverse are subjected to hate, homophobia, transphobia, and heteropatriarchy, and when they die by suicide I believe that hate has played a central role in their deaths. Recently, another of our clients died from suicide. I met with the therapist within a group as part of a supervision practice I call a Solidarity Group (Reynolds, 2010c). When I respond to suicide as a supervisor, I want to see our therapist within a community, not alone. I resist isolating and individuating a counsellor to help them "get over this suicide." We are not going to get over these deaths – that, I believe, is part of our resistance to oppression. We are not going to accommodate ourselves to tolerate deaths connected to hate, because we have ethical obligations to do something about the social con- text in which hate-related deaths occur.

When I met with this team, I interviewed the counsellor – I will call him Elliot – in front of the team. I did not start the interview with questions about how Elliot's client killed himself or how Elliot was affected. Instead I asked Elliot to introduce us all to this person, because we were meeting about a human being, not a "case." I used these questions:

- Teach me who Jonah was. What did you respect about Jonah? What did you appreciate about Jonah?

As a therapeutic supervisor with a social justice ethic, I could not move on and talk to Jonah's therapist about the disappearance of this person if I dis-appeared Jonah by not bringing him fully into the room as a human being.

- How did you honour Jonah's resistance to oppression and hate in his life?

This is very different than, "How did Jonah die?" Instead I would say, "Jonah resisted homophobia and hate, and attacks and gay bashing. How did you bring forward these sites of Jonah's resistance?"

This line of questioning is vital to our sustainability as workers:

- What difference might you have made in Jonah's life?

- When you think about it, here is a person who had been disappeared, killed by hate, not seen as a person, not seen as a human being.

- Did it matter that you actually witnessed who he was? That you talked about how he was treated as a youth? That you took a position on that and said it was wrong? Did it matter? What difference might you have made in Jonah's life in terms of dignifying him, treating him as a human being, treating him with respect?

As an act of accountability, and honouring our clients as our teachers, I asked:

- What difference did knowing Jonah, being a witness to his acts of resistance and his life, make for you? For your life and your work?

I have learned my work on the backs of my clients, and it is the people who have struggled with suicide and lost their lives to it that have informed me. They have offered the most useful teachings that I hold.

The last question is informed by activist practices of re-membering the disappeared:

- How will you keep what Jonah taught you alive in your life and work?

I always acknowledge my teachers: academics, activists, and clients. We reference our teachers as a practice of witnessing and resisting their disappearance, bringing to life the teachings of people who have taught us this work on their backs and to our benefit.

These are the kinds of questions I asked Elliot in front of a group of counsellors. I then interviewed all the witnessing counsellors. I asked them to connect with where they had lost people and where they connected with Elliot – that is, what resonated for them in the dialogue. Jonah was the person who died, Elliot was Jonah's counsellor, and Sara was one of the counsellors who witnessed Elliot's struggles. (These names are fictional, the accounts are not.)

Elliot's Reflection as the Interviewed Counsellor in the Solidarity Group

Our "Remembering Jonah" session today was healing for me as a counsellor and a person. It allowed me to value my work with Jonah in a human, "non-clinical" way. I was trained to examine my reaction to clients in order to provide effective and ethical service. However, none of my training has prepared me for the intense, sometimes overwhelming nature of working with a population of highly marginalized, oppressed clients struggling with mental health and addiction issues. I've often felt my work is a "drop in the bucket" of help and support clients need and deserve. The witnesses reminded me of how precious our relationships with clients can be, how dignity matters. Remembering Jonah's amazing strengths and his resistance against op- pression left me with an honouring view on his life, rather than focusing on the tragedy of the loss of such a beautiful person. Your questions about Jonah's gifts, what he taught me, combat my feelings of helplessness, and this session is going to help me in my work with all my clients.

The structure of the witnessing today (you interviewing me, then the others in the room, and then connecting back to me) allowed me to start feeling my emotions rather than holding on to the safety of numbness. As the supervisor, your transparency helped solidify how important it is to resist overediting our responses in the guise of being "professional." The witnesses shared their responses of pain in their lives and work, and this validated my struggle losing Jonah. The group helped quiet my inner overcritical voice.

On my jog home (more like a walk with a hop than a jog really ...) I saw Jonah's physical features in many people passing me by, and it was a very positive, spiritual experience.

Sara's Reflections as a Witnessing Counsellor in the Solidarity Group

The Solidarity Group Vikki led us in created a space to honour and remember a client in all his humanity. As I listened to Elliot talk about Jonah, I was aware how this stranger transitioned into a man with an identity, soul, and passion. I wished I had known Jonah. Vikki asked Elliot if there was a way that this client's life could enter into Elliot's work so that his death was not forgotten, which reminded me how important it is to honour the intimate knowledge we get from our clients.

My mind wandered to how I bring Brenda, who committed suicide last year, into my clinical practice by sharing what she taught me with clients to combat the blame-game of stigma they are labeled with.

When Vikki turned to me and asked what arose for me from this re-membering process I was overcome with emotion about how real the work we do is and how we as counsellors offer moments of truly seeing our clients for who they are and acknowledging their struggles. I was struck by the privilege of learning from clients and how it has shaped my life and shifted my values.

I was saddened that we did not make more room for Jonah to be in this society because of prejudice. The act of witnessing allowed me to safely question how I fight for marginalized populations and look for acts of resistance in the face of oppression and violence. It reminded [me] that it is okay to hold the faces I love and have lost in my mind in order to fuel and encourage my work.

Thanks Vikki and Elliot for being present and creating a sacred space of remembering for Jonah. I am grateful for the work you both engage in.

Sincerely,

Sara

The purpose of this Solidarity Group and re-membering practice is not to get an accurate account of the crisis, or to guard therapists against vicarious trauma. It is to bring the person who has died to the conversation, to honour their life and their teachings. Whenever I lose a client in any way, I ask myself:

- What difference might I have made in their life?

- What difference did they make in my life? My work?

- What is my commitment to bring their teaching to other clients? To keeping their teachings alive? To acknowledging them as my teacher?

- What is required of me as a citizen, as a social justice activist, to change society so there would have been more room for this person?

This re-membering work does not stop our hearts from breaking, but for me it stops the bleeding. I can continue to work with a broken heart, but I cannot be pumping blood. Doing this re-membering work in a Solidarity Group, in a networked community of others, fosters our collective sustainability and dignifies our client with a witnessing of their humanity.

Inspiring Community Responses to Suicide: "It Gets Better"

I am going to focus on the domain of sexual and gender diverse youth and suicide, not because they are the most oppressed group or the apex of some hierarchy of pain (Reynolds, 2010a), but because there are inspiring and fabulous social justice–informed responses to suicide that merit celebration in these communities. Lesbian, gay, and bisexual youth are twice as likely to think about suicide as heterosexual youth and three times as likely to at- tempt suicide (Silenzio, Pena, Duberstein, Cerel, and Knox, 2007). A staggering statistic is that 41 percent of transgender persons have attempted suicide (National Center for Transgender Equality, 2010). These statistics are most likely underestimates because transgender people who die by suicide are not always recognized and obviously cannot participate in this re- search. This is a devastating situation for our communities. In response to these deaths, American gay author/activist Dan Savage (2010) made a YouTube video called "It Gets Better." Savage does not claim that life will be perfect, but says "try to stick around through this, because *my* life got bet-ter." Hundreds of thousands of people have made It Gets Better videos as part of a collective social media response to hate and suicide.

Youth are not killing themselves. Hate is killing our children. Savage says that "LGBT youth can't picture a future with enough joy in it to compensate for the suffering they're in now." The purpose of the It Gets Better videos is for youth to hear people who reflect who they are, saying "my life is okay." Youth who are sexual and gender diverse and questioning are told, "You're going to be kicked out of your church, you're going to be kicked out of your home, you're never going to have love, you're never going to belong, and you're never going to have a decent life." These folks are sending counter- messages that offer youth images of people who are reflecting their identities, saying we have decent, okay-enough lives.

According to Savage, "the culture says they're ours to torture 'til they're 18, and then they can move to New York City." Youth who survive high school can go to San Francisco, or Vancouver, where they might find some safety, or possible safety. This is the old deal. If you survive as a youth and live to adulthood, that is okay, but you cannot talk to sexual and gender diverse youth. Adults who are sexual and gender diverse cannot talk to children. When they do, heterosexual people like me accuse them of pedophilia, or of recruiting sexually. As a straight person, I can mentor children and people do not think I am trying to have sex with them or trying to make them straight. Social networks and social media mean that Dan Savage does not have to go to a playground to talk to a twelve-year-old. He can put a video up on a website – an act that breaks the old rules and unsettles heteronormative power. But Dan is also calling, as is the whole movement, for us to call events assault when they are assault and to use the legal implements we have to do something about what gets called bullying, the violence of hate.

There is a long history of resistance if we look deeper. One of my heroes, the American transgender author/activist Kate Bornstein (1994), has been especially influential by writing a book called *Gender Outlaw*. She also wrote a book called *101 Alternatives to Suicide for Teens, Freaks, and Other Outlaws* (Bornstein, 2006). The back cover reads: "It gets better." So there are histories of these ideas, just as there are histories of resistance in every domain of oppression. In British Columbia we have an Out in Schools program in which students create antihomophobic videos, because youth videos reaching other youth are effective. Anti-Bullying Day and Pink Shirt Day came from two youth allies in Nova Scotia in response to homophobic-informed bullying at their school (CBC, 2007). We also have the Trevor Project (n.d.), antibullying flash mobs, and multiple examples of communities picking up this inspiring, hope-filled resistance work.

These beautiful and spirited community responses that resist hate and suicide with love and inclusion embody the social divine (Lacey, 2005). The social divine encompasses moments when we are connected, profoundly belonged, and engaged with an ethic of justice-doing. The social divine is present in the profound, sad, and hopeful resistance we engage in collectively to transform an unjust society, where we hold one another up collectively and take action where our government and society have failed. It is hopeful, and spirited, and it demands ongoing commitments for change.

Contesting Simplistic Constructions of "Bullying"

The language of "bullying" decontextualizes and depoliticizes hate and violence and obscures the patriarchy and homophobia that inform bullying. The language of "bullying" individuates events and puts the responsibility for a hateful society on particular young boys and girls. I believe that unjustly spoils the identity of youth who perpetrate bullying. These youth did not invent these ideas. I have worked with youth who have spoiled identities as bullies. They are "othered" too. We can legitimately deny them education and belonging. We are placing the contexts of hate and the responsibility for injustice on the backs of our children and blaming them for these deaths. I am not saying that people are not responsible for their behaviour, but a social justice frame requires us to always examine the social context to understand events.

A newspaper covering the death of a young boy claimed that teasing at school was to blame for his suicide. There are two things wrong with this kind of reporting. First, it constructs as mentally unstable the young boy who died. "Teasing" is neutral and misleading language for the violence of hate. Suicide as a response to teasing is out of proportion. This languaging constructs this youth's identity as mentally unstable, again locating the problem of hate in the mind of the oppressed. Second, reporters name particular boys who bullied him as the reason he died. That is profoundly un- just. Many of us failed this child. All of us who did not transform this society failed this person, not a few youth. I am not saying they are not responsible for their actions; I *am* saying they are not responsible for being socialized to hate. That may seem like a strange position for a feminist to take, but as bell hooks says, "feminism is for everybody" (2001).

Conclusion

I worked with a young woman from Guatemala over twenty years ago who struggled with suicide and substance misuse. She had been told she would be in psychotherapy for the rest of her life given the extent of the political violence she had suffered. She thought I was a pretty good therapist. Eventually, this young survivor grew frustrated with other professional helpers and foster parents telling her she should stay alone, study, and journal. She resisted this professional advice and participated in the Theatre of the Oppressed with fifty other refugee youths, some of them children and grandchildren of the disappeared, who create political theatre together in Spanish. I asked a question from Australian narrative therapist Michael White: "You've said our sessions are pretty good. How many sessions do you think one political activity was worth?" She reflected a bit and said tentatively, "Probably over a hundred." I hold this humbling teaching close: a spirited activist event can be worth a hundred therapy sessions.

We have power. Many helping professionals try to mitigate or equalize power in their work with people. I invite us to embrace our power and be accountable to it. I believe we have an obligation to contest neutrality. We are not neutral about hate. We have the power to move things from private pain to public issue (Tamasese, 2001; McCarthy, 2001; Hanisch, 1970) and to resist the privatization of the pain of suicide. As change agents, I believe we need to "belong" people who have been told by hate that they do not belong on this earth, and we need to participate in delivering justice to them and to all of us. Resisting hate, practising solidarity, and transforming society to be inclusive and just is suicide prevention in its most radical form because social injustice, hate, stigma, and oppression create the conditions that make the horrors of suicide possible.

Dedication

For all the people we have lost to hate and for everyone picking up the hard and necessary work to "belong" all of our children within the human family; most especially Wendy Wittmack and the good people who have served Peak House across twenty-five years.

This writing took place on Indigenous territories that were never surrendered.

Acknowledgments

This chapter is framed from a keynote delivered in October 2011 at the CASP National Conference, "New Conversations on Suicidality." In this keynote I was shouldered up by the important and hard, possibly risky work of others, especially Jonny Morris and Jennifer White. Great appreciation to the CASP conference committee. Respectful thanks to Jonah, Elliot, and Sara, all of whom are real people whose names have been changed. I would like to thank Susan Dermarkar, Lorraine Hedtke, David Newman, Aaron Munro, Colin Sanders, and Jennifer White for generous and helpful readings of this text.

Notes

1. The United Nations Declaration on the Rights of Indigenous Peoples (UNDRIP) is a nonbinding document that recognizes Indigenous people's basic human rights and rights to self-determination, language, equality, and land. It was adopted by the General Assembly of the UN in September 2007. To our shame, Canada, Australia, New Zealand, and the United States were the only four countries to vote against it. In 2010, Canada endorsed it (CBC, 2010).

2. Also see American narrative therapist Lorraine Hedke's excellent website, which outlines these ideas and practices: www.rememberingpractices.com

References

Bornstein, K. (1994). *Gender outlaw: On men, women and the rest of us*. New York: Routledge.

Bornstein, K. (2006). *101 alternatives to suicide for teens, freaks, and other outlaws*. New York: Seven Stories Press.

Buchwald, E., Fletcher, P., and Roth, M. (Eds.). (2004). *Transforming a rape culture* (Rev. ed.). Minneapolis: Milkwood Editions.

CBC. (2007, June 18) Bullied student tickled pink by schoolmates' T-shirt campaign. http://www.cbc.ca/news/canada/bullied-student-tickled-pink-by-schoolmates-t-shirt-campaign-1.682221

CBC. (2009, December 30). PM shuts down Parliament. http://www.cbc.ca/news/politics/pm-shuts-down-parliament-until-march-1.829800

CBC. (2010, November 12). Canada endorses indigenous rights declaration. http:// www.cbc.ca/news/canada/canada-endorses-indigenous-rights-declaration- 1.964779

CBC. (2012, August 17). Refugee health at risk with cuts experts warn. http://www.cbc. ca/news/politics/refugee-mental-health-at-risk-with-cuts-experts-warn-1.1202134

Chronicle Herald. (2010, March 14). Asylum appeal ends in death. http://oppen heimer.mcgill.ca/Asylum-appeal-ends-in-death

Coates, L., and Wade, A. (2004). Telling it like it isn't: Obscuring perpetrator responsibility for violence. *Discourse and Society, 15*(5), 499–526. http://doi.org/10.1177/0957926504045031

Coates, L., and Wade, A.. (2007). Language and violence: Analysis of four discursive operations. *Journal of Family Violence, 22*(7), 511–22. http://doi.org/10.1007/s10896-007-9082-2

Crenshaw, K. (1995). Mapping the margins: Intersectionality, identity politics, and violence against women of colour. In K. Crenshaw, G. Gotanda, G. Peller, and

K. Thomas (Eds.), *Critical race theory: The key writings that formed the movement* (357–83). New York: The New Press.

Gergen, K. (1989). The possibility of psychological knowledge: A hermeneutic inquiry. In R. Addison and J. Parker (Eds.), *Entering the circle: Hermeneutic inquiry in psychology* (pp. 239–58). Albany: State University of New York Press.

Goffman, E. (1963). *Stigma: Notes on the management of spoiled identity.* Englewood Cliffs, NJ: Prentice Hall.

Hanisch, C. (1970). The personal is political. In S. Firestone and A. Koedt (Eds.), *Notes from the second year: Women's liberation, major writings of the radical feminists* (76–77). New York: Radical Feminism.

Harris, C. (2002). *Making native space: Colonialism, resistance, and reserves in British Columbia.* Vancouver, BC: UBC Press.

Harris, C. (2004). How did colonialism dispossess? Comments from an edge of empire. *Annals of the Association of American Geographers, 94*(1), 165–82. http://doi.org/10.1111/j.1467-8306.2004.09401009.x

Hedtke, L., and Winslade, J. (2004). *Re-membering lives: Conversations with the dying and the bereaved.* Amityville, NY: Baywood. http://doi.org/10.2190/RLC

Hill, G. (2010). *500 years of resistance.* Vancouver, BC: Arsenal Pulp Press.

hooks, b. (2001). *Feminism is for everybody: Passionate politics.* Cambridge, MA: South End Press.

Idle No More (n.d.). idlenomore1.blogspot.ca/p/blog-page_11.html

Johnson, H., and Sacco, V. (1995). Researching violence against women: Statistics Canada's national study. *Canadian Journal of Criminology, 37*, 281–304.

Lacey, A. (2005). Spaces of justice: The social divine of global anti-capital activists' sites of resistance. *CRSA/RCSA, 42*(4), 407.

Madigan, S. (1997). Re-considering memory: Remembering lost identities back towards re-membered selves. In D. Nylund and C. Smith (Eds.), *Narrative therapies with children and adolescents* (338–55). New York: Guilford Press.

Marsh, I. (2010). *Suicide: Foucault, history, and truth*. Cambridge: Cambridge University Press.

Martín-Baró, I. (1994). *Writings for a liberation psychology*. Cambridge, MA: Harvard University Press.

McCarthy, I. (2001). Fifth province re-versings: The social construction of women lone parents' inequality and poverty. *Journal of Family Therapy, 23*(3), 253–77. http://doi.org/10.1111/1467-6427.00183

Miller, J.R. (1996). *Shingwauk's vision: A history of Native residential schools*.

Toronto, ON: University of Toronto Press.

Myerhoff, B. (1978). *Number our days*. New York: Simon and Schuster.

Myerhoff, B. (1982). Life history among the elderly: Performance, visibility, and remembering. In J. Ruby (Ed.), *A crack in the mirror: Reflexive perspectives in anthropology* (99–117). Philadelphia: University of Pennsylvania Press.

National Center for Transgender Equality (2010). *Preventing transgender suicide*. http://www.transcentralpa.org/

Regan, P. (2010). *Unsettling the settler within: Indian residential schools, truth telling, and reconciliation in Canada*. Vancouver, BC: University of British Columbia Press.

Reynolds, V. (2002). Weaving threads of belonging: Cultural witnessing groups. *Journal of Child and Youth Care, 15*(3), 89–105.

Reynolds, V. (2008). An ethic of resistance: Frontline worker as activist. *Women Making Waves, 19*(1), 5.

Reynolds, V. (2009). Collective ethics as a path to resisting burnout. *Insights: The Clinical Counsellor's Magazine and News,* (December), 6–7.

Reynolds, V. (2010a). Doing justice: A witnessing stance in therapeutic work alongside survivors of torture and political violence. In J.D. Raskin, S.K. Bridges, and R.A. Neimeyer (Eds.), *Studies in meaning 4: Constructivist perspectives on theory, practice, and social justice* (157–84). New York: Pace University Press.

Reynolds, V. (2010b). Doing justice as a path to sustainability in community work. PhD dissertation., Universiteit van Tilburg.

Reynolds, V. (2010c). A supervision of solidarity. *Canadian Journal of Counselling,* *44*(3), 246–57.

Reynolds, V. (2011a). Supervision of solidarity practices: Solidarity teams and people-ing-the-room. *Context, 116,* 4–7.

Reynolds, V. (2011b). Resisting burnout with justice-doing. *International Journal of Narrative Therapy and Community Work, 4,* 27–45.

Reynolds, V. (2012). An ethical stance for justice-doing for community and therapeutic work. *Journal of Systemic Therapies, 31*(4), 18–33. http://doi.org/10.1521/ jsyt.2012.31.4.18

Richardson, C., and Reynolds, V. (2012). "Here we are amazingly alive": Holding our- selves together with an ethic of social justice in community work. *International Journal of Child, Youth, and Family Studies, 1,* 1–19.

Richardson, C., and Wade, A. (2008). Taking resistance seriously: A response-based approach to social work in cases of violence against Indigenous women. In S. Strega and J. Carriere (Eds.), *Walking this path together: Anti-racist and anti-oppressive child welfare practice* (204–11). Winnipeg, MB: Fernwood.

Sampson, E. (1993). *Celebrating the other: A dialogic account of human nature.* San Francisco, CA: Westview Press.

Savage, D. (2010). *It gets better: Dan and Terry.* https://youtu.be/7IcVyvg2Qlo?feature=shared

Silenzio, V.M., Pena, J.B., Duberstein, P.R., Cerel, J., and Knox, K.L. (2007). Sexual orientation and risk factors for suicidal ideation and suicide attempts among adolescents and young adults. *American Journal of Public Health, 97*(11), 2017–19. http://doi.org/10.2105/AJPH.2006.095943

Tamasese, K. (2001). Talking about culture and gender. In C. White (Ed.), *Working with the stories of women's lives* (15–22). Adelaide, South Australia: Dulwich Centre.

Trevor Project (n.d.). *Preventing suicide among LGBTQ youth: The Trevor Project.* http://www.thetrevorproject.org/

UN Development Fund for Women (2003). *Not a minute more: Ending violence against women.* http://reliefweb.int/report/world/not-minute-more-ending-violence-against-women

Vancouver Sun. (2013). Attawapiskat chief is wrong to blackmail the PM. [Editorial]. *Vancouver Sun,* January 4, A14.

White, J. (2007). Working in the midst of ideological and cultural differences: Critically reflecting on youth suicide prevention in Indigenous communities. *Canadian Journal of Counselling, 41*(4), 213–27.

White, M. (2007). *Maps of narrative practice*. New York: W.W. Norton.

White, M. (2011). *Narrative practice: Continuing the conversation*. New York: W.W. Norton.

EIGHT

The Problem's Not Depression, it's Oppression

I believe what gets understood as mental illness is directed more by pharmaceutical corporations, capitalism, colonization, homo/trans/queer phobia, sexism and racism than by real concern for human suffering. I think its way more accurate to think about people who struggle against exploitation and domination as being *oppressed* not *depressed*. People need justice, not just medication. The problem is not in our minds, our brains, or our neurons, but in the world where privileged people abuse power and destroy lives, Mother Earth, and communities for greed.

Being an activist, acknowledging the suffering of others, unmasking your own privilege, holding a critical analysis of the points of your own oppression and power: All of these things can lead to stuff that looks like Depression. We can start to think we might be crazy (depressed, angry, obsessive, defiant, maladapted...) Hopelessness can make us think we can't do anything about injustice. Political awareness can be paralyzing, overwhelming, and spiritually painful.

Individualism makes us think we're alone, that no one thinks like us.

Our resistance to this political violence, degradation, heartbreak, and terror is to hold each other in sacred and revolutionary love, and to work for justice: that's what solidarity is. Solidarity is belonging. You just need to figure out the best use of you, trust that you will find your people, and work in solidarity with others.

In direct actions, like the homelessness march, I experience the social divine. Belonging with others who struggle and thirst for justice is my solidarity/my spirituality. Activism is my little sanity-making project, my resistance against depression. Activism is not a sign of mental illness, but mental wellness. Survivors of torture have told me a spirited political protest is worth 100 therapy sessions! Happiness is overrated: Social Justice is underrated.

We're not crazy, another world *is* possible. I'm not immature or crazy because I'm 50 and don't own a house, TV, or a car. It's not that I'm idealistic, foolish, or stupid-I mean I have a PhD, a life-partner and (share) a dog. It's that I don't want to participate in consumerism with all of my life. Environmental destruction is suicidal, greed is crazy, and I believe that willfully exploiting the lives of other human beings around the planet is a sign of mental illness. Don't let anybody tell you that because you're heart-broken about the indignities and suffering of most of the world's people you're crazy-that you should go shopping and be happy.

No justice No peace- No peace of mind. A socially just world is a mentally well world. Actions for justice are acts of sanity.

NINE

Resisting and transforming rape culture: An activist stance for therapeutic work with men who have used violence

Introduction

This writing is an attempt to bridge a stance for social justice activism that aims to resist, dismantle and transform rape culture (Buchwald et al, 2004) that exists within a wider culture of violence (hooks, 1984, 2000) and therapeutic work with men who have used violence. This approach to resisting and transforming rape culture requires an ethical stance for justice-doing shouldered up by feminism, anti-oppression analysis and decolonizing practice (Reynolds & polanco, 2012; Reynolds & Hammoud-Beckett, 2012). As therapists and community workers our work with men who use violence happens within the context of rape culture. Working with individual men who perpetrate rape, sexualized violence, and other forms of violence, not unlike working with individual women who have survived rape, does not necessarily take up the social project of transforming rape culture. If work is centered in social change as opposed to only delivering necessary social service (Kivel, 2007) it does not accommodate women to rape culture, only mend individual women, or hold individual man accountable for systemic contexts of violence. Men who use violence are individually responsible for their actions, but not solely responsible for being in rape culture within a broader culture of violence. In this writing I will address the tension of holding the dignity and safety of women and children at the centre when working to hold men responsible for their violence, but also maintaining the dignity and humanity of these men. Our systemic analysis embraces this accountability alongside a collective accountability to resist and transform rape culture. This work requires solid feminist informed supervision and accountability to the victims of men's violence. Work with men who have used violence and work with the women victimized by men's violence do not have to be in competition, as all of us can collectively resist and work to transform rape culture.

An ethical stance for the work: Feminism, decolonization and anti-oppression

A stance for justice-doing positions therapists to respond to our work as activists and to work for socially just structural change alongside our work responding to the suffering of individual clients. This requires critical resistance against neutrality and objectivity (Cushman, 1995) within the helping professions. In work connected to sexualized violence this means resisting and transforming rape culture as part of our ethical stance as practitioners.

I come to this work resisting the violence of men shouldered up by feminism that attends to the intersections of power: Feminist analysis that questions not only patriarchy, but the systemic and structural ways women are marginalized and victimized, addressing the domains of racism, class, religion, colonization, immigration status, sexual orientation, ableism and the myriad ways women are oppressed differentially.

As activists enacting decolonizing practice (Akinyela, 2002; Razack, 2002; Walia, 2012) we begin with accountability to the Indigenous people of the territories we live and work in for all of our organizing. As a white settler, while I am addressing work with men who use violence, I want to respond accountably to colonization and to the traditional people of the land.

I will use the language of men and women to talk about the impact of men's violence in order to have less complicated writing and because I do not want to obscure men's responsibility for men's violence. But I acknowledge and wish the reader to keep in mind that binary understandings of gender that name only men and women erase (Namaste, 2000) and disappear the experiences and lives of people who are transgender and gender variant.

Rape culture

Naming rape culture is not an attempt to be provocative or emotional, but an act of making power transparent and naming violence without euphemisms and minimizing language. Rape culture refers to the normalization of sexualized violence and systemic practices of blaming the victims, particularly women, for being raped (Prochuk, 2014).

I name rape culture because one of three women in Canada will be sexually assaulted in their lives (National Status of Women, 1993). In Canada 6 to 8 % of rape is reported (Statistics Canada, 1993). Forty percent of those reports get charge approval. Two thirds of the 40% go to court, 1.8% of those cases end in conviction, and 0.8% of convicted perpetrators get jail time.

According to the United Nations (2010), "The percentage of women experiencing sexual violence at least once in their lifetime ranges from around 4 per cent in Azerbaijan, 5 per cent in France and 6 per cent in the Philippines, to a quarter or more women in Switzerland (25 per cent), Denmark (28 per cent), Australia (34 per cent), the Czech Republic (35 per cent), Costa Rica (41 per cent) and Mexico (44 per cent)" (pg 13).

There is great debate over these numbers, which purposefully obscures the point. The very real threat of rape and other forms of men's violence serve to control women, and that is not measured by these statistics. This is true despite the fact that women are not victimized and oppressed in the same ways, as many women, including minoritized, marginalized, racialized, disabled, transgender and poor women are at greater risk of violence because of structural oppression. (I use terms 'minoritized', 'marginalized' and 'racialized' for the purpose of naming the power and intention required in the racist and colonial project of re-constructing the majority of the world's people as a collection of minorities). When a man puts his fist through a wall and demands obedience from his family he does not need to hit them. That is violence, but it is not measured or responded to by the state.

American psychiatrist Judith Herman's (1992) writing presents a necessary foundation for most work with psychological trauma. Herman says sexual assault is so prevalent it should not be considered deviant behaviour, but may be more understandable as compliant behaviour. Cloe Madanes (et al,1995), an Argentinean-American strategic therapist, believes that the greatest social issue facing society is the violence of men, in its systemic forms, including what hooks (1984, 2000) calls the culture of violence.

As a society, we ask women why they do not report rape, why they do not speak out, why they do not leave men who are abusive. We are asking questions of the wrong people. Many police forces have published public awareness campaigns on how the potential victims of rape need to behave, shouldering women with the responsibility to not be raped. A poster from the Sussex Police in the UK (Sussex Police, 2011) is entitled "Be smart". "Say no to any sex you do not want" and "Make yourself clearly understood". What has that got to do with rape? Rape and sex are entirely different domains, one is in a consensual intimate domain, one is an act of violence where one person acts violently upon another person because they have the power to do so. When women are told to "say no to any sex you don't want" by the police force in a poster against rape it reveals that systemically the police force cannot or does not want to tell the difference between sex and rape.

Police forces and their consultants are silent on advice to men. Happily, feminists have advice for men. In a poster entitled "Stop rape: 10 top tips to end rape" (Rape Crisis Scotland, 2011) feminists offer an activist inversion of language as resistance. "If you pull over to help a woman whose car has broken down, remember not to rape her." "Use the buddy system. If you're not able to stop yourself from sexually assaulting someone, ask a friend to stay with you when you are in public". Offering parallel advice to men seems ludicrous and patronizing, possibly insulting, and an attack on the culture of accountable men. This fits with what Judith Butler (1997) calls "unspeakable acts." Women do not tell men how to act. But police campaigns saying exactly the same things to women somehow passes. There are no ten tips to men because a rape culture places the responsibility entirely on woman to not get raped. Rape culture teaches 'don't get raped', not 'don't rape', and that feminism is the 'F' word (The 'F' Word Media Collective, 2014).

According to Canadian response-based therapists Linda Coates and Allan Wade (2004, 2007), language can: obscure violence, hide the victim's resistance to violence, hide the perpetrator's responsibilities, and blame victims for violence. If we consider Coates and Wade's four operations of language, we can see how the discourses of rape and sexualized violence invisiblize and disappear the resistance of the victim, as well as obscuring the existence of violence, such as naming rape as making love or sex. The man is often not even in the retelling of the events, as if a woman is raped, yet no man committed the act. Blaming women for being raped is common place and silences many women from naming the events or their attackers. Language is used in relation to men's violence in ways that conflate sex and rape, which is a project of feminist activism that we had hoped we had won.

Legal discourse still investigates whether or not women fight back, collapsing the absence of violent struggle with consent. This erases and disappears the woman's resistance to rape. Every woman, child, man, or transgender person who is raped fights back 100 percent. Resistance is always present when there is oppression and people's resistance is tethered to their access to power. (Wade, 1997; Reynolds, 2010). When a man has a knife at your throat and says "don't scream" and you prudently stay silent it is an act of resistance for your life. It is not *not* fighting back and it is not consent.

Many activists working to dismantle rape culture believe that legal systems cannot deliver safety from rape. The present options from the legal system in responding to sexualized violence are flawed, but they are what we have to work with as we struggle for more just options. Locking individual men up does not dismantle rape culture or deliver safety to women. I do not feel safe because men who are poor, colonized, and marginalized are getting locked up. What that does is violate the dignity and humanity of another man, and that can be dangerous for women, transgender people and other men who have less access to power. Many of the men I work with have been in jail for extensive lengths of time and have been subjected to institutionalization. We are not looking solely to legal systems that American transgender activist Spade (2011) says were "formed by and exist to perpetuate capitalism, white supremacy, settler colonialism, and heteropatriarchy" (pp. 15–16) to resist and transform rape culture. We are looking to each other as women, to accountable men and transgender and gender variant people in community.

"Feminism is for everybody"

bell hooks (2000) a radical black educator from the United States teaches that "feminism is for everybody", women, men, transgender and gender variant people.

I do not see working with women who have survived men's violence and working with men who perpetrate violence against women as a conflict. Despite important differences in some ways it is the same work. I do experience an ethical tension in terms of holding myself accountable in all of my work to the women and children who have suffered men's violence. The collective goal in all facets of this work is to resist, dismantle and transform a rape culture: To have a society where everybody is safe and dignified.

What makes it possible for me to work with men who have used violence?

The culture of accountable men

I believe in the culture of accountable men, meaning that I believe that men can and do choose to be accountable for their particular access to men's power and privilege based on their intersectional identity and sites of both advantage and oppression. I hold the family privilege of being connected to not perfect men but good men, and men who can hold each other to account and men who have made some amends. My father, brothers, and brothers-in-law are committed fathers, my nephews are decent and kind young men, and this amplifies my hope that men can be accountable. This extended family of accountable men and loving strong women is a privilege that resources me. This belief in and experiences of the culture of accountable men shoulders me up in engaging ethically and effectively in work with men who use violence.

Lessons from Death Row

What makes it possible for me to work with men who have been violent is the activism I engaged in against the death penalty in the United States long before I was a therapist. I became involved in work against the death penalty in the United States because when nation states kill their own citizens, they can (and do) kill the innocent, as well as criminalize and execute political opponents and activists. What I learned about men on death row is that people are so much more than the worst thing they have ever done (Reynolds, 2010). Men on death row are not murderers. They are men who murdered someone. They are third base players. They are someone's father. They are somebody's son. They might be guitar players. They are poets. Sometimes they are innocent men, sometimes they are guilty men but they are human beings and there is so much more to a human being than the one act that we use to define who they are. Every man I worked for on death row in the United States was executed. Several of them were innocent.

The United States government has executed innocent people and released many innocent people from death row before their executions, sometimes after 20 years of imprisonment (Cohen, 2012). One of those men was Roger Coleman, who was executed almost twenty years ago. Coleman had committed rape as a young man and served a prison sentence. The fact that he was guilty of rape was used to construct his identity as a monster. In order for a democracy to kill its people you have to construct them as less than human and this is why we must resist using language that calls people 'pedophiles' or 'murderers' or 'rapists' and creates an identity construction of a man as inhuman. This props up the death penalty and the use of violence by the state so we have to take it apart on every level to resist participating in state killings and the culture of violence. The fact that Coleman had been seen as a rapist, constructed as a monster and dehumanized is what made it possible for the state to kill him, despite the fact the state acknowledged he was innocent. One of the things I still shake about is the fact that the state and the prison industrial complex co-opted our resistance against rape to kill this innocent man in the name of women's safety. That is not what feminism wants. That does not serve justice.

We must be careful and critical of how our well intentioned activism may possibly be used to justify and strengthen the structures that we oppose (Smith, 2006; Spade, 2011). For example, feminist activism against a rape culture has been used in some contexts to shift more resources to law enforcement and legal apparatus such as tribunals and inquiries, nominally for women's safety, in the face of widespread cuts to feminist based programs, such as shelters, counselling, and court advocacy.

Attending to power

Addressing power is required in work with men who perpetrate violence, as in all therapeutic work, because the helping professions are immersed in relationships of power. I hold power in these relationships as a therapist and I try to make that public as opposed to mitigating power or minimizing and ignoring it. As an activism informed therapist I aim to resist replicating oppression. Addressing power requires that we look at the intersections of domains of power (Crenshaw, 1995; Robinson, 2005) especially in work alongside men who are poor, racialized and institutionalized.

Brazilian popular education activist Paulo Freire (1970) named dialogue, the space where liberatory practice occurs, as something which can only happen in the absence of oppression. If I am abusing my power with a man we cannot be in dialogue. I work primarily with poor men and institutionalized men who do not have shelter. If we organize our work simply around gender accountability of men to patriarchal power then that client has to be accountable to me. But we meet in the intersections of power and identity. I am housed, I am a therapist. When I am meeting a man who has used violence in relationships in therapy we are in a domain I have competence in, and he is there because he cannot manage his life. That is an intersection of power I need to be accountable to.

I do not start with an understanding of power that says he is a man and has been violent: I am a woman who has been the victim of men's violence, so he needs to be accountable to me. That is not useful or helpful. A stance of therapeutic love (Tomm, 1990) and compassion for this man alongside compassion and accountability to the women he has victimized is at the heart for my work. If I do not have therapeutic love and compassion for this man and I do not believe in the culture of accountable men then I would be unable to do this work. I believe that therapy that does harm to clients is worse than no therapy for many reasons, most especially because it steals hope that any future therapeutic work could be useful. If therapists do harm they do not suffer the consequences, but the women and children in the man's life become more vulnerable. This is especially important because the men I work with are not men who get to hide behind money and dominant culture privilege when they use violence, often they will go to jail.

Another competency that is required in working with men who have used violence is to attend to suicide which is ever near. As practitioners we require the capacity to hold men who have raped their children, men who have hurt their wives, to create some ethical container for the work. Our job is to hold men who have been violent to women and children on this planet, and to help create a place for them as part of an ethic of belonging (Richardson & Reynolds, 2012).

Personal responsibility & Collective accountability

Our collective accountability as therapists with an ethic of justice-doing requires us to work towards changing the structures of social injustice that promote rape culture. When therapists put responsibility for the socially unjust society on the shoulders of individual young men I think that is therapeutic violence and it does not serve that young man, the women he has victimized, or the women and children he may potentially victimize in the future. If we do not help this young man who is willing to talk to us again the consequences will not only be experienced by him but by women he may potentially victimize in the future (Jenkins, 1990). All of our suffering is connected, as all our liberations are connected with each other. So while I want to hold men 100 percent responsible for what they do, they are not responsible for the social context.

Our young men are being raised in a rape culture and then held individually responsible as if they invented misogyny. They did not invent misogyny and patriarchy, they are swimming in it. I think about this in relation to my own position about racism and colonization. I cannot say that I am a non-racist person - that would just be a truth claim I could not back up with facts. I grew up in a racist society in a racist culture. I am a white skinned person of a settler culture in a territory that was stolen from Indigenous people, meaning First Nations people, Metis people and Inuit people, through invasion, occupation, genocide and assimilation (Hill, 2010). The territory is saturated in the blood of Indigenous people in Canada for which there has been no accountability. How can I make a claim to be non-racist in this territory? The most that I can claim is taking a position against racism, colonization and genocide. If I have it set as an intention, and work hard in a given moment to not be racist I may achieve it- but the moment I let down my guard or do not attend to racism I will replicate it. How can I expect a 14-year-old young man to do more and to not replicate a rape culture and a misogynist culture that is the society he swims in and breathes in? And how is it just to leave him alone and individually responsible for that?

When I work with men who have been violent and young men who have been sexually coercive for example, I do not begin with their accountability for violence. I ask them where they learned about violence. I have never met a man who invented violence. Every man I have ever worked with was the victim of violence first, particularly the violence of men. They experienced violence on the body. That is how they were trained up in the ideas of violence. And so we have to start here.

Accountability to women and children who are victimized by men who use violence

Holding work with men who have used violence accountable to women and children that men have victimized is complicated, and requires practitioners to create structures of individual and organizational accountability. In my work with men who have used violence I hold the women and children who are victimized by this man's violence close to me. I bring these women and children into the room with me metaphorically, so that in the whole time that I have a conversation with the man I am reflexively questioning how the woman would critique my therapeutic conversation. How am I honoring and dignifying Julie in my efforts to dignify Joe? We can hold those things in a tension: it is not either-or. Our work with men who have used violence can serve all of us if it is accountable to the larger project of resisting, dismantling, and transforming rape culture.

These questions can be useful in framing individual and organizational responses to structures of accountability in work with men who have used violence:

- How is my work with an individual man held accountable to the people he has been violence against?

- How does my organization assist in this accountability?

- How do I personally attend to this accountability?

- How is our work directed by or informed by the women and children victimized by men who use violence? What structures of accountability can we create to hold this work more closely accountable to the women and children who have suffered from his violence?

- How am I personally and professionally resisting rape culture? How is my organization, professional body, discipline, private practice, training/teaching faculty resisting rape culture? How can I impact the work in all of these domains to be more accountable?

- Who is in solidarity with me in resisting rape culture in these professional domains? Who are my allies? What access to power do we hold in these domains that we can access to promote the hard and ethical work to resist rape culture?

- Are we holding accountability to funding sources higher than accountability to the victims of men's violence? If so, how can we resist this, and what people/communities/organizations can help us get our practices in more ethical alignment with our ethics?

The following is a practice example of what it looks like to be responsive and hold our work with men accountable to women. I served as the supervisor for a center for survivors of torture. Racialized women, refugee women, migrant women and asylum seeking women came to me and said 'you're white, you know how to talk in your language in a way that gets listen to. We need you to talk to police about the fact that they have to understand that men who are the victims of political violence and torture are not necessarily beating their wives when a neighbor phones the police'. These women told me they would never phone the police for protection. It is a site of privilege to think that if you call the police their first interest is your safety. Many people never have that privilege, in particular poor people, racialized and minoritized people and asylum seekers. Sometimes what is happening is a flashback or a psychological experience based on the political violence and torture he has suffered. The police see it as a domestic violence situation, which women describe as being much more complicated than that. If he gets charged, he may lose his asylum or refugee status and the whole family suffers. I want to hold those men 100 percent accountable for what they do. We have to co-create a space of dignity and honour for this man and the violence that he experienced and suffered and how that is part of what is going on in his choices of behavior to hit his wife, and for that he is 100 percent responsible.

Accountable feminist informed supervision

Men who use violence must be accountable to the women and children who are victimized by men's violence. Therapists and organizations working with men who have used violence need to create structures of accountability to these women and children for their work. Feminist informed supervision from women who have the moral courage to challenge even the best of intentions of accountable men therapists is also necessary. What is required is an honest reckoning with male privilege, which we can predict will be discomforting, and possibly require discomfort (Kumashiro, 2004). Canadian critical social worker Barbara Heron (2005) describes 'double comfort' as the comfort that follows when we name our access to privilege, such as holding men's privilege, and then do nothing to mitigate it. Critical supervision will need to disrupt this double comfort with invitations to take actions that require more than naming privilege, and show direct links between therapeutic work and resisting and dismantling rape culture.

These questions are useful in feminist informed supervision in work with men who have used violence:

- How am I holding the safety of the women and children this man has been violent towards at the centre of this work?

- How am I addressing rape culture in my work with this man who has used violence? How am I informed by complex understandings of power and a feminist informed analysis for this work?

- How am I addressing my own access to men's power and privilege in this work? Who is shouldering me up to do this difficult work?

- How do I keep myself open to critique and the possibility that my practice may reveal something other than accountability to the victims of this man's violence?

- What can I pay attention to that might let me know I am working in ways that are not in line with my commitments to do feminist informed accountable work?

- What am I doing to resist, transform and end rape culture? In my work, in my communities, in other aspects of my life?

Gender of the therapist

Johnella Bird (2000) a feminist, narrative-informed therapist in New Zealand, teaches that she asks men what they want, they tell her they want fair and equal relationships and then she holds them to it. I want to honour them and do dignity to them. And because I am a woman I think I am well resourced (Bird, 2006) to do that. Useful questions I am able to ask men are:

- What is it like for you to be able to sit in this difficult conversation with me as a woman and admit that you have done violence against women?

- What does it say about you as a man that you're going to have this conversation with me, a woman? How might our different genders influence what you can say or not say in our work together?

- Am I safe-enough with you in this conversation? What do you know about yourself that has you trusting that you can be a safe-enough man in a difficult conversation with a women?

- Do you think it is possible that you and I could create a respectful relationship between us for all of our work together? What will it take from you as a man to stay respectful with a woman therapist as we talk about your violent actions against other women and children?

- If you and I could have a respectful relationship what might that say about who you are or can be as a man in relationships with women?

When I began as a therapist working with young men who had used violence against their mothers there were questions about whether or not women therapists could effectively and ethically do this work. I do not think it is our gender that qualifies us for the work it is our ethical positioning and feminist informed political analysis.

I believe it is possible for men therapists to be ethical and useful therapists to women who have experienced men's violence. I have supervised some accountable men drug and alcohol counselors and some of their clients were women who had been the victims of men's violence throughout their life. These men had that cold fear in the belly as therapists that they were in some way going to transgress against these women who have been the victims of men's violence. I believe that cold fear in the belly, that terror you have that you may harm a woman is a resource to men therapists, and is actually necessary to work accountably in this situation (Reynolds, 2014). These men responded to this by seeking out feminist-informed therapeutic supervisor.

Living supervision

Our most trustworthy and useful 'supervision' comes from our clients. Despite our best intentions and committed training, I believe that we learn our work on the backs of clients. I use a process I call 'living supervision' (Reynolds, 2014) to centre the client as the expert on the therapeutic relationship, and to provide one structure of accountability for men therapists working with women clients who have experienced men's violence.

In living supervision I have a conversation with the man therapist, and the client, the woman who has suffered men's violence. The man therapist is in a listening position and as the supervisor I interview the woman client about the therapeutic relationship. We are inquiring about the therapeutic relationship, and I ask how the therapeutic relationship has been useful, the ways it has not been useful, and what qualities the therapist brings to the work that the woman speaks of as useful to her. I then interview the man therapist about the relationship, asking what the woman has brought to make it useful, acknowledging that our clients make us better therapists if we are open to listening to their responses in conversation. I ask the man about his hopes for the woman, and for any lived experience he has witnessed that shoulders up these hopes. I ask about his responses to the woman's conversation and what meaning it holds for him, allowing space for the therapist to acknowledge the 'supervision', expertise and critique offered by the client.

In one situation the living supervision conversation revealed that this was the first relationship the woman client could remember with a man where she has been respected and the man has not acted inappropriately or transgressed against her in some way. He has been very careful in fact to open the door for her but always go first so that she does not have to worry that he is checking out her body. This is the first man she remembers who holds her dignity and the care of her at the center of the relationship. She has not been in a relationship like this. This is not to claim that she is safe in the world, or an enactment of applause and gratitude to the male therapist for what is decent and respectful behaviour, but that there is a culture of accountable men. All men are not going to hurt you. The world is not a totally terrifying place that you do not belong in.

Women can work with men who have used violence, and men can work with women who have experienced men's violence with structures of feminist informed supervision and accountability practices. It is not our gender that qualifies us for our work but nor should it disqualify us. Gender variant and transgender workers can also work effectively across genders because they are well positioned to transgress and disrupt gender normative roles that uphold patriarchy and rape culture.

Conclusion

Work with men who have used violence requires feminist informed supervision, accountability to power, and an ability to have compassion and hold the dignity of the man you are working with alongside a compassion and accountability to the women and children he has used violence against.

I do not see my activist and professional work against rape and supporting women who have suffered men's violence and my work with men who have used violence as competing projects, though there is a tension in holding both spaces. There are complexities involved in practicing resistance politics in "an age of co-option and incorporation" (Spade, 2011p. 34), and we can get caught up in the competition over scarce resources that pit services to men and to women against each other. This frame sets us up like dogs under the table fighting over the bones. Our analysis and activism has to embrace ways to address all facets of men's violence without replicating competition between men and women. As an activist I continue to work to try to change the oppressive structures that promote rape culture. It is complicated, difficult and at times painful to hold these things in a tension, a compassionate care for men who have been violent alongside a compassionate and dignified accountability to the women that have been victimized by men's violence. But as activists say, we can walk and chew gum. Our collective project as women, men and gender variant practitioners is to envision another possible world, and to hold all of the facets of our work accountable to resisting, dismantling and transforming rape culture.

Dedication

Respect, honour and love to the women of my extended family and family of choice who have shouldered me up in my life and work: for my sisters Susie and Nancy; and especially our mother, Joan Manuel Reynolds, who is our rock and teacher of a kind of feminism based on strength, intelligence and moral courage.

Acknowledgements

This work and writing occurred on Indigenous territories of the Musqueam, Skxwu7mesh-ulh Uxwuhmixw (pronounced Squamish) & Tsleil Waututh nations which were never surrendered. This work is profoundly collaborative and owes much to a diversity of activists, therapists and community workers, most especially I acknowledge the diversity of women at WAVAW (Women Against Violence Against Women), rape crisis centre where I am counselling supervisor. These women have educated, challenged, critiqued and transformed me. Appreciation to Magin Payet Scudellari for their skilled transcription. This article is framed from my participation on a panel entitled, 'Working with men who use violence' which was created and skilfully facilitated by Maria Losurdo, Manager for

Family Worker Training and Development Program in New South Wales, Australia. My gratitude and respect to the other panelists; Ivan Clarke, Eric Hudson, and Mary-Jo McVeigh. Thanks to Irene Tsepnopoulos-Elhaimer, Sekneh Hammoud-Beckett and Peter Navratil for careful and generative readings which made this a more useful and accountable paper.

References

Akinyela, M. (2002). De-colonizing our lives: Divining a post-colonial therapy. *The International Journal of Narrative Therapy and Community Work*, 2, 32-43.

Bird, J. (2000). *The heart's narrative: Therapy and navigating life's contradictions.* Auckland, New Zealand: Edge Press.

Bird, J. (2006*). Constructing the narrative in supervision*. Auckland, New Zealand: Edge Press.

Buchwald, E., Fletcher, P. & Roth, M. (1993). *Transforming a Rape Culture.* Minneapolis: Milkwood Editions.

Butler, J. (1997). *Excitable speech: A politics of the performative.* New York, NY: Routledge.

Coates, L., & Wade, A. (2004). Telling it like it isn't: Obscuring perpetrator responsibility for violence. *Discourse and Society*, 15, 499-526.

Coates, L., & Wade, A. (2007). Language and violence: Analysis of four discursive operations. *Journal of Family Violence*, 22, 11-522.

Cohen, A. (2012, May 14). Yes America we have executed an innocent man. *The Atlantic*. http://www.theatlantic.com/national/archive/2012/05/yes-america-we-have-executed-an-innocent-man/257106/

Crenshaw, K. (1995). Mapping the margins: Intersectionality, identity politics, and violence against women of colour. In K. Crenshaw, G. Gotanda, G. Peller, & K. Thomas (Eds.), *Critical race theory: The key writings that formed the movement* (pp. 357-383). New York, NY: The New Press.

Cushman, P. (1995). Constructing the self, constructing America: A cultural history of psychotherapy. Reading, MA: Addison Wesley.

The "F" Word Media Collective. (2014). *The "F" word*. Retrieved from http://www.coopradio.org/content/f-word

Freire, P. (1970). *Pedagogy of the oppressed*. New York, NY: Continuum.

Herman, J. (1992). *Trauma and recovery*. New York, NY: Basic Books.

Heron, B. (2005). Self-reflection in critical social work practice: Subjectivities and the possibilities of resistance. *Journal of Reflective Practice, 6*(3), 341-351.

Hill, G. (2010). *500 years of Indigenous resistance*. Vancouver, Canada: Arsenal Pulp Press.

hooks, b. (1984). *Feminist theory: From margin to center*. Cambridge: South End Press.

hooks, b. (2000). *Feminism is for everybody: Passionate politics*. Cambridge: South End Press.

Jenkins, A. (1990). *Invitations to responsibility: The therapeutic engagement of men who are violent and abusive*. Adelaide: Dulwich Centre Publications.

Kivel, P. (2007). Social service or Social change, in INCITE! Women of color against Violence, (Eds.), *The Revolution will not be funded: Beyond the Non-Profit industrial complex*. 21-40. Cambridge, MA: South End Press.

Kumashiro, K. (2004). *Against commonsense: Teaching and learning towards social justice*. New York, NY: Routledge.

Madanes, C., Keim, J., & Smelser, D. (1995). *The violence of men: New techniques for working with abusive families: A therapy of social action*. San Francisco, CA: Jossey-Bass.

Namaste, V. (2000). *Invisible lives: The erasure of trans-sexual and transgendered people*. Chicago, IL: University of Chicago Press.

Prochuk, A. (2014). *What is rape culture?* www.wavaw.ca/what-is-rape-culture/

National Status of Women, (1993). *Evaluation Report of the Women's Program (Appendix B)*,   Retrieved from www.swc-cfc.gc.ca/account-resp/pr/wpeval-evalpf/wpe-epf-eng.pdf

Rape Crisis Scotland (2011). *Stop rape: 10 top tips to end rape*. http://www.rapecrisisscotland.org.uk/

Razack, N. (2002). *Transforming the Field: Critical Antiracist and Anti-Oppressive Perspectives for the Human Service Practicum*. Halifax: Fernwood Publishing.

Reynolds (2014) Centering ethics in therapeutic supervision: Fostering cultures of critique and structuring safety. *The International Journal of Narrative Therapy and Community Work*. No. 1, 1-13.

ative
ative
 ativeative
ativeive

Reynolds, V. & Hammoud-Beckett, S. (2012). Bridging the worlds of therapy and activism: Intersections, tensions and affinities. *International Journal of Narrative Therapy & Community Work*. No. 4, 57-61.

Reynolds, V. & polanco, m. (2012). An ethical stance for justice-doing in community work and therapy. *Journal of Systemic Therapies*. 31(4) 18-33.

Reynolds, V. (2010). Doing justice: A witnessing stance in therapeutic work alongside survivors of torture and political violence. In J. Raskin, S. Bridges, & R. Neimeyer (Eds.), *Studies in meaning 4: Constructivist perspectives on theory, practice, and social justice*. New York, NY: Pace University Press.

Richardson, C., & Reynolds, V. (2012). "Here we are amazingly alive": Holding ourselves together with an ethic of social justice in community work. *International Journal of Child, Youth and Family Studies* 1:1-19.

Robinson, T. (2005). *The convergence of race, ethnicity, and gender: Multiple identities in counselling* (2nd Ed.). Boston, MA: Pearson Education.

Smith, A. (2006). Heteropatriarchy and the Three Pillars of White Supremacy: Rethinking Women of Color Organizing. In INCITE! Women of Color Against Violence (Eds.), *Color of Violence: The INCITE! Anthology* (p. 66-73). Cambridge, MA: South End Press.

Spade, D. (2011). *Normal life: Administrative violence, critical trans politics, and the limits of law*. Brooklyn, NY: South End Press.

Statistics Canada, (1993). *Juristat: Canadian Centre for Justice Statistics*. Catalogue no 85-002-XIE, 19(3).

Sussex Police, (2011). *Be smart*. http://www.psni.police.uk/be_smart_female_postcard.pdf

Tomm, K. (1990). *Ethical postures in family therapy*. Paper presented at the annual meeting of the American Association for Marriage and Family Therapy. Philadelphia: PA.

United Nations, (2010). *Violence against women*. Retrieved from http://unstats.un.org/unsd/demographic/products/Worldswomen/WW2010%20Report_by%20chapter%28pdf%29/violence%20against%20women.pdf

Wade, A. (1997). Small acts of living: Everyday resistance to violence and other forms of oppression. *Journal of Contemporary Family Therapy*, 19(l), 23-40.

Walia, H. (2012). *Decolonizing together: Moving beyond a politics of solidarity toward a practice of decolonization.* http://briarpatchmagazine.com/articles/view/decolonizing-together

Trauma and Resistance: 'Hang Time' and Other Innovative Responses to Oppression, Violence and Suffering

This writing presents activist-informed ways of responding to suffering in persons who have been oppressed and harmed. This approach centers on witnessing their prudent and creative acts of resistance (Reynolds, 2010; Reynolds, Bahman, Hammoud-Beckett, Sanders, & Haworth, 2014). A witnessing approach requires that we situate personal suffering in its sociopolitical context and resist the individualization and medicalization of suffering. Activist practices of witnessing are enacted through an ethical stance for justice-doing, which includes the duty of the witness to work to change the social contexts of oppression, and engage a true reckoning with power (Reynolds & polanco, 2012).

To foreground the practice of witnessing acts of resistance (as opposed to assessing, diagnosing, and treating trauma symptomology), I share a compilation of stories from working with youth who have given me permission to share their experiences. The stories from practice shared below contain threads from various youth's stories; I have woven these threads together in order to structure safety for youth who are indeed co-creators of this work, and to make the practice clearer. This requires holding a tension between acknowledging youth wisdom and necessarily protecting identifying details.

Decolonizing Practice and Justice-Doing

As an activist and therapist, I work to bridge the worlds of social justice activism with community work (Reynolds, 2019; Reynolds & Hammoud-Beckett, 2018). My people are Irish, Newfoundland, and English folk, and I am a white settler with heterosexual and cisgender privilege. I am still immersed in the on-going work of un-settling myself as a white settler (Regan, 2010), despite my commitment to be decolonizing in all of my paid and unpaid work.

Decolonizing practice is not a metaphor (Tuck & Yang, 2012); it means commitments to Indigenous governance and land return. In all my activism, community work, and organizing, I aim to be directed by Indigenous people (Manuel & Derrickson, 2015). As a settler I have set intentions to stay implicated in the ongoing catastrophes (Kouri & Skott-Myers, 2016) of colonization and genocide (Brave Heart, & DeBruyn, (1998). I am informed by Metis trauma counsellor/researcher/activist Natalie Clark (2016) who writes of trauma as the 'New Colonial Frontier'. As an adjunct professor and therapeutic supervisor, I resist interpreting Indigenous resistance to ongoing colonization and state violence as a symptom of trauma, a therapeutic act of harm that Response Based practitioners Nick Todd and Allan Wade (1994) name with the neologism: *psycolonization*. In *The Wretched of the Earth*, (1963) Frantz Fanon wrote specifically of the psychopathology of colonization directly related to France's use of political terrorism and wide spread torture to suppress the Algerian struggle for Independence. Fanon proposes that psychology as a euro-centric colonizing force is used to pathologize the colonized, but that we should centre our inquiry on the mental unwellness of the colonizer. Fanon's teachings were absent from all 27 years of my education, and I am confident that erasure was connected to white supremacy, anti black racism in the academy, and to silencing diverse voices of dissent. Here I am informed by black, American therapist Makungu Akinyela (2002; 2014) and Travis Heath (2018) and their work to decolonize from a black, anti-colonial perspective addressing the soul wound (Duran, 2006) of slavery (Hardy, 2017b). As a white settler therapist, I am inextricably related to the project of psychology that systematically psycolonizes Indigenous people; I can't distance myself from these practices, but must continue to resist them in practice and theorizing.

This practice also requires justice-doing. Justice-doing goes beyond the scope of anti-oppressive practice, which aims to not replicate oppression, but entails actually being just and ethical with people, which requires engaging the activist project to transform the social contexts in which suffering and oppression occur, and to do this in ways led by persons and with accountability to their communities. One reflexive question I continually puzzle with is: "How am I attending to power in this moment, in this interaction, with this person?"

This work is an anti-perfection project in part because we have not delivered on a just society. The practice of engaging in a purposefully messy and imperfect process (Reynolds, 2014) is informed by queer theory (Butler, 1990), critical trans theory (Spade, 2011), and anti-authoritarian social justice activism (Chomsky, 2005; Buechler, 2005; Shantz, 2011) where we aim to respond immediately to all oppressive and abusive acts. It requires that we take overt positions for justice-doing, defy neutrality, and have the moral courage to face up to and repair the consequences of imperfect actions.

As scholars and cultures of resistance teach, we must continually and fluidly attend to the intersections of domains of identity connected to both power and disadvantage (Crenshaw, 1995). This practice is informed by women of color feminism (Smith, 2006), in particular black feminists such as bell hooks (1984), and Patricia Hill Collins (1998). Ideas of diversity and inclusion, although useful, are also limiting and are being problematized and transformed by communities of resistance and by activists with marginalized voices (Ahmed, 2012). The structural inequities that promote suffering demand complex collective responses.

Trauma: Psychology language that obscures more than it reveals

Trauma, as conceptualized and defined by the mainstream field of psychology, is a medicalized term that obscures violence and human suffering. The language of psychology centres on descriptions of individuals' brokenness which hides the structural violence that promotes suffering. Legislative poverty, ableism, developer-created homelessness, on-going colonial violence, racism, anti-black racism (Hardy, 2017a), white supremacy, the prison industrial complex (Maynard, 2017), cisnormativity, heteronormativity, and rape culture – specifically, the structural state violence that fosters the murder and disappearance of Indigenous women that is tied to the rape of the earth through resource extraction and enacting ongoing colonization (Hunt, 2016) — all of these forms of structural violence are excluded from and concealed by psychological conceptualizations of trauma. A complex analysis helps us resist the psychological project, which reduces political and structural violence into personal deficiency (de Finney et al, 2018a): the perfect storm of victim-blaming.

Here I am accompanied by many scholar-practitioners who have offered well-considered critiques of the language of trauma (Sutherland et al., 2016; Strong & Busch, 2013; Allan Wade, personal communication). Specifically, how it locates our interest as workers in symptoms and diagnoses that are personalized, individuated, and constructed as the responsibility of the person, as if their personal strengths or resiliency are the issue, and as if the material world of power and oppression can be mitigated by neutrality and objectivity

Persons share complex stories and experiences from their lives, in which there is suffering, hardship, resistance, and responses that are insightful and intelligent. Practitioners too often side with *psychocentrism* (Defehr, 2016), reducing this complexity into simplicity, redefining people's complex responses and acts of resistance to fit narrowly defined categories of trauma criteria and symptomology. This moves the focus from a person's autonomous responses and unique acts of resistance to professional assessment and psychological templates of mental wellness. Experiences defined as trauma are often better understood as exploitation and oppression rooted in the political inequities of our unjust societies (Reynolds et al., 2014; Richardson & Reynolds, 2014). Persons' responses to harm and abuses of power are often better understood as acts of resistance.

Psychology has long been curious about parenting as the site of harm, focused on abusive or neglectful families, and actively constructs those families as the source of mental unwellness. People with childhoods characterized by abuse and neglect are construed as lacking parents who are as benevolent and competent as those who don't experience these harms: but what they lack is justice. Poverty – which is legislated and predictable in capitalist neo-liberal societies – causes harms to families by manufacturing precarious lives and limiting life choices such as employment, housing, and education. This is neglect. Colonization, ableism, transphobia, racism, femicide, misogyny, and anti-black racism are abusive. This is not a matter of individual personal resiliency, but of structural oppression. Conceptualizations of personal dysfunction and trauma not only obscure more than they reveal, but actively contribute to blaming individuals and families for their own suffering (Coates, Bonnah & Richardson, 2019).

"The Connective Power of Politicizing Trauma"

Indigenous Two Spirit therapist Riel Dupuis-Rossi, who identifies as Kanien'keha:ka (Mohawk), Algonquin and Italian, writes of "the connective power of politicizing trauma" (Dupuis-Rossi & Reynolds, 2018, pg. 305). Dupuis-Rossi works alongside other Indigenous people in resisting the colonial and institutional state violence that is most often re-inscribed as trauma or inter-generational trauma:

"Trauma is understood politically...and the responsibility for it is handed back to its rightful source, the Settler government and other historical and contemporary colonial forces. [...] Politicizing trauma creates an opening that allows the client to create a new relationship to her suffering (Duran, Firehammer, & Gonzalez, 2008). Kluane understands her experiences as historical, political, social, and specific to a colonial agenda, as opposed to being experiences that reflect her worthlessness, unloveableness, rejection, and abandonment. Kluane realizes that it is not because she is unworthy or unlovable that she has existed in a perpetual state of deprivation and pain; rather, she has been subjected to a genocidal political agenda that is dehumanizing. With the help of traditional wisdom and teachings, she is able to see herself as having been a child who was deserving of love, care, and protection. The deprivation is connected to an external context, the foster home and colonialism, as opposed to being understood as a result of personal deficits" (Dupuis-Rossi & Reynolds, p. 305).

Politicizing trauma is always useful, as all contexts exist within relationships of interpersonal and structural power. I am, however, quoting Dupuis-Rossi extensively here as their words provoke a required discomfort for me and my fellow settler and non-Indigenous practitioners who might otherwise *settle* ourselves into identities as 'the good guys' in struggles against the trauma industry, which indeed sustains our privileges as settler-practitioners, as we are inextricably connected to psychology as a colonial force.

A Witnessing Stance

I describe my stance as witnessing with an aim to bridge the worlds of activism and therapy. There is a rich theory of therapeutic practices oriented around witnessing, specifically in the narrative and constructivist traditions (Myerhoff, 1982; Weingarten, 2000; White, 2002), as well as testimony work by Akinyela (2002; 2014). Of particular interest and relevance is the work of Indigenous women such as Cathy Richardson (2012), who identifies as Metis and Cree, and Barbara Wingard (2001), who is Aboriginal from Ghana people; their witnessing work emerges from their cultural locations as Indigenous women. My approach is informed by decades of fellowship in social movements and activist practices of witnessing, which hold governments and other bodies to account for abuses of power. These abuses include executions, torture, and other violent strategies that silence, dissent, and terrorize populations into submission. The presence of an international activist community is a profound act of faith in the power of witnessing (Amnesty International, 2000; Reynolds, 2010).

Witnessing also serves to resist the individualization and isolation of persons who have survived violence. El Salvadoran Liberation psychologist and Jesuit Priest, Martín-Baró (1990; 1994), worked to bring Liberation Theology to psychology, teaching that in order for psychology to be liberating it must first be liberated. In 1989 a Salvadoran death squad, which was American trained, executed him, alongside his Jesuit brothers, a homemaker, and her daughter. Martín-Baró teaches that political violence is best understood from a perspective that is both psychological and sociopolitical. This means that the path to liberation lies not in the individual psyche of the victim, but within social relations. The meanings given to the acts of political and state terror are social, not individual.

State oppression, such as 'residential schools', legislated poverty, and developer-designed homelessness, dis-members, dis-connects, and removes people from their sites of belonging. In resistance to this dislocation, witnessing work is situated within networked communities. Witnessing engages an ethic of belonging that re-connects, paying particular attention to cultural meanings and practices that *belong* persons in community. I believe, along with many others across time, that culture is a site of healing (de Finney et al, 2018b; Hardy, 2017a; Richardson & Wade, 2008), and that justice-doing can promote healing.

A commitment to witnessing in activist cultures includes the duty of the witness to move beyond hearing individual pain into collective accountability to take actions against injustices. Witnessing exists in relationships of solidarity, meaning shared ethics across points of connection, and it requires an overt position for justice-doing, which requires the witness to respond by taking actions to change the conditions that support and promote abuses of power with action.

Acts of Resistance

As an activist, it has never felt useful, accountable or respectful to question persons who have experienced torture about their humiliation and harm. It has always been useful to talk of how they managed to survive, to stay human in situations outside of human understanding—situations that are perpetrated by government agents acting with impunity to suppress dissent with political terrorism. These teaching led me to seek stories of resistance to suffering, instead of psychologizing and medicalizing their experiences of torture and interpreting their acts of resistance as criteria for mental illness and trauma. My understandings of resistance owe much to asylum seekers and refugees who have survived torture and political violence whom I have worked alongside over the past three decades; and particularly, Indigenous persons from Turtle Island who have survived and continue to resist the political violence of colonization, genocide and assimilation.

Resistance refers to all of a person's or peoples' responses against abuses of power and oppression, and the many ways that they maintain their dignity and move towards justice. Allan Wade's article, *Small acts of living: Every day resistance to violence and other forms of oppression* (1997), provides a comprehensive analysis of working with resistance in this way. Wade took the title for his article from Sociologist Erving Goffman (1961), who wrote in *Asylums* about people's resistance to being held in "total institutions" (p.181), such as psychiatric institutes and prisons, where power is overt and where the holders of power dictate most behaviour. Goffman witnessed people's responses to these institutions and their nuanced and small forms of resistance, such as sticking out their tongue, walking slowly, and pretending to be unintelligent. Goffman's ideas are important because they challenge what usually gets attended to as resistance, which is socially constructed as fighting back and speaking up. Instead he amplified these 'small acts of living' to describe the nuanced and multiple ways people resist violence and humiliation and work to restore their dignity.

Overt acts of resistance against oppression are the least common forms of resistance, as the adverse consequences of such resistance can be extreme (Scott, 1985). Often, people who are subjected to abuses of power cannot safely and openly protest abuse. People fight back against oppression in multiple ways, but not always in ways that are easily noticed or understood as resistance (Richardson & Wade, 2008).

The following are the Understandings of Resistance that scaffold my work with people suffering from and struggling against oppression:

1. Wherever there is oppression and abuses of power there is always resistance;

2. Resistance ought not to be judged by its ability to stop oppression, rather;

3. Resistance is important for its ability to maintain a person's relationship with humanity, especially in situations outside of human understanding.

We witness resistance, not because it stops the abuses of power, but because attending to resistance amplifies the person's sense of autonomy and adds grip to the fingerhold they have on their dignity (Richardson & Wade, 2010). As practitioners, we serve as witnesses to the person's resistance despite the success or failure of the struggle, as resistance helps people stay connected to humanity: their own, and the wider sense.

Acts of resistance are most often not able to stop oppression. It is important not to fetishize or romanticize resistance, as our collective purpose is to promote possible lives of justice, not to have rich practices of resistance. Not all responses are acts as resistance, and acts can only be understood as resistance if the person performing them would describe them as such (Wade, 1997).

Making Resistance Visible: Troy's Story of 'Hang Time'

As part of a Living Supervision practice, I participate in sessions alongside therapists I supervise (Reynolds & Larcombe, 2016). In my role as Clinical Supervisor at Peak House, a live-in substance-misuse program for youth of all genders, I met with Troy, a white youth who lives under guardianship of the state. I was invited into the therapeutic relationship between the therapist, who I will call Julie, and the youth, who I will call Troy, because Troy's intake form – which included information from diverse and historic records – was complex and disconcerting. After seeking Troy's consent to participate with him and Julie, I asked him if he was aware of the descriptions of him in the file, to which he mumbled affirmation. So, I began to ask his understandings of these descriptions, specifically being an alcoholic, an addict, and having a diagnosis of Addictive Personality Disorder. He was also ascribed, through various professionalized assessments from different domains, an identity with a possible learning disorder, trauma, and dissociative symptomology. He was reported to be a liar, and someone who had made false allegations of sexual abuse. This was quite an overwhelming picture, which was why I was invited in. He said that it was pretty much what he was told, and wondered what I made of it, and, acknowledging that we'd called in the 'big guns' (me as the supervisor), if he was "too messed up to help." I believe as practitioners we are ethically required to be the bringers of hope, and to build trust-worthy-ness; as such, I never lie to youth. I let Troy know why I had been called in, and I also let him know that I had hope for him based on youth who had taught me how to be useful over two decades at Peak House.

After structuring safety (Reynolds et al., 2014; Richardson & Reynolds, 2014), and beginning to co-construct our relationship of respect and dignity, I asked Troy if he described himself as an addict, if he knew Addictive Personality Disorder is not a credible diagnosis, and what he thought of being called an alcoholic. He thought for a while and responded that he pretty much drank until he blacked out. Here, I resisted the usual addiction counselling protocol, such as: What is your drug of choice? How much do you use? Who do you use with? How do you get your drugs? Instead I asked, "What are you blacking out?" Troy named his "foster father's attacks".

This changes everything. Nowhere in the assessment are the foster father's attacks against Troy named. Instead we have a litany of explanations for all that is going on with Troy due to his mental health, addiction, and moral failings. Coates and Wade (2007) describe how language can be used to hide violence, obscure the perpetrator's responsibility, blame the victim, and hide the victim's resistance to the abuse and violence. The language in Troy's file accomplished all of these things: it concealed the violence that beset him, revoked responsibility from the abusers for the suffering at hand, perpetuated an undignified story about Troy's identity that blamed him for his own suffering, whilst erasing and subverting any possible descriptions of his agency and his resistance.

My intention as a therapist is to make the person's acts of resistance visible (not to interpret it as symptoms of trauma) so I asked Troy what he did when this man attacked him. I resisted asking questions about the nature of the violence, specific degrading acts, or his feelings about this. He said he didn't do much, and that there was no way he could fight a big strong angry man as the attacks started when he was a boy. I asked what he *did* do. There was profound silence and palpable connection. Troy moved towards me, and said that I was going to find this weird. I told him I've heard lots of ways that people fight back that are *way out there*, so he asks, if I know who Michael Jordan is, and if I know what 'Hang Time' is. After a lot of discussion about basketball, including tales of the two games I saw Jordan play, we get out of our chairs and compare our vertical leaps, his is impressive, mine, not so much. Troy tells me he has Michael Jordan's iconic 'Hang Time' poster, which is a life-sized portrayal of the perhaps-greatest-basketball-player-of-all-time flying through the air, palming the ball, poised to slam dunk. Following an animated, embodied discussion on both sides in which we discuss Jordan's 'Hang Time' – and how I, as a white 5'3 middle-aged woman even know this stuff –Troy describes his acts of resistance:

Troy has this almost life-size poster of Jordan flying through the air taking up the whole wall of his small basement room. When he hears his foster father's steps coming down the stairs, and anticipates an attack, Troy leaves his body and joins Michael Jordan in 'Hang Time'. He hangs, suspended in time, and experiences himself as out-of-time. Following the assault, when the man leaves his bedroom, and Troy judges it is safe-enough for him to reappear, he slam-dunks the basketball ball, actively ending the suspension of time, and simultaneously comes back into his body.

Troy's words evoke a profound and meaningful silence. The conversation was quiet and slow, and we were drawn closer together physically connected by the social poetics (Katz & Shotter, 2004) of all that was spoken between us in the spirited and embodied language that exists beyond words. We were inhabiting 'spaces of justice' (Lacey, 2005) co-created relationally by our points of connection, momentary solidarity, and intentions to centre and witness Troy's acts of resistance.

Troy's use of 'Hang Time' is a classic example of dissociative behaviour, and yet we resist this description as it hides his act of resistance and youth wisdom. I ask him how he thought of this. If he thought it might be a useful way of trying to be safe without physically fighting back? What it might mean to Michael Jordan that he is accompanying Troy in ways that have Troy feeling safer? What qualities this act of resistance speaks to? How this has been useful to Troy? Troy spoke of thinking it might be "thinking quick, being smart, moving fast, and finding someone safe to not be alone."

We go on to have a conversation about how this is connected to a possible 'learning disability' and if Troy might not be going into 'Hang Time' in his science class because the teacher's voice scares him. I ask if he thinks the teacher will harm him like the foster father and he says no, and we strategize how to not use 'Hang Time' when it isn't needed.

I asked about his relationship to drinking, specifically 'drinking 'til he blacks out'. He responds that now that he's thinking of 'Hang Time' and his creativity, intelligence, and connection to Jordan – maybe he doesn't need to black out. Troy thinks he'll be more able to resist 'drinking 'til he blacks out' with help from the crew of Peak House.

While Troy and I focused on his many creative, insightful, inspiring and courageous acts of resistance, acknowledging that at times he 'sacrificed himself' for his siblings, it is important to hold these celebratory revelations in a tension alongside a knowing that he was not even remotely able to keep himself safe from this man's attacks, or his family safe from state apprehension. Witnessing these acts of resistance was extremely useful to Troy though, as it honoured his ability to 'stay human' in an environment of fear, degradation and suffering.

In my work with Troy, I resisted an intrusive-curiosity that could probe both what is wrong in Troy's mind and the mind of the man who perpetrated sexualized violence against him. Here, I am informed by Jewish scholar Hannah Arendt's work on the 'Banality of Evil' (1994), which invites us to resist centering our inquiry on people who perpetrate violence, especially our societal histories of constructing despotic rulers and actors as 'evil geniuses'. I am, however, committed to an ethical-curiosity that seeks to bring forward Troy's acts of resistance to abuses of power so these acts can be witnessed as expressions of his youth wisdom.

Necessary Assumptions: Making Sense and Seeking Safety

Witnessing resistance requires us to create relationships of dignity and respect across differences of privilege. It is the task of therapists to build a bridge across the differences of power and to meet the person where they are at. From this dignifying relationship, we invite persons to take responsibility where they have actual choices and access to power available to them, but not for the debilitating oppression, violence, and marginalization they have experienced nor for the social context that promotes and sustains their suffering. We collaborate with persons and assist them in making any changes they prefer to make to alter their relationship to suffering. As therapists enacting justice-doing, we are further required to use our specific social locations and access to power to work to change the social contexts in which suffering and structural violence occurs.

There are two necessary assumptions for witnessing resistance that I am unable to work without:

1. Persons' behaviour makes sense.

2. Persons are trying to be safe.

These assumptions invite me to resist diagnosing persons' behaviour and responses as symptoms of trauma, and to resist seeing persons as being unsafe and not trustworthy with their own lives.

Un-housing as an Act of Resistance

I work in the Downtown Eastside of Vancouver—the poorest neighbourhood in Canada, off Indigenous reserve. In Vancouver, even a family of four with two adults working full-time at minimum wage is unhoused, both because they cannot afford housing and because housing is unavailable. In the context of supervising a housing outreach worker, I was asked to assist the worker and their organization with the following situation: a mother who is sole-parenting two children lives in a car. When she is offered the prospect of housing from an outreach worker who approaches her on the street as she exits the car in the morning with her children, she quietly and laconically complies with the interview. The worker returns over the next days for follow-up, with the mandatory housing assessment forms, to find the woman and family gone, the car moved. The meaning and assessment the worker gives to this is that the mother is pre-contemplative, not ready for change or housing, and possibly self-defeating. This assessment is upheld by the dominant parlance of the helping professions, which blames this purportedly inept mother for poverty, a lack of housing and the resulting neglect that is linked to abuses of structural power.

In a supervisory conversation we engaged a critical analysis of justice-doing where we worked to meet this woman where she is at in the world; we looked for her behaviour to make sense and we tried to see her attempts to create safety for her family. When the worker was able to actually meet this woman in the material political world she exists in, the worker was able to see their actions as a threat to the family, putting the children at risk of apprehension by the state. Again, the mother's behaviour is not evidence of faulty logic, multigenerational trauma, attachment disorder, or an inability to trust due to Borderline Personality Disorder, (all of which were considered to make sense of her behaviour), but an astute intelligence and resistance to state apprehension. This was not a refusal to be housed, but an attempt to keep her family together. What was required of the worker was that they be accountable to their individual power and their access to structural institutionalized power, which they cannot abdicate. This requires collective accountability and solidarity with other workers as opposed to blaming other workers for systemic failures when we have, as a society, failed and refused to create more just and dignifying options and responses to suffering and oppression. The task, from there, became how to actually be a safe-enough resource for this woman to trust, and that began with acknowledging our power as workers, and being accountable for the reality that being housed can make families more vulnerable to surveillance and apprehension, as their where-abouts are known, and workers can and have been used to report on the family's behaviour. This is not a quick fix or a matter of semantics. When state-sponsored fostering receives more money than families would need to keep their own children, what is required is actually working to dismantle these systems, while simultaneously responding to suffering with the flawed and limited resources we have

Instead of judging this woman for putting her children at risk, we look for how a woman's responses make sense and how women are trying to keep their children safe, especially in ways that aren't easily recognizable, especially when we structurally hold mothers responsible for men's violent behaviour.

Conclusion

The psychological language of trauma obscures persons' acts of resistance, often reinterpreting resistance to criteria of mental illness. The language of trauma obscures violence and resistance to oppression by pathologizing people, which blames them for their own suffering and limited life choices. Justice-doing and a stance for decolonization help us address suffering that is inextricably linked to structural oppression and resists pathologizing and individualizing people's responses to oppression. Witnessing as enacted in social justice movements creates a space for resistance to be revealed and requires that practitioners are responsible to work toward changing social structures of oppression in which suffering occurs. When we create relationships of respect and dignity, we truly meet people where they are at and their acts of resistance become visible, inviting a witnessing of their intelligence, strength, and courage. We don't diagnose people as mentally ill, and we don't accuse them of being self-sabotaging, but enter their world where their actions towards dignity and safety (Richardson & Wade, 2010) become visible to us.

Dedication

For Cori Kelly (who identifies as Blackfoot/Irish) who I am humbled to name as a mentor, for her big-hearted presence, brilliant analysis, and whose moral courage to offer wise critique and invite fierce accountability is a gift to so many of us, and to me specifically as a white settler. Cori shoulders up immeasurable numbers of folks with her spirited presence that *belongs* so many of us in the power of her love and the warmth of her circle.

Acknowledgments

This writing and work took place on the traditional and unceded ancestral lands and territories of the Coast Salish (xʷməθkwəy̓əm [Musqueam], Sk̲wx̲wú7mesh [Squamish], and Səl̓ílwətaʔ [Tsleil-Waututh] nations, which were never surrendered.

Heartfelt gratitude to my Solidarity Team for this project: Cori Kelly, Tara *Danger* Taylor, Janet Newbury, Sacha Medine, Stefanie Krasnow, and Riel Dupuis-Rossi.

Revolutionary love and solidarity for the Response Based Practice folks: Cathy Richardson whose Cree name is Kinewwsquao, Linda Coates, Allan Wade, and Shelly Bonham. This writing weaves our connections of witnessing resistance while maintaining the important differences in our work, specifically the origins of the theorizing and practice, which comes from different influences, mine from direct action activism, and the RBP from critical and complex analysis of language. I honour these differences while acknowledging the influence RBP has had throughout my articulation and transformation of this work. If other folks can't tell our work apart, well, I'm humbled and honoured by that.

Mr. Peaslee helped again.

References

Ahmed, S. (2012). *On being included: Racism and diversity in institutional life.* Durham and London, UK: Duke University Press.

Akinyela, M. (2002). Decolonizing our lives: Divining a postcolonial therapy. *International Journal of Narrative Therapy and Community Work*, (2), 32-43.

Akinyela, M. (2014). Narrative therapy and cultural democracy: A testimony view. *Australian and New Zealand Journal of Family Therapy*. No 35. 46-49.

Amnesty International (2000). *Torture worldwide: An affront to human dignity.* New York: Amnesty International Publications.

Arendt, H. (1994). *Eichmann in Jerusalem: A report on the banality of evil.* New York, N.Y., U.S.A: Penguin Books.

Reynolds, Vikki (2019). Setting an intention for decolonizing practice and justice-doing. In Collins, S (Ed.) *Embracing Cultural Responsivity and Social Justice.* (pp. 615–630). Victoria: Counselling Concepts.

Reynolds, Vikki (2014). A solidarity approach: The rhizome & messy inquiry. In Simon, G. & Chard, A. (Eds.) *Systemic Inquiry: Innovations in Reflexive Practice Research.* London, UK: Everything Is Connected Books

Reynolds, Vikki (2010). Doing justice: A witnessing stance in therapeutic work alongside survivors of torture and political violence. In J. Raskin, S. Bridges, & R. Neimeyer (Eds.), *Studies in meaning 4: Constructivist perspectives on theory, practice, and social justice* (pp. 157–184). New York, NY: Pace University Press.

Reynolds, Vikki , "Bahman," Hammoud-Beckett, S., Sanders, C. J., & Haworth, G. (2014). Poetic resistance: Bahman's resistance to torture and political violence. *International Journal of Narrative Therapy and Community Work*, 2, 1–15. http://dulwichcentre.com.au/publications/international-journal-narrative-therapy/

Reynolds, Vikki & Hammoud-Beckett, S. (2018). Social justice activism and therapy: Tensions, points of connection, and hopeful scepticism. In C. Audet & D. Paré (Eds.), *Social justice and counseling: Discourse in practice* (pp. 3–15). New York, NY: Routledge.

Reynolds, Vikki & Larcombe, A. (2016). Living Supervision in Practice: Structuring accountability with men therapists working alongside women and gender-variant persons with precarious lives, in I. McCarthy & G. Simon (Eds.), *Systemic therapy as transformative practice*. London: Everything is Connected Press, 125-138.

Brave Heart, M. Y. H., & DeBruyn, L. M. (1998). The American Indian holocaust: Healing historical unresolved grief. *American Indian and Alaska Native Mental Health Research, 8*(2), 60-82. http://doi.org/10.5820/aian.0802.1998.60

Buechler, S. (2005). New social movement theories. *Sociological Quarterly*, 36(3), 441-464.

Butler, J. (1990). *Gender trouble: Feminism and the subversion of identity.* New York, NY: Routledge.

Chomsky, N. (2005). *Chomsky on anarchism*. B. Pateman (Ed.). Edin: AK Press.

Clark, N. (2016). Shock and Awe: Trauma as the New Colonial Frontier. *Humanities*, 5,14,1-16.

Coates, L., Bonnah, S., & Richardson, C. (2019). Beauty and the Beast: Misrepresentation and social responses in Fairy-tale Romance and Redemption. *International Journal of Child, Youth and Family Studies, 10*(1), 119–136. https://doi.org/10.18357/ijcyfs101201918809

Coates, L., & Wade, A. (2007). Language and violence: Analysis of four discursive operations. *Journal of Family Violence*, 22, 511–522. http://doi.org/10.1007/s10896-007-9082-2

Crenshaw, K. (1995). Mapping the margins: Intersectionality, identity politics, and violence against women of colour. In K. Crenshaw, G. Gotanda, G. Peller, & K. Thomas (Eds.), *Critical race theory: The key writings that formed the movement* (pp. 357–383). New York, NY: The New Press.

Defehr, J. (2016). Inventing Mental Health First Aid: The problem of Psychocentrism. *Studies in Social Justice*. 10(1), 18–35.

Defehr, J. N. (2017). Navigating psychiatric truth claims in collaborative practice: A proposal for radical critical mental health awareness. *Journal of Systemic Therapies*, 36(3), 27-38.

de Finney, S., Palacios, L., Kaur Mucina, & Chadwick, A. (2018a). Refusing Band-Aids: Un-Settling "Care" Under the Carceral Settler State. *CYC-Online* September 2019. ISSN 1605-7406, pp. 28-38.

de Finney, S., Moreno, S., Chadwick, A., Adams, C., Sam, S. R., Scott, A., & Land, N. (2018b). Sisters rising: Shape shifting settler violence through art and land retellings. In C. Mitchell & R. Moletsane (Eds.), *Young people engaging with the arts and visual practices to address sexual violence*. Rotterdam, The Netherlands: Sense.

Dupuis-Rossi, R. & Reynolds, Vikki (2018). Indigenizing and decolonizing therapeutic responses to trauma-related dissociation. In Arthur, N (Ed.) *Counselling in Cultural Contexts Identities and Social Justice*. Switzerland: Springer.

Duran, E. (2006). *Healing the soul wound: Counseling with American Indians and other Native Peoples*. New York, NY: Teachers College Press.

Duran, E., Firehammer, J., & Gonzalez, J. (2008). Liberation psychology as the path toward healing cultural soul wounds. *Journal of Counseling & Development*, *86*, 288–295. http://doi.org/10.1002/j.1556-6678.2008.tb00511.x

Fanon, F. (1963). *The wretched of the earth*. New York: Grove Press.

Goffman, E. (1961). *Asylums*. New York: Doubleday.

Hardy, K.V. (2017a). *Race through a trauma lens.* In K.V. Hardy & T. Bobes (Eds.), Promoting   cultural sensitivity in supervision: A Manual for practitioners. New York, NY: Routledge. P.19-21.

Hardy, K.V. (2017b). Soul work: Healing racial trauma. Soul-work: Healing racial trauma; A two-day conference for people of color and white allies. Stampford, June 2-3, 2017.

Heath, T. (2018). Moving beyond multicultural counselling: Narrative therapy, anti-colonialism, cultural democracy and hip-hop.

Hill Collins, P. (1998). Fighting words: Black women and the search for Justice. University of Minnesota Press.

hooks, b. (1984). Feminist theory: From margin to Centre. Boston, MA: South End Press.

Hunt, S. (2016). *Decolonizing the roots of rape culture*. Retrieved from: https://ccsvconference.wordpress.com/2016/09/26/decolonizing-the-roots-of-rape-culture/

Katz, A., & Shotter, J. (2004). On the way to "presence": Methods of a "social poetics." In D. Pare & G. Larner (Eds.), *Collaborative Practice in Psychology and Psychotherapy*. New York: Haworth Clinical Practice Press.

Kouri, S., & Skott-Myers, S. (2016). Catastrophe: a transversal mapping of colonialism and settler subjectivity. *Settler Colonial Studies*, *6*(3), 279–274, http://doi.org/10.1080/2201473X.2015.1061967.

Lacey, A. (2005). *Spaces of justice: The social divine of global anti-capital activists' sites of resistance.* CRSA 42 (4).

Manuel, A., & Derrickson, R. (2015). *Unsettling Canada.* Toronto, ON: Between the Lines Press.

Martín-Baró, I. (1994). *Writings for a Liberation Psychology.* Cambridge: Harvard University Press.

Maynard, R. (2017). *Policing Black lives: State violence in Canada from slavery to the present.* Halifax, NS and Winnipeg, MB: Fernwood Publishing.

Myerhoff, B. (1982). Life history among the elderly: Performance, visibility and remembering. A crack in the mirror. *Reflexive Perspectives in Anthropology*, 99-117.

Regan, P. (2010). *Unsettling the settler within: Indian residential schools, truth telling, and reconciliation in Canada.* Vancouver, BC: UBC Press.

Reynolds, V. & polanco, m. (2012). An ethical stance for justice-doing in community work and therapy. *Journal of Systemic Therapies*, *31*(4), 18–33. http://doi.org/10.1521/jsyt.2012.31.4.18

Richardson, C. (2012). Witnessing life transitions with ritual and ceremony in family therapy: Three examples from a Metis therapist. *Journal of Systemic Therapies*, 31(3), 68–78.

Richardson, C., & Reynolds, Vikki (2014). Structuring Safety in Therapeutic Work alongside Indigenous Survivors of Residential Schools. *Canadian Journal of Native Studies*, XXXIV (2), 147-164.

Richardson, C., & Wade, A. (2008). Taking resistance seriously: A response-based approach to social work in cases of violence against Indigenous women. In S. Strega & J. Carrière (Eds.), *Walking this path together: Anti-racist and anti-oppressive child welfare practice.* Winnipeg, MB: Fernwood.

Richardson, C., & Wade, A. (2010). Islands of safety: Restoring dignity in violence-prevention work with Indigenous families. *First Peoples Child and Family Review*, 5(1), 137–155. Retrieved from http://journals.sfu.ca/fpcfr/

Shantz, J. (2011). *Active anarchy: Political practice in contemporary movements.* Lanham, MD: Lexington Books.

Smith, A. L. (2006). Heteropatriarchy and the three pillars of white supremacy: Rethinking women of color organizing. In INCITE! Women of color against violence (Eds.), *Color of violence: The INCITE! Anthology* (p. 66-73). Cambridge, MA: South End Press.

Spade, D. (2011). *Normal life: Administrative violence, critical trans politics, and the limits of law*. Brooklyn, NY: South End Press.

Strong, T. & Busch, R. (2013). DSM-V and evidence-based family therapy. *Australian and New Zealand Journal of Family Therapy, 4*(2), 90–103.

Sutherland, O., Coulture, S., Silva, J., Strong, T., Lamarre, A. & Hardt, L. (2016). Social Justice Oriented Diagnostic discussions: A Discourse Perspective. *Journal of Feminist Family Therapy, 28*(2-3), 76–99.

Todd, N. & Wade, A. (1994). Domination, deficiency and psychotherapy. *The Calgary Participator, 4*(1), 37–46.

Tuck, E. & Yang, K. W. (2012). Decolonization is not a metaphor. *Decolonization: Indigeneity, Education & Society, 1*(1), 1–40. Retrieved from http://jps.library.utoronto.ca/index.php/ des

Wade, A. (1997). Small acts of living: Everyday resistance to violence and other forms of oppression. *Contemporary Family Therapy, 19*, 23-49. Retrieved from https://link. springer.com/journal/10591

Weingarten, K. (2000). Witnessing, wonder and hope. *Family Process, 39*(4), 389-402.

White, M. (2002). "Definitional ceremony and outsider witness responses." Workshop notes: www.dulwichcentre.cau, August 23rd 2002.

Wingard, B. (2001). Introductions and Stories of Life. In: Wingard B, Lester J (Eds.), *Telling our stories in ways that make us stronger*. Adelaide,, Australia: Dulwich Centre Publications.

ELEVEN

Social Justice Activism and Therapy.

Tensions, Points of Connection and Hopeful Scepticism

Vikki Reynolds & Sekneh Hammoud-Beckett

This writing invites a critique of the tenuous, strained, yet hopeful relationship between social justice activism and therapy (Reynolds & Hammoud-Beckett, 2012). It addresses the tensions of therapy replicating oppressive practices, and invites a critique of our practice with an aim to move us more in line with our collective ethics for justice-doing (Reynolds, 2009; Reynolds & polanco, 2012). This critique entails addressing our positioning in relation to power, privilege, and dis- advantage; resisting neutrality and taking overt positions for justice-doing; naming and beginning to respond to white supremacy and colonialism in our traditions of practice; problematizing our relationship to social control and social change in our work; and resisting competition as affronts to our solidarity. A critical engagement with reflective practice will be offered (Freire, 1970; Tomm, 1985), inviting a hopeful scepticism (Kvale, 1996; Ricoeur, 1970) about our practice enacting the ethics we espouse. Our hope is to breathe life into our ethical engagement with practice, and move towards justice-doing in our work.

Our analysis occurs on the shoulders of women of color feminism (Smith, 2006), critical race theory (Crenshaw, Gotanda, Peller, & Thomas, 1995), queer theory (Butler, 1990), critical trans theory (Spade, 2011), decolonizing practice (Fanon, 1961; Lawrence & Dua, 2005; Walia, 2012, 2013), and anti-authoritarian social justice activism (Buechler, 2005; Chomsky, 2005; Shantz, 2011). Our hope is to contribute to the rich histories of scholarship and activism regarding the pre- carious relationship of justice-doing and the helping professions (Razack, 2002; Rodriguez, 2007; Rossiter, 2006).

Sekneh is a woman of color from a Muslim background with a family experience of migration to Australia. Vikki is a working-class woman and a Canadian-born white settler, whose people migrated to Canada from Ireland, England, and Newfoundland. The analysis that follows is the basis for **all** of our therapeutic work, not only work with people from oppressed locations. For example, all of our praxis addressing colonization is relevant and required in all of our work on Indigenous territories, whether we are working with Indigenous people or settlers.

We offer reflection questions in each section with the hope of unsettling our complicity and re-newing our ongoing commitment to work with intention and accountability. We invite you to take a moment and identify a social issue you have encountered in your work that you would like to explore through a lens of justice- doing. We expect that not all questions can be readily answered, but we see such instances as an opportunity for readers to identify areas for further reflection and action.

Addressing Power and Privilege

To enact a decolonizing anti-oppression stance we need to reflect, as Sontag (2003) says, on how the suffering of others is systemically mapped onto the privileges we hold as helping professionals. These privileges are often made invisible by the obscuring of power. Kvale (1996) warns that an investigation into our practice, and our ability to enact the ethics we espouse, might reveal transgressions we neither intended nor accepted responsibility for.

Addressing our privilege foments discomfort that is both predictable and necessary (Kumashiro, 2004) in terms of unsettling our relationships to power and opening us up to accountability. These reflexive questions, that can never be fully answered, provide a frame for beginning to address our access to power and responding accountably in relationships of power:

- What are the intersections (Crenshaw, 1995; Truth, 1851) of my own power and privilege with the locations of my disadvantage? How am I accountable for unearned privileges?

- How do I resist positioning myself in my locations of disadvantage when serving suffering others? That is, when we are in the power position of therapist, how do we resist positioning ourselves as the oppressed person in the relation- ship due to some other site of disadvantage? How do we get our own sites of disadvantage out of the way if they are not useful?

- How am I responding to power both moment to moment and contextually in this interaction?

- How am I resisting righteousness, posturing, and the double comfort (Heron, 2005) of naming privilege righteously, but doing nothing to mitigate it-such as naming white privilege, and then dominating the space?

- How can I invite, embrace, and hold the discomfort required to accountably address my access to power?

- Who is in solidarity to shoulder me/us/our organizations up in malting space for discomfort, accountability, and repair of power relations? What ideas, practices, and lived experience helps me/us in doing this?

- How are we holding ourselves as professionals, as well as holding our teams, organizations, and professions, to account for transgressions of power? How are clients invited in safe and trustworthy enough ways to name transgressions? What structures and practices are in place to make this naming possible and useful consistently and predictably across time?

Resisting Neutrality and Taking Overt Positions for Justice-Doing

A stance for justice-doing creates a position for therapists to respond to our work alongside suffering others (Sanders, 2007) as activists and to work for socially just structural change. In activism, it is the duty of the witness to do more than respond to suffering, and to take up the project of resisting and transforming the structures in society that create the conditions for oppression and exploitation.

This requires a critical resistance towards neutrality and objectivity (Cushman, 1995; Dyer, 2002) within the helping professions. As therapists there is a risk that we can participate in deconstructing and naming transgressions of power without taking on the social project of transforming the societies in which we live. As Maori researcher Linda Tuhiwai Smith (1999) says in *De-Colonizing Methodologies,* deconstruction is a useful practice, "but it does not prevent some-one from dying" (p. 3).

Simultaneously, as practitioners, we must be careful and critical of how our well- intentioned activism can be used to justify and strengthen the structures that we oppose (Smith, 2006; Spade, 2011). For example, feminist activism against a rape culture (Buchwald, Fletcher, & Roth, 1993) has been used in some contexts to shift more resources to police, nominally for women's safety, in the face of widespread cuts to feminist-based programs, such as shelters, counseling, and court advocacy. We also need to be cautious of using the rhetoric of social justice (Wade, personal communication) to engage in competition, appropriate cultural knowledges, and enact empty posturing.

These questions invite a questioning of our relationship to objectivity, neutrality, and being silent in the face of oppression:

- Despite our overt ethical stances for justice-doing, what positions are we not taking or are being silent about? What promotes this silence: ignorance, tired- ness, discomfort, lack of moral courage, not knowing what to say and how to say it so it can be heard as critique and not attack, concern for career or advancement? Or is silence promoted by histories of being unsupported, victims of backlash, lack of allies, precarious employment, lack of safety as opposed to discomfort, lack of privilege, power, and solidarity? Conversely, when can we take up silence as resistance (Hammoud-Beckett, 2007a) to oppression? How can we discern when it is safe-enough and we are required to speak, and when we need to build more solidarity as a tactic to make effective change?

- How are the politics of neutrality and objectivity mapped onto the legacies of white supremacy and colonization in the helping professions? How are professional objectivity and neutrality connected to other sites of oppression and exclusion; such as homophobia, transphobia, ableism, and stigma against mental illness?

- How do we resist the particular discourses of professionalism that are barriers to justice-doing and maintain our required and useful connections within these disciplines?

- Harlene Anderson teaches that we invented our professions and their codes of ethics, and when they are not just it is our obligation to challenge and trans- form them (Everett, MacFarlane, Reynolds, & Anderson, 2013). Who is along- side us, and what organizations and communities are in solidarity with us when we challenge, resist, and transform our professional bodies?

- How do we hold these positions against neutrality and for justice-doing alongside requirements from funding bodies that side with and maintain structural oppressions?

Naming and Responding to White Supremacy and Colonization

European and Anglo-colonialism in Canada and Australia (and elsewhere) originated in political violence against Indigenous peoples in attempts to steal and exploit Indigenous land, wealth, resources, and children and place Indigenous peoples into a class of servitude. Words such as "torture;' "genocide;' "racism;' and "white supremacy" are omitted from the discourse used to describe this deliberate violence against Indigenous people (Chrisjohn & Young, 1997; Logan, 2001; Richardson & Reynolds, 2014).

Indigenous warrior Gord Hill (2010) describes colonialism as comprised of invasion, occupation, genocide, and assimilation. "Residential schools" in Canada worked to violently assimilate the children whose families survived genocide. Between 48 percent and 70 percent of the children were sexually abused (Feldthusen, 2007). In some schools this figure was as high as 100 percent. The non-sexual physical abuse was often barbaric and indicates that the violence was systemic and deliberate, that those in charge were aware and acted with impunity (Feldthusen, 2007). In Australia, the "Stolen Generations" (Read, 1981) refers to the government kidnapping of between 1 in 10 and 1 in 3 Aboriginal children who were taken to missions or adopted to white families (Knightley, 2000).

In response to the Truth and Reconciliation process in Canada, and the "non- apology" of the federal government (Coates & Wade, 2009) that failed to take full responsibility and did not offer repair, non-Indigenous academic Paulette Regan (2010) asks what it would mean in concrete terms for the settler majority to shoulder the collective burden of the history and legacy of residential schools.

The helping professions are inextricably linked with these violent histories and current oppressions, and practice within contexts of colonization. Indigenous people are often pathologized and described by professionals as mentally ill, traumatized, and addicted, as opposed to seeing their behavior as resistance and naming that they are more often oppressed than depressed. A decolonizing ethical stance requires an inquiry into the relationship of therapy and community work and white supremacy (Akinyela, 2002; Smith, 2006). It also calls for an examination of the professions' (and professionals') participation in colonization (Gergen, 2005; Hammond-Beckett, 20076), what Todd and Wade (1994) name as "psycholonization" and McCarthy (1995) describes as "benevolent colonization:'

Sekneh and Vikki have different migration paths and therefore connected but different accountabilities to the Indigenous peoples whose territories we live on. We struggle with how we collectively decolonize ourselves, our families, communities, and organizations from our specific migration histories. Accountability for land theft, and histories of atrocities against Indigenous people, is complex. We struggle:

- What accountabilities can we enact in order to ethically identify as more than settlers and migrants?

- As settlers and migrants, how can we embrace our nuanced experiences of identity, honoring our histories of migration and honoring our ancestors, and the precarious journeys they embarked on?

- How can we resist centering our own migration experiences, or alternately resist the paralysis of guilt? How, instead, can we intentionally center account- ability, openness, and responsibility to address colonialism?

- Practitioners who identify as white are further required to examine the interconnectedness of colonialism, euro-centrism (Said, 1979), and white supremacy (Said, 1993; Smith, 2007), and to resist and dismantle these oppressions. The following questions offer a frame for therapists who are non-Indigenous to begin to investigate their relationships to colonization and accountable responses to it:

- How am I positioning myself, individually and collectively, on Indigenous territories? How might I act in accord with protocols of the Indigenous communities whose land I live and work on?

- How might I hold all of my work accountable to colonialism, keeping such accountability at the forefront consistently rather than sporadically or not at all-even when working with other non-Indigenous people?

- How might we (as individual practitioners, organizations, and professions) address the colonialism entrenched in the traditions of therapeutic and com- munity practice?

- How might we be directed by and accountable to Indigenous people **in** our work?

- What can we do to actually enact inclusivity (Sin & Yan, 2003) and authentic partnerships and not tokenism in including Indigenous people?

- How might we strategically name and resist colonialism **in** interactions with funders and governing bodies? What is our role and ethical obligation as non-Indigenous workers in resisting, dismantling, and transforming systemic oppressions that make space for our voices at tables with funders/government/ academia at the expense of Indigenous people and voices?

- How are we (as practitioners, organizations, and professions) participating, overtly, covertly, unintentionally, or with ethical blindness, in the psycholonization of indigenous people? How might we be doing this in ways that perpet- rate colonialism and oppression and construct Indigenous people, families, and communities as unwell, broken, and incapable?

Problematizing Our Relationship with Social Control and Doing

Social Change Work

Social justice educator and activist Paul Kivefs (2007) excellent and troubling chapter "Social service or social change" poses foundational questions for workers and non-profit organizations regarding the ethical stance for our work. Are we taking up the project of resisting oppressions and transforming societies, or are we "serving" people who are oppressed and exploited, possibly accommodating them to oppression? As Andrea Smith (2011), a member of the Women of Color Collective says, "You can't heal your way out of patriarchy:' For example, we need to see women who have experienced sexual assault individually in therapy to assist with their personal recovery and simultaneously engage the wider community in the social project of resisting and transforming a rape culture. We need to both walk alongside people who are working to change their relationships to suffering, and work with them for social change directly related to the systemic oppressions that are the root of suffering.

Practitioners who are not working in non-profit organizations or government agencies are not outside of these struggles, but also need to reflect on their role in making social change, and on the accessibility of their services. We need to be strategic about the parts of our work where funding restrains and directs us in ways that replicate the structures of inequity we are responding to and trying to dismantle. Addressing funding needs accountably requires that we navigate com- plex terrains. Non-profit organizations struggle with the diverse implications of funding and ethical obligations to maintain funding to keep their doors open to people who need them.

We acknowledge that we hold this critical analysis along with accountability for our community work being inextricably linked to these tensions. The following reflexive questions invite an inquiry into the ethical stance of our social service work and its connection to the project of social change and transformation of our unjust societies:

- Are we accommodating people to individual lives of suffering, or are we taking on the project of changing the social structures that promote oppression?

- Are we rigorously questioning our possible role (as workers, teams, and organizations) in maintaining social control and increasing surveillance that fall on "over policed and under protected" (Kushnick, 1999) people and communities?

- How can we establish trustworthiness that we are not acting as agents of state control and additional surveillance of our society's most disadvantaged people? (For example, how do we protect migrant people without status who need our care but who do not trust any government-funded agency not to report them to governments who attack and transgress their human rights to refuge?)

- How are we, our teams, and agencies taking on the task of resisting and trans- forming oppressive social structures within our organizations and government agencies that create and uphold the suffering of the people we aim to serve? (For example, how are we working to take on rape culture, hire people from minoritized and marginalized locations?)

- Are we holding accountability to funding sources higher than accountability to the people we aim to serve? If so, how can we resist this, and what people/ communities/organizations can help us get our practices more aligned with our ethics?

- How can workers and non-profit organizations participate in accountable ways with funding bodies, especially as funders may restrict critiques of governments and social policies?

- How can we, as communities of workers and non-profit organizations, stay in strained relationships of solidarity when we are set up for financial competition against each other for scarce resources? How do we decline invitations to division and competition and shoulder each other up in order to collectively take up the project of changing society and responding to the suffering of the people we work with?

- How can we sustain ourselves as workers, organizations, and movements in these messy terrains? What points of connection give us enough wiggle room to be in these spaces of capitalism and social control and maintain our ability to do dignity, and enact our collective ethics?

- While we hold onto and work for our shared vision of a just society in the future, how do we continue to enact ethics within flawed systems? How can we know we are not being co-opted or complicit? How do we resist cynicism and continue our struggles to transform the organizations and government structures we work with and in?

Resisting Competition as an Affront to Our Solidarity

The capitalist context of our work requires that we are in competition with each other, as individual workers and organizations, for resources. Some 30 years of Western democracies' relationship to neo-liberalism and the dismantling of the social net has left people with precarious lives (Butler, 2004; Walia, 2013) and also placed workers in the context of a scarcity of resources amid an abundance of need. This scarcity of resources is of course a myth (Rosenthal, 1999), as evidenced by limited government funding of social work as opposed to seemingly limitless funding to aid corporations (Klein, 2007), militarization (Dawson, 2014), and the prison industrial complex (Davis, 1998; Rodriguez, 2007). Workers and organizations are pitted against each other like dogs fighting over bones.

As workers we are not immune to this competition, despite our explicit claims to the ethics of collaboration and solidarity. We are recruited into the ideas and practices of competition, often replicating the competitive discourse of the sporting realm, whereby the other is positioned as an opponent who can be vanquished through domination and superior strength and skill. If our mandates and collective ethics espouse the desire to change society towards justice-doing, this competition is counter-productive: We know that we need each other in order to resist and transform the structural oppressions that promote people's suffering.

For example, in work against the violence of men, competition invites comparisons and negative judgments of this work as vying for the same resources as work supporting women who have suffered men's violence. But we know we have to take on oppression on all fronts, and that work with people who use violence and people who are victimized are interconnected. Resisting and transforming a rape culture requires we work with all women, men, and gen- der-variant people suffering from and performing violence (Reynolds, 2014a). As bell hooks (2000) teaches, "Feminism is for everyone:' A useful line of questions might include:

- How can we resist competition and enact solidarity in our work with both people who have used violence and people who have experienced violence?

- What practices can we create to hold all of this work accountable to people who have suffered from violence (Hammoud-Beckett, 2007a)?

- How can the safety of people subjected to violence be held at the center of all of this work?

- Our solidarity is required for our collective liberation. Australian feminist Elspeth Probyn (1993) addresses the challenges to feminist solidarity and the power differences that exist between white feminists and women of color feminists. She acknowledges the moral courage required for women of color to speak of racism, and names this act "speaking with attitude" (p. 140). This is not the act of speaking about oneself or the other, rather it is "speaking within the space between myself and another self" (p. 140). Because feminism is a movement, not an individual project, she reminds us to recognize that "without her I am nothing" (p. 163).

- Here are some questions to frame an inquiry into our complicity with competition and to make our solidarity more intentional and public:

- How can we hold onto a believed-in respect for the work of others, based on an understanding of our collective ethics? How can we create dignifying relationships of respect across organizations and domains of practice with an aim to be of use to people we aim to serve?

- How can we resist competition related to funding? How can we prioritize promoting social change, holding the needs of the people we aim to serve at the center? What collaborations or solidarity can we offer to other workers and organizations as we resist disrespectful competition that requires we denigrate their work and reputations, and specifically their ability to be of use?

Conclusion

We hope that this critical investigation into our ethical stances for justice-doing in our collective work unsettles our complicity and renews our ongoing commitment to work with intention and accountability. We want to unsettle a sense of normalcy or "professional competency;' and embrace the discomfort necessary for an ongoing invitation to a hopeful scepticism that invites us to rigorously critique the claims to ethics we hold (Reynolds, 2014b). As we have not delivered on a just society we cannot envision what doing justice would fully look like in practice (Chomsky, 2005), and we join other activists, practitioners, and community members in the hard work required to develop authentic and believable ethical stances that are both decolonizing and anti-oppressive.

We are shouldered up in this project by Arab writer Joumana Haddad (2012), who challenges patriarchy and a myriad of intersecting oppressions. In solidarity, we honor her acknowledgment of the multiplicity of silenced and uninvited voices, and we commit to carving out spaces for these people and voices in our classrooms, organizations, supervision, and societies, and to ongoing resistance against their erasure (Namaste, 2000) and disappearance:

> I owe all these anonymous women and men [sic] a great debt of gratitude. I keep on hearing their beautiful, hijacked voices echoing in my head, inspiring me and pushing me beyond my limits day after day, word after word. You deserve to hear them too ... I am neither a lonely voice in the wilderness, nor an extraordinary exception. My microphone simply works, theirs is broken. But one day it will be fixed. And oh how will they roar when that day finally comes. (Haddad, 2012, p. 157)

Dedication

For Cheryl White and David Denborough, who brought us together, and continue to create spaces that inspire and challenge us in the doing and questioning of just practice in community work. For the people and voices shut out and missing from our teams, organizations, and classrooms: We acknowledge our complicity in these disappearances.

This work and writing occurred on Indigenous territories on Turtle Island (which includes North America) and Australia.

Acknowledgments

This work is truly collaborative. We acknowledge the moral courage and intelligence of our many teachers, most especially students, supervisees, activists, and people we have consulted with who chose to gift us with their critique, questioning, and sometimes just anger, to our benefit, at their cost, across huge divides of privilege. Katy Batha, Riel Dupuis-Rossi, and Aaron Munro, our cultural consultants, contributed to the usefulness of this chapter. Mr. Peaslee helped again.

References

Akinyela, M. (2002). De-colonizing our lives: Divining a post-colonial therapy. *The International Journal of Narrative Therapy and Community Work, 2,* 32-43.

Buchwald, E., Fletcher, P., & Roth, M. (1993). *Transforming a rape culture.* Minneapolis, MN: Milkweed Editions.

Buechler, S. (2005). New social movement theories. *Sociological Quarterly,* 36(3), 441-464. doi: 10.l111/j.1533-8525.1995.tb00447.x

Butler, J. (1990). *Gender trouble: Feminism and the subversion of identity.* New York, NY: Routledge.

Butler, J. (2004). *Precarious life: The powers of mourning and violence.* London: Verso. Chomsky, N. (2005). *Chomsky on anarchism.* B. Pateman (Ed.). Edinburgh: AK Press.

Chrisjohn, R., & Young, S. (1997). *The circle game: Shadow and substance in the residential school experience in Canada.* Penticton, BC: Theytus Books.

Coates, L., & Wade, A. (2009, August). "For this we are sorry": A brief review of Canada's most recent non-apology to Aboriginal Peoples. Presented at Under the

Volcano Festival of Art and Social Change Program. Vancouver, BC.

Crenshaw, K. (1995). Mapping the margins: Intersectionality, identity politics, and violence against women of color. In K. Crenshaw, G. Gotanda, G. Peller, & K. Thomas (Eds.), *Critical race theory: The key writings that formed the movement* (pp. 357-383). New York, NY: The New Press.

Crenshaw, K., Gotanda, G., Peller, G., & Thomas, K. (Eds.), *Critical race theory: The key writings that formed the movement.* New York, NY: The New Press.

Cushman, P. (1995). *Constructing the self, constructing America: A cultural history of psycho- therapy.* Reading, MA: Addison Wesley.

Davis, A. (1998, September 10). Masked racism: Reflections on the prison-industrial com- plex. Color Lines. Retrieved from www.colorlines.com

Dawson, T. (2014, August 19). Military policing in Canada under scrutiny following Ferguson protests. *Edmonton Journal.* Retrieved from http://edmontonjournal.com

Dyer, R. (2002). The matter of whiteness. In P. S. Rothenberg (Ed.), *White privilege: Essential readings on the other side of racism* (pp. 9-14). New York, NY: Worth.

Everett, B., MacFarlane D., Reynolds, V., & Anderson, H.(2013). Not on our backs: Supporting counsellors in navigating the ethics of multiple relationships within queer, Two Spirit, and/or trans communities. *Canadian Journal of Counselling and Psychotherapy, 47*(1), 14-28. Retrieved from http://cjc-rcc.ucalgary.ca

Fanon, F. (1961). *The wretched of the earth.* New York, NY: Grove Weidenfeld.

Feldthusen, B. (2007). Civil liability for sexual assault in Aboriginal residential schools: TI1e balcer did it. *Canadian Journal of Law and Society, 22(1),* 61-91. doi: 10.1017/ S0829320100009121

Freire, P. (1970). *Pedagogy of the oppressed.* New York, NY: Continuum.

Gergen, K. (2005). *An invitation to social construction.* Thousand Oaks, CA: Sage.

Haddad, J. (2012). *Superman is an Arab: On God, marriage, macho men and other disastrous interventions.* London: Westbourne Press.

Hammoud-Beckett, S. (2007a). Nurturing resistance and refusing to separate gender, cul- ture and religion: Responding to gendered violence in Muslim Australian communities. In C. White & A. Yuen (Eds.), *Conversations about gender, culture, violence and narrative practice.* (pp. 43-51). Adelaide, Australia:

Dulwich Centre Publications.

Hammond-Beckett, S. (2007b). Azima ila Hayati-An invitation in to my life: Narrative conversations about sexual identity. *The International Journal of Narrative Therapy & Community Work, 1,* 29-39. Retrieved from http://dulwichcentre.com.au/ international-journal-of-narrative-therapy-and-community-work

Heron, B. (2005). Self-reflection in critical social work practice: Subjectivities and the possibilities of resistance. *Journal of Reflective Practice, 6*(3), 341-351. doi: 10.1080/14623940500220095

Hill, G. (2010). *500 years of Indigenous resistance.* Vancouver, BC: Arsenal Pulp Press. hooks, b. (2000). *Feminism is for everybody: Passionate politics.* Cambridge, England: South End Press.

Kivel, P. (2007). Social service or social change? In INITE! Women of color against violence (Eds.). *The Revolution will not be funded: Beyond the non-profit industrial complex.* (pp. 129-150). Cambridge, MA: South End Press.

Klein, N. (2007). *The shock doctrine: The rise of disaster capitalism.* Toronto, ON: Knopf Canada.

Knightley, P. (2000). *Australia: A biography of a nation.* New York, NY: Vintage.

Kumashiro, K. (2004). *Against common-sense: Teaching and learning towards social justice.* New York, NY: Routledge.

Kushnick, L. (1999). "Over policed and under protected": Stephen Lawrence, institutional and police practices. *Sociological Research Online, 4*(1).

Kvale, S. (1996). *Inter-views: An introduction to qualitative research interviewing.* London: Sage.

Lawrence, B., & Dua, E. (2005). Decolonizing antiracism. *Social Justice, 32*(4), 120-143.

Logan, T. (2001). *The lost generations: The silent Metts of the residential school system.* Winnipeg, MB: Southwest Region Manitoba Metis Federation.

McCarthy, I. (1995). Serving those in poverty: A benevolent colonisation? In J. van Lawick & M. Sanders (Eds.), *Gender and beyond.* Amsterdam, Netherlands: L.S. Books.

Namaste, V. (2000). *Invisible lives: The erasure of trans-sexual and transgendered people.*

Chicago, IL: University of Chicago Press.

Probyn, E. (1993). *Sexing the self: Gendered positions in cultural studies.* London: Routledge.

Razack, N. (2002). *Transforming the field: Critical ant/racist and anti-oppressive perspectives*

for the human service practicum. Halifax, NS: Fernwood.

Read, P. (1981). *The stolen generations: The removal of Aboriginal children in New South Wales 1883 to 1969.* Department of Aboriginal Affairs (New South Wales government).

Regan, P. (2010). *Unsettling the settler within: Indian residential schools, truth telling, and reconciliation in Canada.* Vancouver, BC: UBC Press.

Reynolds, V. (2009, December). Collective ethics as a path to resisting burnout. *Insights: The Clinical Counsel/or's Magazine & News,* 6-7.

Reynolds, V. (2014a). Resisting and transforming rape culture: An activist stance for therapeutic work with men who have used violence. *Ending Men's Violence against Women and Children: The No to Violence Journal,* Spring, 29-49.

Reynolds, V. (2014b). Centering ethics in therapeutic supervision: Fostering cultures of critique and structuring safety. *The International Journal of Narrative Therapy and Community Work, 1,* 1-13. Retrieved from http://dulwichcentre.com.au/ international-journal-of-narrative-therapy-and-community-work

Reynolds, V., & Hammoud-Beckett, S. (2012), Bridging the worlds of therapy and activism: Intersections, tensions and affinities. *International Journal of Narrative Therapy & Community Work, 4,* 57-61. Retrieved from http://dulwichcentre.com.au/ international-journal-of-narrative-therapy-and-community-work

Reynolds, V., & polanco, m. (2012). An ethical stance for justice-doing in community work and therapy. *Journal of Systemic Therapies, 31(4)* 18-33. doi: 10.1521/jsyt.2012.31.4.18

Richardson/Kinewesquao, C., & Reynolds, V. (2014). Structuring safety in therapeutic work alongside Indigenous survivors of residential schools. *The Canadian Journal of Native Studies,* 34(2), 147-164. Retrieved from www.brandonu.ca/native-studies/cjns

Ricoeur, P. (1970). *Freud and philosophy: An essay on interpretation.* New Haven,

CT: Yale University Press.

Rossiter, A. (2006, October). Innocence lost and suspicion found: Do we educate for or against social work? *Critical Social Work,* 2(1), Retrieved from wwwl.uwindsor.ca/ criticalsocialwork

Rodriguez, D. (2007). The political logic of the non-profit industrial complex. In INCITE! Women of Color against Violence, (Eds,), *The revolution will not be funded: Beyond the non-profit industrial complex* (pp. 21-40). Cambridge, MA: South End Press.

Rosenthal, S. (1999, January 1). The myth of scarcity. Retrieved from www.susanrosenthal. com

Said, E. (1979). *Orienta/ism.* New York, NY: Vintage Books.

Said, E. (1993). *Culture and imperialism.* New York, NY: Vintage Books.

Sanders, C. J. (2007). A poetics of resistance: Compassionate practice in substance mis- use therapy. In C. Brown & T. Augusta-Scott (Eds.), *Narrative therapy: Making meaning, making lives* (pp. 59-77). London: Sage.

Shantz, J. (2011). *Against all authority: Anarchism and the literary imagination.* Exeter, UK: Imprint Academic.

Sin, R., & Yan, M. (2003). Margins as centres: A theory of social inclusion in anti-oppression social work. In W. Shera (Ed.), *Emerging perspectives on anti-oppression social work* (pp. 25-41). Toronto, ON: Canadian Scholar's Press.

Smith, A. L. (2006). Heteropatriarchy and the three pillars of white supremacy: Rethinking women of color organizing. In INCITE! Women of Color against Violence (Eds.), *Color of Violence: The INCITE! Anthology* (pp. 66-73). Cambridge, MA: South End Press.

Smith, A. L. (2011). Andrea Smith at Women's World 2011. https://youtu.be/eCZY78dbiD0

Smith, C. (2007), *The cost of privilege: Taking on the system of white supremacy and racism.* Fayetteville, NC: Camino Press.

Sontag, S. (2003), *Regarding the pain of others.* New York, NY: Picador.

Spade, D. (2011). *Normal life: Administrative violence, critical trans politics, and the limits of law.* Brooklyn, NY: South End Press.

Todd, N., & Wade, A. (1994). Domination, deficiency and psychotherapy. *The Calgary Participator,* 37-46.

Tomm, K. (1985). Circular interviewing: A multifaceted clinical tool. In D. Campbell &

R. Draper (Eds.), *Applications in systemic therapy: The Milan approach*. London: Grune &Stratton.

Truth, S. (1851). *Ain't I a woman? Civil rights and conflict in the United States: Selected speeches* (Lit2Go Edition). Retrieved from http://etc.usf.edu/lit2go

Tuhiwai Smith, L. (1999). *Decolonizing methodologies: Research and Indigenous peoples*. London: Zed Books,

Walia, H. (2012, January 1). Decolonizing together: Moving beyond a politics of solidarity toward a practice of decolonization, *Brlarpatch Magazine*. Retrieved from http://briar- patchmagazine.com

Walia, H. (2013). *Undoing border imperialism*. Oakland, CA: AK Press

SOLIDARITY, COLLECTIVE CARE AND SUSTAINABILITY: RESISTING BURNOUT

An Ethical Stance for Justice-Doing in Community Work and Therapy

with response from marcela polanco

Abstract

This writing illuminates a possible stance for an ethic of justice-doing as a frame for community work and therapy. This approach to justice-doing is offered as an imperfection project, and while incomplete and necessarily flawed, it has been helpful to groups of workers striving to practice more in line with our collective commitments for social justice. This approach is profoundly collaborative and informed by decolonizing practice and anti-oppression activism. I will describe the intentions that guide this stance, which include striving towards centering ethics, doing solidarity, addressing power, fostering collective sustainability, critically engaging with language, and structuring safety. Even an imperfect orientation towards justice-doing can open our work to transformations for ourselves, the people we work alongside and our communities and society, and offer the potential for experiencing the social diving. This article is framed from a keynote delivered at the Winds of Change Conference held in Ottawa, Ontario in June, 2012. I acknowledge the Algonquin people whose territories we met on.

Finally, marcela polanco (2011), who describes her work as a therapy of solidarity, will offer a reflection on my position for an ethic of justice-doing.

Introduction

My work is profoundly collaborative and informed by decades of solidarity with direct action activists, and in particular my work alongside survivors of torture in several countries, here I include Indigenous peoples who have survived the political violence of what is called 'residential schools'. I have been informed and transformed by my work. This work comes from a decolonizing and anti-oppression stance, which is not to say it is correct or safe. I embrace this work very much as an anti-perfection project.

I am inviting you to lean into the stance I lay out for justice-doing, and see where there are points of connection in our work, and where we are in imperfect solidarity. I would like you to hold on to the important differences in our work as well. There are many paths to justice-doing, and I have respect for yours, as I outline mine. In my work promoting the care, sustainability and usefulness of teams of community workers and therapists, I ask myself these recursive questions: How can we stay alive and of use working in contexts of social injustice? How can we do this work in accord with our collective ethics (Reynolds, 2009), and our commitments to social justice? How can we hold on to solidarity in political contexts that set us up against each other? How can we experience sustainability and transformation collectively across time? An ethic of justice-doing is my response to these reflexive questions I hold close, struggle with, never fully answer, and never silence.

Our work occurs in contexts that lack social justice because we have not delivered on a just society. The issues of mental illness, addiction, and trauma, are medicalized and sanitized in language that hides human suffering and affronts to dignity. As workers and clients, we are collectively up against the privatization of pain and the criminalization of suffering, such as the criminalization of homelessness, poverty and dissent.

bell hooks (1994), evokes a spirited solidarity when she writes:

> I came to theory because I was hurting — the pain within me
> was so intense that I could not go on living. I came to theory
> desperate, wanting to comprehend — to grasp what was

happening around and within me. Most importantly, I wanted to make the hurt go away. I saw in theory then, a location for healing. (p. 59)

Inspired by hooks, I recognized that theorizing is required for activism, which led me to feminist, queer, and anarchist theory. I am also presently immersed in decolonizing practice and critical trans politics. But there are limits to theory. Liberatory theory is fabulous, but we have not delivered on the promises of a just society (Tuhiwai Smith, 1999). I am also informed by American anarchist theorist Noam Chomsky (2005), who writes:

Social action cannot await a firmly established theory of man [sic] and society, nor can the validity of the latter be determined by our hopes and moral judgments. The two — speculation and action — must progress as best they can, looking forward to the day when theoretical inquiry will provide a firm guide to the unending, often grim, but never hopeless struggle for freedom and social justice. (p. 116)

 Building a just society is a collective responsibility that requires frontline workers to become activists for social change, both in their work with clients and in their lives. Social justice includes all domains of social life. It is beyond the more narrow scope of human rights and justice systems, which primarily uphold laws. Indian author/activist Arundhati Roy (2005), speaks of attacks on social justice, and draws important distinctions between social justice and human rights:

Today, it is not merely justice itself, but the idea of justice that is under attack. The assault on vulnerable fragile sections of society is at once so complete, so cruel, and so clever — all encompassing and yet specifically targeted, blatantly brutal and yet unbelievably insidious — that its sheer audacity has eroded our definition of justice. It has forced us to lower our sites, and curtail our expectations. Even among the well-intentioned, the expansive, magnificent concept of justice is gradually being substituted with the reduced, far more fragile discourse of 'human rights'". (p. 331)

Trans activist Dean Spade (2011) speaks of the limits of human rights, particularly in activism when legal privileges become central. A good example of this is the struggle for gay marriage. There is an understanding that we are working for gay and lesbian human rights, but the message is that we will come back for you trans and gender variant folks later. This is part of a trickle-down discourse of human rights. Spade (2011) says social justice trickles up. People in the margins make more space for everybody. Social justice endeavors that work to improve the life choices of more marginalized folks such as single lesbian racialized undocumented mothers in poverty, improve social justice for gay white men with money privilege. The inverse is not true.

Spade (2011) illustrates how critical race theory, women of color feminism, queer theory, and critical disability studies, highlight the ineffectiveness of the discrimination principle as a method of identifying and addressing oppression, and how ideas of equality are too often tools for maintaining unjust social structures. Part of the complexities involved in practicing resistance politics in what Spade (2011) calls, "an age of co-option and incorporation" (p. 34), requires we reconsider assumptions of human rights and legal strategies. Queer and trans theorists suggest a more transformative approach which includes human rights reforms, but is not centered in them. Social justice activism makes demands that exceed what can be won in a legal systems that Spade (2011) says was, "formed by and exists to perpetuate capitalism, white supremacy, settler colonialism and heteropatriarchy" (pp. 15-16).

So in practice, what would justice-doing look like? There is a poster on the wall in my office which is from Amnesty International, and relates to refugee work in Eastern Europe called 'The return'. It is a sepia-toned picture of a dozen refugees at the moment of embrace, people stepping towards each other with open arms, coming together upon finding each other after the separation of war and political violence. The sense of belonging, joy-filled re-connection and love is palpable — it takes my breath away. One man in the foreground wears a dark coat. This man could be a refugee survivor of torture I worked with. We did not get his family out. He did not kill himself. I guess people say we were successful, as his death was a near thing. But it is the belonging and re-connection depicted in Amnesty International's poster that we really wanted to deliver. This is justice, this is belonging. In our imperfect way, we delivered therapy, we used medication, and we brought everything we had to the circle to help this man, but we could not deliver the possibility of return to his home country, reconnection, accountability, and justice. This is what I want to try to deliver, as an ethic of justice-doing.

How do we do that? Just theory and just practice are not enough. What is required is that we enact our ethics. I am offering a possible and imperfect ethical stance for justice-doing in community work. I utilized Deleuze and Guattari's (1987) concept of the rhizome, for the guiding intentions that comprise my stance for justice-doing. Deleuze and Guattari (1987), offer the rhizome concept to describe horizontally linked, non-hierarchical forms of social organization, thought, and communication. The spirit of the rhizome is illustrated beautifully by Canadian anarchist and liberatory educator Scott Uzelman (2005):

> Running bamboo often gives rise to unwitting bamboo gardeners. A single innocent shoot can stand alone for several years and then suddenly an entire field of bamboo begins to sprout. This leaves the unsuspecting gardener with a new bamboo garden that stubbornly resists attempts to get rid of it. While on the surface each shoot appears to be an individual, related but separate from its neighbors, underground all are connected through a complex network of root-like stems and filaments called a rhizome. During the years the gardener watched a single bamboo shoot grow tall, underground the bamboo rhizome grew horizontally, spreading throughout the yard, storing nutrients in anticipation of a coming spring. Like the bamboo garden, social movements are often rhizomatic organisms growing horizontally into new terrains, establishing connections just below the surface of every day life, eventually bursting forth in unpredictable ways. (p. 17)

The guiding intentions which comprise the ethical stance for justice-doing are different than principles, which are clear and precise. The guiding intentions coexist in relationship to each other, much as the filaments of a rhizome. They are linked, overlapping, living, and fluid. For example, all of the guiding intentions are inextricably linked to structuring safety, and yet structuring safety is itself a guiding intention. Like a rhizome, they are rough around the edges, disorderly, not of equal size, and resist mathematical precision. I will extract each of the guiding intentions in an attempt to describe them. But I offer a caution. In practice and in action, it is not possible or required to completely separate any guiding intention from another. The six guiding intentions are: centering ethics, doing solidarity, fostering collective sustainability, addressing power, critically engaging with language, and structuring safety (Reynolds, 2010a).

Centering ethics

The first guiding intention in my ethical stance for justice-doing is centering ethics. I believe that if we are able to enact our ethics, we can be sustained in the work. When we are not able to enact our ethics, we experience spiritual or ethical pain. This spiritual pain is a discrepancy between what feels respectful, humane, generative, and working in contexts that call us to violate the very beliefs and ethics that brought us to community work. This spiritual pain can be a resource to us, letting us know we are transgressing our ethics. It calls for attention and repair. Collective ethics are those important points of connection that are the basis for the solidarity that brought us together and can hold us together. Our collective ethics speak to the values, intentions and commitments at the heart of our shared work.

What is most important is that we enact our ethics, as it is in the doing that ethics are revealed. Kvale's (1996) hermeneutics of suspicion is informed by Paul Ricoeur's work (White, 1991). This hopeful skepticism invites us to hold our claims to ethics in abeyance, until the practice can be shown to reveal the theory. A hermeneutics of suspicion invites a hopeful yet skeptical position, which requires that we stand in critical distance from the claims to ethics we make, and opens us to the possibility that our practice may reveal something other than our intention. For example, when teams tell me they are client centered, I ask how every action is holding clients at the center of the work, and what clients would say about that claim. This hopeful skepticism invites us to continually ask how we are ethically "walking our talk", as activists say.

Doing solidarity

My understandings of solidarity are derived from time-honoured activist traditions of envisioning collective ethics, looking for connective practices of resisting oppression, and promoting justice-doing. Solidarity speaks to an understanding that just ways of being are interconnected, as are our struggles and sites of resistance. We are meant to do this work together. The work of justice-doing is profoundly collaborative and there are many paths. We do this work on the shoulders of others, and we shoulder others up. When I call my work a Supervision of Solidarity (2010a), I envision a spirit of solidarity that embraces clients, workers and the supervisor.

The Zapatistas are people in an Indigenous movement in Chiapas Mexico, who have inspired a generation of activists. The Zapatista movement is particular to the Indigenous peoples of Chiapas, but they see themselves as connected to communities and people involved in all struggles for social, environmental, and economic justice. Zapatistas call, "We are you", and global justice activists respond "I am Zapatista". This is the doing of solidarity. Subcomandante Marcos (Klein, 2002), illuminated solidarity as the wheel driving the Zapatista movement, when he identified himself in these diverse yet connected ways:

Marcos is gay in San Francisco, black in South Africa, an Asian in Europe, a Chicano in San Ysidro, an anarchist in Spain, a Palestinian in Israel, a Mayan Indian in the streets of San Cristobal, a Jew in Germany, a Gypsy in Poland, a Mohawk in Québec, a pacifist in Bosnia, a single woman on the Metro at 10:00 P.M., a peasant without land, a gang member in the slums, an unemployed worker, and of course a Zapatista in the mountains. (p. 116)

Solidarity invites us to be allies to each other across the differences of access to power that can divide us. When we experience being the subjects of power, we accept allies because we need them, and we cannot be romantic or sentimental about this. We accept allies, not because it is safe or because we have reasons for perfect trust. We invite good enough allies, despite past acts that are not trustworthy, as imperfect allies are required when the stakes are high and risk is near. Fluidity makes room for imperfect allies, momentary allies, moment to moment alliances, which are flawed, not safe, but required and of use.

Fluidity is a gift from queer theory (Butler, 1997), and informs the work of fluid and imperfect allies (Reynolds, 2010b). Fluidity invites imperfect solidarity, which resists unity and looks for points of connection "intersecting oppression and uniting resistance" (No One Is Illegal, n.d.). Being in solidarity with other workers requires resisting injurious division between workers, because it never benefits clients. Some mental health workers have told me of the heartbreaking work they do, at times taking a person's autonomy and admitting them against their will to mental hospitals and psychiatric wards. The rest of us can wash our hands, saying that we would never do that, as if mental health workers are personally responsible for the lack of dignified options. Here, we need to resist blame and lean in, resist judging others, and collectively work for more just options. We need to look for the ethics of the other. I remind myself that no one came to this work to hurt people, and I lean in looking for our collective ethics as a first point of connection and a place for solidarity to begin to grow (Reynolds, 2011a).

Addressing power

A reflexive question I am always asking is: How am I responding to power in this moment? Power is always present in our work, and abuses of power are often at the centre of community work. I am not neutral about power relations, and always take an overt stand for social justice in relation to power. Addressing power requires contesting neutrality, holding a complex analysis of power, attending to the intersections of privilege and oppression, witnessing both acts of resistance and justice-doing, and collective accountability.

I am informed by the work of Crenshaw (1995), and other critical race theorists who articulate intersectionality (Robinson, 2005). Here we look at our access to privilege and power, and the places we are subject to the power of others. The convergence of different domains of identity such as gender, class, and culture, construct this intersectionality. At a RainCity Housing shelter in Vancouver's Downtown East Side where I was consulting, Aaron Munro showed me a sign put up in the shelter. It was a map of the Vancouver area which was stenciled with the message, 'Racism sexism and homophobia are not permitted in this area'. The shelter folks said, "You use lots of big words" and spray painted 'no hate' on the shelter wall. This is the doing of intersectionality.

Witnessing resistance is at the heart of my work. There is always resistance to oppression (Wade, 1996, 1997; Reynolds, 2010b), and addressing power requires we create finely tuned attention to acts of resistance, and sites of resistance, where people are acting for justice, and to maintain a finger hold on dignity.

Collective accountability requires that I be responsible for more than my personal individual acts. This is in resistance to capitalism and individualism, which only require personal responsibility. For example, if my white brother enacts racism, I do not distance myself saying, "I'm not that white guy". I lean in and help my white brother. This is my work to do as a white person. I sometimes refer to racism as the perfect crime, because I acknowledge that I do not have to enact racism in order to benefit from it.

Fostering collective sustainability

In the helping professions, burnout is constructed as an individual problem of workers, which measures whether or not we are tough enough for this work. Burnout is backed up by ideas that our clients hurt us. My clients do not hurt me or harm me; they inspire critique, teach, and inform me. Burnout denies that it is social structures of inequity, and lack of social justice, that harm us in the work. The problem is not in our heads or our hearts, but in the social world where clients live and struggle alongside workers against structures of injustice. The prescription for this individual weakness of burnout is often self-care. I know self-care is important in order for us to bring hope to the helping relationship, and to keep clients at the centre. But it is a limiting idea. I do yoga and drink water, and I have not created one unit of housing in my homeless city. Self-care does not change the context of social injustice, which is where clients live and we work (Reynolds, 2011b).

When I speak of sustainability, I am speaking to an ongoing aliveness, a genuine connectedness with people, and a presence of spirit. Solidarity and collective ethics invite us to collective care, and resisting the individualism that burnout constructs. It invites collective accountability, where I am accountable for more than my individual actions.

Paulo Freire (1970) and the popular education folks, speak of a revolutionary love that is an act of courage and commitment to others (1970). We do not conflate love and sex. We know we need to be careful about language in the work we use with clients, but I do not believe that love is truly absent from our work.

Sustainability requires we have a knowing-in-the-bones that our work matters. This requires that we attend to the things that are not measured in our work. This is what I call immeasurable outcomes, the ineffable, intangible, and untraceable. Our work in the margins goes unmeasured because of the lack of an instrument of measure, or because what we do is not prioritized, or recognized as having value. I track and name our immeasurable outcomes so our work is not disappeared. The important parts of our work that I am calling immeasurable outcomes include such things as doing dignity, and fostering safety and belonging. Immeasurable outcomes also include 'unhappenings', which are the things that do not happen, or situations that do not get measurably worse because of the work we do. For example, and elder who does not repeatedly return to the emergency ward because street nurses got them their medication; or a young man who does not attempt suicide because he is connected to an outreach worker.

Borrowing from the 12 Step traditions of 'giving it back' (Alcoholics Anonymous, 2001), I connect with other workers on the differences their work makes in the lives of the people we work alongside. This is not a nice thing to do — it is an ethical obligation for our collective sustainability. It is not the job of our clients to esteem or dignify us. We must take responsibility for this community-making practice. Here is a story of a 'giving it back' practice from my work in the Downtown East Side of Vancouver:

Joe, a First Nations elder with shaggy hair and an uncertain smile, shows up at my counselling office and I almost fall off my chair. Outreach workers have been looking for him because his health is so risky, he is homeless again, and he hasn't checked in with his parole officer. Everyone is concerned for his life. We are beginning to suspect that he is either dead or in jail.

I say, "Joe! How are you?"

He catches me up on the hell he has crawled through. I ask him to teach me how he "crawled through hell".

He says, "Julie, a worker at detox, kept me alive". Joe says he puked on her twice and she just kept cleaning him up. When he was thinking of leaving detox, she followed him to the door, telling him she would miss him. He was 'nic-ing out' and she found him a cigarette. He said he was rude to her and she refused to take it personally, and told him she knew he could be more respectful.

I said, "That is amazing, have you told her that? Let's call her!" We place a call to detox and actually get Julie on the speakerphone.

I say, "Julie, Joe is here and he's just told me that you are a reason he is still alive."

Julie cuts me off excitedly, "Joe is alive?" She is amazed.

I say, "Yeah, yeah, he is right here and he says that you are a reason he is alive."

In a shaky voice, Joe says, "She remembers me?"

Julie responds, "Of course I remember you Joe, you puked on me twice!"

I ask Julie what it means to her that Joe is saying that she is a reason that he is alive.

She responds, "Man, I can go to work for five years on this!"

I ask Joe what it means to know that he is going to help Julie go to work for the next five years. In a dignified voice Joe says, "Maybe I'll help her keep a couple more guys alive" (Richardson & Reynolds, 2012, p. 2).

Critically engaging with language

No language is neutral, as power is always in play. My understandings of critically engaging with language lean heavily on the analysis of Canadian response based therapists Linda Coates and Allan Wade (2004; 2007), and particularly their work illuminating the following four operations of language in relation to power. According to Coates and Wade (2004; 2007), language can: obscure violence, hide the victim's resistance to violence, hide the perpetrator's responsibilities, and blame victims for violence. I am now going to use the language around rape to illustrate the importance of language and how it operates in powerful ways.

I work as the clinical supervisor at WAVAW (Women Against Violence Against Women), a rape crisis centre in Vancouver. We are living in a rape culture. I am not using the language of rape culture to be provocative or emotional, both of which are used as backlash against feminist voices. I am naming a rape culture as an act of making power transparent, and as Allan Wade would say, putting words to deeds. I use the language of rape culture, because one of three women in Canada will be sexually assaulted in their lives (National Status of Women, 1993). The BC government cut 100% of funding to rape crisis centres in 2002. None of this funding has been returned.

According to Statistics Canada (1993), 6 to 8% of rape is reported to police. Forty percent of those reports get charge approval. Two thirds of the 40%

go to court, 1.8% of those cases end in conviction, and 0.8% of convicted perpetrators get jail time. As a society, we ask women why they don't report rape, why they don't speak out, why they don't leave. We are asking questions of the wrong people. The police and the government need to answer to these numbers, and explain why we are in a rape culture, and how they plan to help us get out of it. We need to ask questions of the perpetrators, not the victims. We live in a society that says "don't get raped", not "don't rape", and where feminism is the 'F' word. Given the math, it is not hard to defend the claim that rape is functionally legal. Judith Herman (1992) alluded to this in her book, *Trauma and Recovery,* when she said that rape was possibly more complicit than deviant behavior.

In response to rape, police offer advice to whom? The victim. And they talk to women about their responsibilities not to be raped. Many police forces have published public awareness campaigns on how the potential victims of rape need to behave. One such poster from the Sussex Police in the UK (2011), says, "Be smart. Say no to any sex you don't want. Make yourself clearly understood". If we consider Coates and Wade's four operations of language, we can see how this language obscures violence, and blames the victims. It also conflates sex and rape, which is a project of feminist activism that we had hoped we had won. Police and their consultants are silent on advice to men.

Happily, feminists have some advice for men regarding rape. In a poster entitled "Stop rape: 10 top tips to end rape", feminists offer an activist inversion of language as resistance. "If you pull over to help a woman whose car has broken down, remember not to rape her". "Use the buddy system. If you're not able to stop yourself from sexually assaulting someone, ask a friend to stay with you when you are in public" (Rape Crisis Scotland, 2011). Offering parallel advice to men seems ludicrous and patronizing, possibly insulting, and certainly fits with what Judith Butler (1997) calls 'unspeakable acts'. Women do not tell men how to act.

Critically engaging with language also requires that we contest normalizing language such as suicide and trauma. Here medicalization is used to cover-up oppression and violence in the context of social injustice and human suffering. We now have symptoms and medication, when what we require is justice. The medicalized language of suicide, for example, constructs a person's death by suicide as an individual act they are solely responsible for. I believe that hate kills. No one kills themselves in a vacuum. When 43% of trans gendered and gender variant people make attempts to commit suicide (National Centre for Transgender Equality, 2010), it speaks more to hate in society than to mental illness in a particular community. Similarly, using a term like suicide when a survivor of torture dies, blames the victim of torture for their own death, which lets torturers, governments, and corporations who profit from the torture off of the hook. We need to contest the neutrality and hidden power in this kind of language.

Liberatory language practices serve our commitments to justice-doing by making power public, contesting domination, attacks on dignity, and oppression. Excellent examples of liberatory language practices are found in the binary-busting language of queer theory that contests the male/female binary. Here is an illuminating example from Queen and Schimel (1997), who describe 'pomosexuality':

Pomosexuality lives in the space in which all other non-binary forms of sexual and gender identity reside — a boundary-free zone in which fences are crossed for the fun of it, or simply because some of us can't be fenced in. It challenges either/or categorizations in favor of largely un-mapped possibility and the intense charge that comes from transgression. It acknowledges the pleasure of that transgression, as well as *the need to transgress limits that do not make room for all of us*" (p. 23, my emphasis).

This is what I think Dean Spade means when they say social justice 'trickles up'. Trans and queer folks in the margins create more space for all of us. I have huge respect for transformative teachings from these communities.

Structuring safety

Most of what I have learned about structuring safety comes from my work with refugees who are survivors of torture and political violence, where the risks of transgressing safety are huge (Reynolds, 2010c). There are no perfectly safe helping relationships, as there are always risks of transgressing safety. We contest the binary of 'safe or unsafe', when we co-create relationships of 'enough-safety' with our clients (Bird, 2000, 2006). I work to create 'some-safety', 'enough-safety', or a 'safe-r' conversation and relationship. All conversations across difference are risky, because power is always at play. Doing harm by replicating oppression is always a potential risk. This is true despite our commitments to social justice and our collective ethics.

Structuring Safety describes the practices of negotiating or co-constructing conditions, structures, and agreements that will make space for 'safe-enough' work. Therapeutic relationships that are experienced as safe are not capricious, natural, or random. They require intentional practices that create consistency, predictability, and set the space for *safe-enough* conversations. Structuring Safety is not something therapists do to get ready for the real work; it *is* the real work (Reynolds 2010c, 2010d).

Developing a capacity for Structuring Safety requires skill, a complex analysis of power, moral courage, compassion, and critical supervision. In all anti-oppression activism, we strategize against an anticipated backlash. There is always the risk of transgression, and the need for repair. Structuring safety is comprised of acknowledging that we are involved in risky conversations, resisting replicating dominance, acknowledging the limits of accountability, and being open to a critique of our most closely held ideas and theories.

Despite our best intentions and our commitments to social justice, we are going to be imperfect. For example, attending to intersectionality can distance us at times from decolonizing practice (Walia, 2012; Lawrence & Dua, 2005; Richardson & Reynolds, 2012). Canadian activist and journalist Linda McQuaig (2011), offered a lovely analysis of the 'Occupy' movement which she said was amazingly successful, despite being flawed, in that it got everyone, including corporate media, to question greed as our highest value. 'Occupy' is flawed and imperfect and useful. There is a lovely poster that came from the 'Occupy' movement that shows an Indigenous woman in the background and the text reads: 'Take back Wall Street. Occupied since 1625'. We can't occupy occupied land. In taking on capitalism, rampant consumerism, and greed, activists risked losing sight of colonization, and invisiblizing Indigenous issues at best, and participating in colonization at worst. In his book, *500 Years of Indigenous Resistance*, Indigenous warrior Gord Hill (2010) outlines how colonization includes invasion, occupation, genocide, and assimilation. Our failures to make 'Occupy' perfect are not a reason to despair, but an opportunity for us to make repair and to engage in decolonizing practice in our imperfect solidarity.

Conclusion

I have outlined six guiding intentions which formulate an ethical stance for justice-doing. They include centering ethics, doing solidarity, addressing power, fostering collective sustainability, critically engaging with language, and structuring safety. The practices are emergent from these ethics. We don't create a practice and try to bring ethics to it. All of my solidarity practices, Solidarity Teams, Solidarity Groups and a Supervision of Solidarity (Reynolds, 2010a, 2011c) , like marcela polanco's Therapy of Solidarity (2011), are emergent from an ethical stance of justice-doing.

It is important that an ethical stance for justice-doing be put back into the context of the rhizome, where it can be open to change. This stance is a part of social justice activism, no more and no less. The stance must be returned back to the networked communities that fostered it (Lacey, 2005), where all of our work finds points of connection, and counter informs and inspires us collectively.

As an activist, I am enlivened by participating in the spontaneous co-creation of spaces of justice-doing, and embodied connections with unknown others, who embrace me with spirited solidarity in direct action struggles against oppression. These moments amplify my hope for change on many fronts, and inspire me in my community work with people who are marginalized. I am going to finish up with a story that speaks to the heart of my own relationship with justice-doing and the social divine:

> It is April 2009. The Olympics, which will cost seven to nine billion dollars, are still a year away, and while homelessness hasn't yet tripled, it will. The 'March Against Homelessness' starts in three different parts of Vancouver. People collect and march towards each other, where we will merge and arrive at a site for a rally. I am marching alongside the people of the Downtown East Side, walking with some guys who are pushing shopping carts, smoking cigarettes, and drinking from bottles wrapped in paper bags. Three First Nations women safety-pin a piece of cloth to my back, upon which are the words 'Homes not Games'. We are a spirited and skeptical crew. A homeless man with stringy hair, who is walking beside me, is making up his own responses to chants, which have us laughing alongside and enjoying his wit. At the moment we come up the incline of Robson Street, we see a crowd of people from the West Side coming towards us.   No shopping carts or jerry-rigged wheelchairs, but lots of all-terrain baby strollers and expensive raingear.   It is the convergence of two very different communities. The guy beside me stops walking. I am elated, moved, my body expansive. I feel palpably connected to him. This relational moment between me and this man, connecting with all of the West Side marchers, is a moment of the social divine. Our differences back-grounded, not invisiblized: Our connections of imperfect solidarity fore-grounded. He looks at me and through a genuinely surprised smile says, "They're here for us" (Reynolds, 2011b, p. 42).

There are no accidents that we are all here today, not in unity (Bracho, 2000), but in a networked community, of imperfect solidarity and collective ethics. We have been brought together at The Winds of Change Conference because we have a shared commitment to justice-doing in our work. Social justice activism is a part of our work, for many of us here it is the heart of our work.

We know that a socially just world is a mentally well world. No justice, no peace. No peace of mind.

Acknowledgements

I hold huge gratitude for the imperfect solidarity of fellowships of activists, co-workers, and 'clients' across several decades, who have informed this work. My continued respect to David Paré who invited this keynote and has continually carved out space for me in my tension-filled relationship with academia. As always, heartfelt thanks to my editor Coral Payne, who continues to make complex ideas accessible. This writing occurred on unceded Indigenous territories, which were never surrendered.

****

Response

marcela polanco:

A response to Vikki Reynold's Ethic of social justice-doing

In the early morning of May 24th 2012, Rosa Elvira Cely, a 35 year old Colombian woman, was found at the National Park in Bogotá, Colombia after she had called the emergency number as she was being brutally raped. She was found shaking, naked, with bruises on her face and neck, and a stab wound in her back. She died at a hospital four days later. Rosa Elvira was a street vendor in Bogotá; she had an 11 year-old daughter, and was finishing her high school studies. She had aspirations of becoming a psychologist as reported by the Colombian newspaper El Tiempo (Gordillo, 2012). Rosa Elvira is one among millions of other women in Colombia, and other parts of the world, who became subjected to horrific and deadly acts of men's violence for having been born women.

Vikki's "imperfect" and "fluid" proposal for a path to work collectively from a position of an ethic of social justice-doing resonated with me as a proposal to shape possible responses to femicide, sexual violence, or other expressions of oppression, marginalization, and discrimination against women.

As a Colombian woman and immigrant in the U.S., when working with women, I face the impossibility of being impartial or indifferent to the profound implications of these kinds of expressions of gender disparity. Instead, I feel concern to act in solidarity with the hundreds of Colombian men and women who took the streets of Bogotá to keep the memory of Rosa Elvira alive, to protest against femicide, and to demand justice. It is a concern with the necessary political awareness that events such as this call to overcome the traditions of impunity, solitude, silence, and amnesia that are often put in place by responses of patriarchal systems of justice. In Vikki's words, I could consider such acts as *doing justice* alongside *doing dignity,* and contesting pretenses of neutrality.

Vikki's ethic of social justice-doing, guided by a requirement of naming power to identify injustices, in this case, make visible the historically rooted gender disparities in my Colombian culture, which, as well as other expressions of social disparities, carries implicit binary thinking. As Indigenous women from Antioquia, Colombia said they suffer marginalization three times: By being Indigenous, poor, and women (Gauma, Pancho & Rey, 2009). Taking a path to attend to intersectionalities, as Vikki proposes, allows entrance into spirited relationships of solidarity when responding to injustices and by abuses of power. In Gloria Anzaldúa's (1987) words, I take this to mean working in the borderlands, men and women together, which requires

...a shift out of habitual formations: from convergent thinking, analytical reasoning that tends to use rationality to move toward a single goal (a Western mode), to divergent thinking, characterized by movement away from set patterns and goals toward a more whole perspective, one that includes rather than excludes. (p. 101)

Vikki's proposal, which I take as an inspiring invitation of inclusion to continue reimaging our worlds, arrives from a land foreign not only to Rosa Elvira's but mine as an immigrant. Yet, its organic and imperfect frame makes visible the cultural gaps among us that seem to intersect at a location from where we could stand in their borderlands alongside one another to sustain our work in our differences, in a virtual collective to contribute to what I hope results in the delivery of more just worlds.

References

Alcoholics Anonymous, (2001). *The Big Book* (4th Ed.). New York, NY: AlcoholicAnonymous World.

Anzaldúa, G. (1987). *Borderlands La Frontera: The new Mestiza.* San Francisco, CA: Aunt Lute Books.

Bird, J. (2000). *The heart's narrative: Therapy and navigating life's contradictions.* Auckland, New Zealand: Edge Press.

Bird, J. (2006). *Constructing the narrative in supervision.* Auckland, New Zealand: Edge Press.

Bracho, A. (2000). An institute of community participation. *Dulwich Centre Journal*, 2000 (3).

Butler, J. (1997). *Excitable speech: A politics of the performative.* New York, NY: Routledge.

Chomsky, N. (2005). *Chomsky on anarchism*. B. Pateman (Ed.). Edinburgh, Scotland: AK Press.

Coates, L., & Wade, A. (2004). Telling it like it isn't: Obscuring perpetrator responsibility for violence. *Discourse and Society*, 15, 499-526.

Coates, L., & Wade, A. (2007). Language and violence: Analysis of four discursive operations. *Journal of Family Violence*, 22, 11-522.

Crenshaw, K. (1995). Mapping the margins: Intersectionality, identity politics, and violence against women of colour. In K. Crenshaw, G. Gotanda, G. Peller, & K. Thomas (Eds.), *Critical race theory: The key writings that formed the movement* (pp. 357-383). New York, NY: The New Press.

Deleuze, G., & Guattari, F. (1987). *A thousand plateaus: Capitalism and schizophrenia*. London, United Kingdom: Athlone Press.

Freire, P. (1970). *Pedagogy of the oppressed*. New York, NY: Continuum.

Gauma, L., Pancho, A. & Rey, E. (2009). Historias de vida de mujeres: Las indígenas hablan [Women life stories: Indigenous women speak up]. In E. Rey (Ed.),*Antigua era más duro: Hablan las mujeres indígenas de Antioquia* [Antigua was more difficult: Indigenous women from Antioquia speak up] (pp. 112-148). Bogotá, D.C., Colombia: Centro de Cooperación al Indígena   Cecoin.

Gordillo, V. (2012, May 29). *Autoridades continúan con la búsqueda de autor de brutal violación. El Tiempo*, Retrieved from http://www.eltiempo.com/colombia/bogota/ARTICULO-WEB-EW_NOTA_INTERIOR-11904904.html

Herman, J. (1992). *Trauma and recovery*. New York, NY: Basic Books.

Hill, G. (2010). *500 years of Indigenous resistance*. Vancouver, Canada: Arsenal Pulp Press.

hooks, b. (1994). *Teaching to transgress: Education as the practice of freedom*. New York, NY: Routledge.

Klein, N. (2002). The unknown icon. In T. Hayden (Ed.), *The Zapatista reader* (pp. 216-217). New York, NY: Thunder's Mouth Press/Nation Books.

Kvale, S. (1996). *Inter-views: An introduction to qualitative research interviewing*. London, United Kingdom: Sage.

Lacey, A. (2005). Networked communities: Social centres and activist spaces in contemporary   Britain. *Space and Culture: The Journal*, 8(3), 286-299.

Lawrence, B., & Dua, E. (2005). Decolonizing antiracism. *Social Justice,* 32(4), 120-143.

McQuaig, L. (2011, October 25). *Occupy movement makes unbridled greed controversial*.Rabble.ca. Retrieved from http://rabble.ca/columnists/2011/10/occupy-movement-makesunbridled-reed-controversial

National Status of Women, (1993). *Evaluation Report of the Women's Program (Appendix B)*, www.swc-cfc.gc.ca/account-resp/pr/wpeval-evalpf/wpe-epf-eng.pdf

National Centre for Transgender Equality (2010). *Preventing transgender suicide*. http://transequality.org/PDFs/NCTE_Suicide_Prevention.pdf

No One Is Illegal Vancouver (n.d.). Retrieved from http://noii-van.resist.ca

polanco, m. (2011). *Autoethnographic means to the ends of translating/ decolonizing narrative therapy: The birth of terapia solidaria [therapy of solidarity]* (Unpublished doctoral dissertation). Nova Southeastern University, Ft. Lauderdale, Florida.

Queen, C., & Schimel, L. (Eds.). (1997). *Pomosexuals: Challenging assumptions about gender and sexuality.* San Francisco, CA: Cleis Press.

Rape Crisis Scotland (2011). *Stop rape: 10 top tips to end rape.* http://www.rapecrisisscotland.org.uk/workspace/uploads/files/rcs%5Btopten%5 Dposta4fi.pdf

Reynolds, V. (2009). Collective ethics as a path to resisting burnout. *Insights: The Clinical Counsellors' Magazine & News*, Winter (1), 6-7.

Reynolds, V. (2010a). A supervision of solidarity. *Canadian Journal of Counselling*, 44(3), 246-57.

Reynolds, V. (2010b). Fluid and imperfect ally positioning: Some gifts of queer theory. *Context: Magazine for Family Therapy & Systemic Practice UK*, 111, 13-17.

Reynolds, V. (2010c). Doing justice: A witnessing stance in therapeutic work alongside survivors of torture and political violence. In J. Raskin, S. Bridges, & R. Neimeyer (Eds.), *Studies in meaning 4: Constructivist perspectives on theory, practice, and social justice.* New York, NY: Pace University Press.

Reynolds, V. (2010d). *Doing justice as a path to sustainability in community work.* http://www.taosinstitute.net/Websites/taos/Images/PhDProgramsComplete Dissertations/ReynoldsPhDDissertationFeb2210.pdf

Reynolds, V. (2011a). The role of allies in anti-violence work. *Ending Violence Association of BC Newsletter*, 2, 1-4. http://www.endingviolence.org/files/uploads/EVABC_NL_Winter11_v2_FINALlo wRes_copy.pdf

Reynolds, V. (2011b). Resisting burnout with justice-doing. *The International Journal of Narrative Therapy and Community Work*, (4), 27-45.

Reynolds, V. (2011c). Supervision of solidarity practices: Solidarity teams and people-ing-the-room. *Context: The Magazine for Family Therapy and Systemic Practice in the UK.* August 2011, 4-7.

Richardson, C., & Reynolds, V. (2012). "Here we are amazingly alive": Holding ourselves together with an ethic of social justice in community work. *International Journal of Child, Youth and Family Studies*, 1, 1-19.

Robinson, T. (2005). *The convergence of race, ethnicity, and gender: Multiple identities in counselling* (2nd Ed.). Boston, MA: Pearson Education.

Roy, A. (2005). *An ordinary person's guide to Empire.* New Delhi, India: Viking by Penguin Books.

Spade, D. (2011). *Normal life: Administrative violence, critical trans politics, and the limits of law.* Brooklyn, NY: South End Press.

Statistics Canada, (1993). *Juristat: Canadian Centre for Justice Statistics.* Catalogue no 85-002-XIE, 19(3).

Sussex Police, (2011). *Be smart.* http://www.psni.police.uk/be_smart_female_postcard.pdf

Tuhiwai Smith, L. (1999). *Decolonizing methodologies: Research and indigenous peoples.* London, United Kingdom: Zed Books.

Uzelman, S. (2005). Hard at work in the bamboo garden: Media activists and social movements. In A. Langlois, & F. Dubois (Eds.), *Autonomous media: Activating resistance and dissent* (pp. 17-27). Montreal, Canada: Cumulus Press.

Wade, A. (1996). Resistance knowledges: Therapy with aboriginal persons who have experienced violence. In P.H. Stephenson, S.J. Elliott, L.T. Foster, & J. Harris (Eds.), *A persistent spirit: Towards understanding aboriginal health in British Columbia.* Canadian Western Geographical Series, 31, 167-206.

Wade, A. (1997). Small acts of living: Everyday resistance to violence and other forms of oppression. *Journal of Contemporary Family Therapy*, 19(I), 23-40.

Walia, H. (2012). *Decolonizing together: Moving beyond a politics of solidarity toward a practice of decolonization.* Retrieved from http://briarpatchmagazine.com/articles/view/decolonizing-together

White, E. (1991). Between suspicion and hope: Paul Ricoeur's vital hermeneutic. *Journal of Literature and Theology*, 5, 311-321.

Supervsion of Solidarity Practices
Solidarity Teams and People-ing-the-room

In this writing I will describe a Supervision of Solidarity which is informed by social justice activism and an ethic of justice-doing (2010a, 2010b). I will outline the supervision practices of Solidarity Teams and People-ing-the-room, and connect with the intentions and theorizing that provide the scaffolding for these practices.

A Spirit of Solidarity

Solidarity speaks to the interconnections of our collective movements towards social justice, and in resisting oppression. This spirit of solidarity has been beautifully articulated by Lily Walker (n.d.), an Australian Aboriginal women's leader, speaking to non-Aboriginal activists at a land rights protest: "If you come here to help me, then you are wasting your time. But if you come here because *your liberation is bound up in mine*, then let us begin."

While the language of solidarity may be new to many therapists, the spirit of solidarity is alive and well in our work with each other and with clients. I am borrowing this term from social justice movements as part of my hope in bridging the worlds of therapy and activism. Using the language of solidarity here is not loose language, posturing, or an attempt to alienate less politically located folks! I am purposefully inviting therapists to engage with the rich traditions of solidarity that hold us together.

No language is neutral (Brand, 1991) and like much language from social justice movements the word solidarity is problematic. I align myself with Wittgenstein's (1953) idea that the meaning of a word is in its use, and I engage the term solidarity to mean that our collective liberation, and struggles towards something *just*, are interwoven. Engaging with a spirit of solidarity means that we see all of our work towards justice as inter-connected, and that we have ethical commitments to recursively carry and sustain each other and act in line with our collective ethics (Reynolds, 2009).

A Supervision of Solidarity

A Supervision of Solidarity speaks to an ethical positioning for justice-doing in therapeutic supervision. I supervise therapists who work amidst structures of injustice where death is ever-near, alongside people whose experiences of marginalization are extreme, and whose suffering is unconscionable. As a supervisor I need to respond to the desperation, risk and isolation experienced by clients, as well as the spiritual pain held by therapists who can experience work in contexts of injustice as shoveling water.

The creation of the supervision practice of Solidarity Teams was my response to these reflexive supervision questions:

- How can I help therapists be more accompanied and less alone when working with clients who have a finger-hold on dignity, and are suffering experiences of social and political injustice and exploitation?

- How can I make myself more available to therapists struggling with despair, paralysis, or feelings of incompetence in the face of grave problems?

- How can I *belong* therapists within a community of others who work in accord with our collective ethics, embrace a spirit of solidarity, and see our collective work as justice-doing?

My interest in building community and creating rooted and fortifying connections in supervision has to do with my belief that, over time, isolation and individualism loom as great threats to our sustainability. Our pre-existing unity, shared hopes, and commonly held ethics speak to the fact that we are already doing solidarity with each other.

Solidarity Teams

A Solidarity Team is a group of people who serve as a networked community (Lacey, 2005) of support which shoulders-up a therapist and accompanies them in the difficult contexts of their work. This practice was developed in my early work alongside survivors of torture and political violence. It was immediately apparent that I would need to build a team in order to be sustained and useful in the work. The purpose of the Solidarity Team is to contest the isolation and individualization of the therapist by positioning them within community. In supervision I invite therapists to build their own Solidarity Teams by choosing specific people from their lives, and carrying that team into their work in imagined and actual ways.

Being positioned within a community of choice allows therapists to access all of who it is possible for them to be in order to be of use to clients. The question for therapists is not, "what would my supervisor say now", but rather;

- If I were to position myself in solidarity alongside my supervisor, how might I respond more usefully with this person?

- If I engage with the spirited solidarity of my Solidarity Team how might I be resourced to be the most useful therapist I can be in this moment, with this person, in this context?

The Solidarity Team exists fluidly, across time, and is comprised of people both real and imaginary, who are alive or who have passed on. Solidarity Team members may be intimate to the therapist or be public figures. When I began working alongside doctors, I put Che Guevera on my Solidarity Team because he was a revolutionary doctor committed to the struggle for global justice. Che invites me to act in solidarity with doctors despite different locations of power because we work alongside marginalized people and my solidarity is required.

Solidarity Team members can invite us to collective accountability for the gaps in our work: those spaces in between our privileged locations and the marginalized locations of clients or other therapists (Reynolds, 2010d). For example, I invite therapists working with men who have been violent in relationship to hold a Solidarity Team member who has suffered rape alongside them. This can position the therapist in community with a greater capacity to attend to the tension of compassion for him, alongside an invitation of responsibility for his actions. I ask these supervisory questions:

- How might your work with this man who has used violence be different if this Solidarity Team member was in on all of your conversations with him?

- How might you be better resourced not to lose track of the victims of violence by being accompanied by this Solidarity Team member?

My Solidarity Team includes Warren Williams, who identifies as Black, and whose imagined, re-membered, and sometimes physical presence invites me to be accountable to my location as a member of the dominant culture (and where I live in Canada that means a member of white culture). I position myself alongside Warren to borrow on his knowings of working accountably alongside minoritized and marginalized person. Warren's solidarity is also useful to me when I work alongside my people from the dominant culture as his imagined-presence helps me invite them/us to accountability. I invited Jesse P., a transgendered person from my family of choice, to be on my Solidarity Team. I hold him close in all my supervisory work, reminding myself that I can never really know who anyone is. I do not want to close space for anybody's identity - therapists or clients. This is true not solely regarding issues of gender, but in all domains of identity (Crenshaw, 1995) where what passes for normal is socially constructed and subject to my power in the supervisory relationship.

These Solidarity Team members inform me to engage with these reflexive questions:

- How is Warren's spirited presence in this conversation inviting me to account for my privilege and access to power? How is Warren's solidarity shouldering-up my active resistance to transgressing against this person's dignity?

- If Jesse were alongside me now, how might I open more space for all of this person's preferred identity and ways of being to be welcomed into our relationship?

- How can our Solidarity Teams resource us to resist replicating disrespect, harm, dominance and oppression in all of our work across differences of power (Wade, 1997; Reynolds, 2010c)?

Cathy Richardson, who identifies as Métis, engaged with the practice of the Solidarity Team in a unique way as she gave the opening lecture at a conference. She put three chairs on the stage behind the podium. She invited her colleague, Allan Wade, who is a white man, well published and holds a Ph.D., to sit in the middle chair. On either side of him she placed a book written by other white men who are also well published and held Ph.D.s. Cathy made public to all of us that her purpose was to show that white people, with authenticated and privileged voices, were saying the same things that she was saying as a Métis person. Cathy let us know that she was doing this to remind herself that she knew the facts, and that they were correct. Allan's presence, sitting down behind her, reminded her that she was not crazy, and that there were allies who would back her up when she named colonization and genocide.

In supervisory conversations I use the following questions to invite therapists to explore the possibilities of creating, embodying and accessing their own Solidarity Teams:

- Who would you invite to be on your Solidarity Team?

- What qualities do they hold which qualify them to be on your Solidarity Team?

- What qualities, resources, ideas, and collective ethics connect you with this person/these folks? (individually and as a group)

- What is your history of solidarity with these folks?

- How will you invite these folks onto your Solidarity Team?

- What are the expectations and responsibilities of this position as a Solidarity Team member?

- How will you embrace Solidarity Team members with whom you have no physical contact, such as mentors who have passed on, such as your grandmother, a former hockey coach. Or people whom you have not met - Neil Young, Emma Goldman...

- How might you access your Solidarity Team in your work? When might you invite particular members to be in solidarity with you? When might you have the whole team? Are there times when you would not invite a particular member into conversation with you?

- In what circumstances will you invite the spirit of members of your Solidarity Team, and when might you actually invite another person to a conversation, or make physical contact with a person?

- Consider your relationship with a particular Solidarity Team member. How will being in solidarity with this team member make it possible for you to be of use to clients, and more in line with your ethics? If I were to ask this Solidarity Team member about their particular experiences and knowings of your relationships with ethics, how would they respond? If I were to ask this Solidarity Team member how you have been in solidarity with them, how would they respond?

- How will you hold yourself accountable to the members of your Solidarity Team? How will you catch them up on their usefulness to you and to clients, for moments they cannot know about? What difference will belonging in this Solidarity Team make
  - For you?
  - For the people you've invited to be in solidarity with you?
  - For the people you work alongside?

Solidarity Teams offer the possibility of an ever present witness to the epiphanies, small miracles, and moments of meaning and beauty in our work, that may otherwise be lost. Invitations to Solidarity Team members can make explicit our permissioning of each other to connect without fear of judgment, whether things are going well or poorly. Having a plan of who to call in a crisis is a foot up against despair. In moments of despair, when we are lacking in spirit, Solidarity Teams can accompany us, in physical and spirited ways, and re-member (Myerhoff, 1982; Madigan, 2011) us with experiences of competency and usefulness.

People-ing-the-room

The practice of People-ing-the-room invites therapists to bring forward the spirit of their Solidarity Team members and is informed by Karl Tomm's ideas of the internalized other (1985). Karl uses this practice in couples counselling where he interviews one partner as their internalized other, meaning their experience of the other person they carry with them. He then checks in with the partner to see if the person has had an accurate experience of them. To use a heterosexual couple as an example, a woman is interviewed as her partner and responds, speaking in first person, as him. The man is then interviewed to see if he feels that the woman has understood him. Karl would then interview the other member of the couple as their internalized other: the man would then be interviewed as the woman and speak in first person as her. The woman would be called by the man's first name to invite her into the experience.

I began to expand on the practice of the internalized other when I started working with refugees who were survivors of torture and political violence. Many survivors live in extreme isolation in which they have no one to share meaningful greetings in their language or ever touch them in kindness. In an effort to help these survivors re-member sites of belonging, I invite them to People-the-room. I interview the survivor as one of their internalized others in order to help them re-member some part of themselves that has been stolen through the violence of torture and displacement.

I worked with a survivor of torture from northern Africa who felt that he had lost touch with his courage.

When I asked who would be a good witness, and could re-member him as a person in connection with courage, he introduced me to his mother as an internalized other. He then responded as her to my questions about him. Interestingly, his mother (speaking in a different language) thought that grandmother was a better person to tell the story. We People-d-the-room with his grandmother. In a third language, she told a beautiful story of this man as a baby, giggling and happily waving at a dangerous snake that had everyone else horrified.

In preparing for this survivor's refugee hearing, which was daunting and terrifying, we engaged with the practice of people-ing-the-room evoking his community and family to be alongside him in the courtroom. This practice held him in a profound and embodied love, making it possible for him to withstand the indignity and risks of the re-tellings of torture's story of him. (This survivor gave his permission for me to use our work together in teachings and writings. His hope in sharing his story was to be of use to me, and help therapists be more useful alongside refugees.)

I then expanded the practice from clients to therapists. When we lost a survivor of torture to what euphemistically gets called "suicide", I immediately surrounded myself with members of my Solidarity Team by People-ing-the-room. I remember the immediate sensation of being accompanied in my tiny, now-crowded and still-empty office. Because I was facing a death, I called forward the members of my Solidarity Team who have been alongside me at executions in anti-death penalty work. I also evoked members who I sensed would best accompany me in this dark moment. I moved fluidly from the experience of feeling accompanied by my Solidarity Team to picking up the phone and methodically attempting to make real-time contact. Stephen Madigan, a member of my Solidarity Team, was the first person I was able to speak with. He asked about the care of my team, and offered to come to us immediately. We declined his offer, but in this conversation he was of further use to me in terms of helping me make an immediate plan that included canceling my morning appointments. In my isolation, I was not able to see that I could not be useful in that moment with survivors of torture, many of whom were struggling with suicide.

In contexts of social injustice therapists can become burdened, terrified and paralyzed. In supervision I invite therapists to plan for these likely possibilities, and create strategies to People-the-room with allies from their Solidarity Team when needed. For example, facing fear, therapists can borrow on the moral courage allies hold in order to centre the client and offer containment and enough-safety (Bird, 2004, 2006). My aim is for therapists to be embraced with revolutionary love, re-minded of their relationships with competency and more able to be present.

People-ing-the-room positions the therapist *within* a community of concern (Madigan & Epston, 1995), and offers a way to engage with the spirit of their Solidarity Team. It is also a resource that we can share with clients so that they are not alone in their struggles.

Conclusion

"Self-care" and competency are not enough to ensure the sustainability and usefulness of therapists working within contexts of social injustice. Practices informed by the ethics of a Supervision of Solidarity invite us to hold our competency alongside a rich interconnectedness. Solidarity practices invite a critique of and resistance to the influence of individualism, and promote inter-dependence over independence. The supervisory practices of Solidarity Teams and People-ing-the-room can breathe life into a Supervision of Solidarity, making it palpable, embodied and useful.

This article is dedicated to Warren Williams & Jesse P. for teachings, revolutionary love & solidarity.

Acknowledgments

This writing is profoundly collaborative. I honour the communities of activists who have mentored and critiqued me, held me in solidarity, and made these ideas/practices speakable. This work is informed, inspired and shouldered-up by the folks who have provided excellent supervision throughout my work: Michele Maurer, Heather Elliott, Stephen Madigan, Colin Sanders, Johnella Bird, David Epston, Cathy Richardson and Allan Wade. Many of their ideas and ineffable contributions live as shadows throughout my work and this writing, and can't be nailed-down-enough in references.

References

Bird, J. (2004). *Talk that sings: Therapy in a new linguistic key*. Auckland, NZ: Edge Press.

Bird, J. (2006). *Constructing the Narrative in Supervision*. Auckland, New Zealand: Edge Press.

Brand, D. (1991). No Language is Neutral. *University of Toronto Quarterly*: 61(1), p. 64. Coach House Press.

Crenshaw, K. (1995). Mapping the margins: Intersectionality, identity politics, and violence against women of colour. In K. Crenshaw, G. Gotanda, G. Peller, & K. Thomas (Eds.), *Critical race theory: The key writings that formed the movement* (pp. 357-383). New York: The New Press.

Lacey, A. (2005a). Networked communities: Social centres and activist spaces in contemporary Britain. *Space and Culture: The Journal*. 8(3), 286-299.

Madigan, S., & Epston, D. (1995). From 'spy-chiatric gaze' to communities of concern: From professional monologue to dialogue. In S. Friedman (Ed.). *The reflecting team in action: Collaborative practice in family therapy* (pp. 257-276). New York: Guilford Press.

Madigan, S. (2011). *Narrative Therapy*. Washington: American Psychological Association.

Myerhoff, B. (1982). Life history among the elderly: Performance, visibility, and remembering. In J. Ruby. (Ed.). *A crack in the mirror*. Philadelphia: University of Pennsylvania Press.

Reynolds, V. (2010a). *Doing Justice as a Path to Sustainability in Community Work.*

Reynolds, V. (2010b). A Supervision of Solidarity. *Canadian Journal of Counselling*, 44(3), 246-257.

Reynolds, V. (2010c). *Doing justice*: A witnessing stance in therapeutic work alongside survivors of torture and political violence. In J. Raskin, S. Bridges, & R. Neimeyer (Eds.), 157-184. *Studies in meaning 4: Constructivist perspectives on theory, practice, and social justice*. New York: Pace University Press.

Reynolds, V. (2010d) Fluid and Imperfect Ally Positioning: Some Gifts of Queer Theory. *Context*. October 2010. Association for Family and Systemic Therapy, UK, 13-17.

Reynolds, V. (2009). Collective ethics as a path to resisting burnout. *Insights*, Dec. 2009, 6-7.

Tomm, K. (1985). Circular interviewing: A multifaceted clinical tool. In D. Campbell & R. Draper (Eds.), *Applications in systemic therapy: The Milan approach*. London: Grune & Stratton.

Wade, A. (1997). Small acts of living: Everyday resistance to violence and other forms of oppression. *Journal of Contemporary Family Therapy*, 19(l), 23-40.

Walker. L. in Sinclair, R. (n. d.). Participatory action research. In *Aboriginal and Indigenous Social Work.*

Wittgenstein, L. (1953). *Philosophical investigations*. Oxford, England: Blackwell.

FOURTEEN

The F Word:
An Interview with Vikki Reynolds on the Politics of Forgiveness

Conducted by Natasha Sanders-Kay

VIKKI REYNOLDS is an activist and therapist who works from a Decolonizing and Justice-doing framework. As a consultant, facilitator and supervisor she has worked with refugees, survivors of torture—including Indigenous survivors of state violence in Canada—mental health and substance use counsellors, rape crisis counsellors, frontline and housing workers and QT2SBIPOC communities. Her specialties include 'Trauma' and Witnessing Resistance to Violence and Oppression and a Supervision of Solidarity. Vikki is the author of *Justice-Doing at The Intersections of Power: Community Work, Therapy and Supervision* (Dulwich Centre Publishing, 2019). She conducts her work on the unceded territories of the xʷməθkwəy̓əm (Musqueam), Skwxwú7mesh (Squamish), and Səl̓ílwətaʔ/Selilwitulh (Tsleil-Waututh) Nations.

On August 2, 2022, *subTerrain* spoke with Vikki on Zoom about forgiveness. What follows are excerpts from our conversation. Catch the full video interview at https://vikkireynolds.ca/media/

subTerrain: In your experience, what makes forgiveness possible?

Vikki: I remember being taught by Johnella Bird from New Zealand, she said forgiveness is the 'F' word in therapy. So much of therapy was about sending people— in particular women and non-binary people who'd been harmed by, for the most part, men—therapy was about getting them ready to go back into the world and face more abuse and shit and violence, and forgive the perpetrators; that that was the goal of therapy. And a lot of the talk was if you don't forgive, they own a part of you and all this stuff. So I started off not being very enamoured of the idea of forgiveness. But, aside from being a therapist, I'm a prison abolitionist, and I worked against the death penalty. And that really informed my thinking, not necessarily about forgiveness, but about repair, and restoring humanity to people, and to the complexity of seeing people beyond just being perpetrators. Forgiveness itself is pretty problematic when it's decontextualized and weaponized against really oppressed and harmed people. It's very political, who is required to forgive and who is allowed to withhold forgiveness as a virtue. That's always gendered, classed, racialized. When you can have accountability and repair, then I believe people can have something that might smell like forgiveness.

subTerrain: What does a genuine apology look like?

Vikki: I've been really informed by the transformative justice folks, women of colour in particular; I'm thinking about Mariame Kaba, Angela Davis, groups like INCITE! Women, Gender Non-Conforming, and Trans people of Color Against Violence, and Mimi Kim of Creative Interventions, and Rachel Herzig of Creative Resistance. So all of what I'm going to talk about is really informed by direct action activism and all of these brilliant people. The first thing I do in moving towards an apology, is you've got to acknowledge the structural violence that incident happened in. No guy I worked with ever invented violence. We need to start with the context. People need to be accountable for their actions. I believe 100% in accountability, but people are *not* accountable for the contexts in which those actions occur. Meaning poverty, colonization, racism; we need to think about necro-politics, about Mbembe's work about policies that actually kill people—that's the real violence and strategic abandonment of people, what abolitionist Ruth Wilson Gilmore describes as organized abandonment. I've given you a long answer, but to get to a real apology, the first thing is you have to *name what you did*. In real language. The second thing is you have to take responsibility not just for what you did but for *the potential impact and consequences that you made possible in this world*. If a man hits a woman and her head hits the table, she could be dead. He's not only responsible for hitting her, he's responsible for very potentially killing her. You have to really map out all those potential consequences. It's very tender to do that work because that's where I worry that, in particular, men who are trying to take responsibility might think about suicide. Because if you truly map out how much consequence there is here, it's enormous. That's what we have to repair. And I'm willing to walk alongside men to repair all of that. When you involve the police and you go to the justice system, they're only responsible for that one act. And it all becomes about punishment, there is no repair. So that third piece is about *working to make repair*. How do we start to repair, and we start with, ethical practice, for me, means, you track vulnerability. Say "Who's the most vulnerable?" and centre those persons. Often people want forgiveness. That's not up to you. It's up to the person who has experienced the harm to decide whether forgiveness is a piece of what's important for *them*. We've all been in experiences, whether it's a person talking to us or whether we've transgressed and just go, "Oh you have *got* to forgive me! My way back to my humanity, to my picture as a decent person integrated in society, is all hinged on your forgiveness"— that's not okay. That's an abuse of power. That's actually demanding something of someone that you harmed; you don't get to make the demands now. They might make demands of what is required for a repair. But that's not hinged on "And then I'll forgive you." They might never forgive you. A lot of the men I've worked with have often really hurt their children and female partners—and their kids never want to see them again. Then part of the accountability is making sure you're never near those people again. So you do the work to make repair. Then you have to *have a real plan to not do it again*. The fifth one is *you have to not do it again*.

subTerrain: What kinds of power and privilege relations need to be kept in mind when we forgive, or choose not to? Or when we want to be forgiven?

Vikki: If we move with forgiveness, what happens is in our society under patriarchy and all those other power structures is—you have to forgive *and forget*. I teach young women to *not* forget. Young women have a knowing in the bones—a wisdom of the body that comes from experienced violence. I don't want them to forget that. I want them to hold on to everything I call their 'spidey sense.' Everything that lets you know this is not going okay. When we do forgive and forget, we never talk about this stuff again, pretend it didn't happen—that's gaslighting. Especially the imperative, you know, young women and non-binary people—especially of colour, poor, Black, Indigenous—are really *required* to forgive. That's your big job, you start forgiving before you even understand oppression or have any analysis of that. And in that forgiving, how much is forgotten? That actually sets people up again. We've got to make sure the real work is being done so that forgiveness doesn't happen at the cost of moving in a just way. Again, if we're going to use an ethical map and centre most vulnerable people, forgetting is a really dangerous act that doesn't centre people who've been harmed.

subTerrain: Who is forgiveness for? What's its value and potential?

Vikki: I think when forgiveness is weaponized it's always to stop repair, to stop accountability, but also to stop transformation of our societies, right? Like the imperative to forgive as young women, in particular, stops us fighting rape culture and stops us from the creation of a consent culture which benefits everybody. That's the real cost of the weaponization of forgiveness. But for some people—as a therapist I know this, I've worked with survivors of torture, right—for some of them, they wanted to forgive the people who'd harmed them. I'll give you one example. I was seeing a guy who was a political activist, he was a Communist, he was a direct-action activist, he had risked everything, and he ended up going to jail and was

252

tortured. He needed to forgive those people. Because of his own political analysis which said they were also just workers. His thing was, if he continued to think of this torturer as his Satan—that he was letting the oppressive state apparatus off the hook. So forgiveness *can* make space to hold *more* accountability, know what I mean?

subTerrain: What are some of the biggest lessons you've learned about forgiveness, doing the work that you do?

Vikki: How it's weaponized. It's absolutely devastating to be with so many young women, who are harmed in so many ways, and yet they are informed, by social workers, probation officers, family members, all these other things, that they are *required* to forgive. And they come to therapy doing everybody else's work. And just the load that is carried by oppressed people.

But the other thing I would say is—'cause it's lovely to speak about that one man who was a survivor of torture—you know, that experience humbled me. *I* wasn't willing to forgive any torturer. And it was absolutely liberatory for him. In my own life, I'm sixty-one now, I've moved to forgiveness for people who haven't done the hard work to do repair. Because *I* didn't want to be angry anymore. It was good. But it didn't change anything. Because people don't do the work, it's not a *transformative* forgiveness. A forgiveness that is tied to accountability and people having done the work, *then* you can forgive with an open heart, thinking "I'm actually part of transforming the world"; that's really something to celebrate.

THIRTEEN

The Zone of Fabulousness

Resisting vicarious trauma with connection, collective care and justice doing in ways that centre the people we work alongside

The Zone of Fabulousness: A person centered approach to "Burnout"

This work offers an alternative approach to understanding the ways we as workers are harmed in the work, and our collective resistance to these harms, that is different than Vicarious Trauma or Burnout. Instead of looking at workers' traumatic symptoms we look at how we treat people we work alongside (persons), and if we are able to create relationships of respect and dignity. Are we in staff-centered teams, or person-centered teams? If so, how are persons at the centre of all we do? As workers, are we responding to the heart-breaking work with disconnection where we are moving too far away from persons, taken with negativity and moving into cynicism; or are we moving in too close, with heroic posturing, becoming enmeshed and enacting transgressions of intimacy and 'specialness'? If we are able to hold persons at the centre of our work and care, and stay with connection, resisting Disconnection and Enmeshment, we are more able to resist Burnout and create collective sustainability. The Zone of Fabulousness is the space of connection, where persons are at the centre, we are connected as workers in our collective ethics with collective care (as opposed to self-care), the bringers of a believed-in hope as an ethical obligation, collaborative and creative, messy, imperfect but accountable, and shouldering each other up.

Where I am standing: Decolonizing and unsettling

While my aim is to enact justice-doing and decolonization in all of my paid and unpaid work, I am immersed in the on-going work of un-settling myself as a white settler (Reynolds & Hammoud-Beckett, 2018). Tuck & Yang (2012) teach that decolonization is not a metaphor, and means commitments to Indigenous governance and land return. I aim to be directed in all my activist work and organizing by Indigenous people (Manuel & Derrickson, 2015).

Resisting Burnout with Justice-Doing

Resisting Burnout with justice-doing reflects an activist position for staying alive in our work (Reynolds, 2011a). Ideas of Vicarious Trauma are based in ways persons' pain infects us with hopelessness, yet often persons inform, transform, educate, provoke and educate us. The harms in our work are most often from structures that are oppressive and do not allow for the resources and practices needed to respond to human suffering with dignity. Four decades of neo-liberalism, the destruction of the social net of care, and mean-spirited and hate-filled politics must be understood as the context of our work and inextricably linked to our struggles for sustainability as workers. Our resistance to these contexts of structural oppression and horror is to enact our collective ethics which are the values that drew us to this work and the fabric of the solidarity that can hold us together in acts of collective care. Self-care is a required, but limited response. Self-care is essential so that we can de-centre ourselves as workers, and truly hold the person at the centre of our care. Working against our ethics leads to spiritual pain or ethical pain, and workers have taught me across decades that spiritual pain is a better way to understand the harms workers experience than Burnout. If we can enact collective care, as opposed to only self-care, sustainability becomes possible, and we can act in solidarity as activists to change the social context, and shoulder each other up in resistance to the dark spaces of our work.

From a justice-doing lens 'Vicarious Trauma' inventory measures are more accurately revealed as measures of the privileged locations of practitioners. Workers with more access to power and life choices can measure up as more profession, more 'mentally well'. I believe a better measure of practitioner wellness is how we treat the persons we are working alongside, if persons are centred in the work, and if we are enacting our collective ethics.

There are two main ways that what gets called Burnout shows up with workers: Enmeshment and Disconnection. As workers we either move too close into persons enacting transgressions of intimacy, or too far away enacting negativity and Disconnection.

Enmeshment

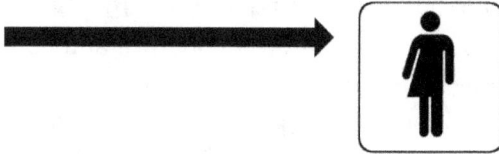

When workers enact Enmeshment we move in too close and transgress the boundaries of persons. We position ourselves as heroes, moving outside of what is humanly possible. Heroic posturing leads to isolation in efforts to hide actions we know will invite critique. We create 'special' relationships with persons, not unique, lovely, generative, connective relationships. 'Special' relationships replicate the conditions of sexual abuse, and are a threat to the safety of the community. Sexual abuse is most often not a stranger jumping out from a bush with a knife, but usually happens in intentional, well nurtured exploitative relationships. For example, a young person is required to go with their uncle in his car, even though they know he is going to abuse them and then buy them ice cream, under the guise of a 'special' relationship. Whenever we replicate special relationships, we replicate these conditions, which ruptures the safety of the community.

Workers enacting Enmeshment say things like: "I'm the only one that cares. I'm the only one that really gets it," situating ourselves as saviours. We are taken with guilt, but also righteousness, and full of 'should'. "You know, what this organization should do is they should be doin' this. You should be doin' that. Everybody should be doin' that." We feel incompetent, thinking we are personally responsible for fixing persons' lives. We abandon our teams, work in isolation, setting the team up with inconsistencies and special favours. We also set persons up, because they are then required to join in these transgressive, precarious and scary special relationships. Enmeshment can lead to workers losing their jobs because they convince themselves it is reasonable and required to do things like taking persons home. Enmeshment leads to transgression and intrusion, losing our collective ethics that centre persons and the collective responsibility of our teams.

Disconnection

Burnout can also show up as workers enacting Disconnection and moving too far away from persons. As workers we start to disconnect and detach. This does not usually lead to us losing our jobs, but coasting along the fringes of what has plausible deniability. We experience diminished empathy, and alarmingly and at times astonishingly situate ourselves as the victims of our jobs, organizations and of persons. As workers we disconnect from our own bodies, emotions, persons and teams. When taken with Disconnection we police other workers. We do not have broken hearts because we do not bring our hearts to work. When a person dies and you are crying, an embodied emotional experience, a disconnected worker slams you on the back and says, "If you're gonna cry every time someone dies, you're never gonna make it here." To which my response is, "If I don't cry every time I'm involved in a person's death, I've lost my humanity." We side with cynicism, and claim we are merely devil's advocates while the barrage of negativity and negative judgement encourages the staff to organize around their own struggles with each other. Cynicism does not require that workers only reject innovation or working harder, we have to squash everybody else, steal the hope of fellow workers, and take everybody out at the knees. New workers come in with innovation and energy saying, "Look, I think this is what we're gonna do. I think we're gonna start new groups, I think we need to see a lot more people." Disconnected workers cut those folks off saying, "Listen, here - Everything you've thought of we've thought of. Everything you wanna try we've tried. None of it works. Go ahead with your idea." Meanwhile, everybody else quietly bemoans the interaction as audience not participants: "Oh no, there they go again" like they are merely unkind. It is not unkind, or a personality problem: It is bullying hidden behind cynicism. When we disconnect, we start to situate ourselves as martyrs of the work, construct staff-centered teams, mitigate and mutualize bullying and massive negativity, and persons are lost.

Connection: The Zone of Fabulousness

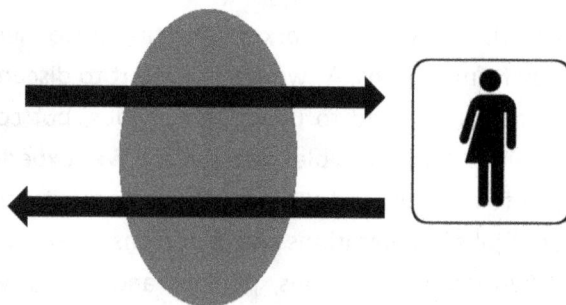

When we get harmed in the work, responding to the spiritual pain of being unable to do justice with persons, we can either get enmeshed and way too close to persons, or we get disconnected and too far away. We need to prioritize being person-centered teams not staff-centered teams. We want to be in the Zone of Fabulousness - because we are fabulous. Fabulousness happens when we enact collective ethics, and are collaborative, innovative, and justice-doing. We can be heartbroken but as workers we are not the center of the heartbreak. We understand that this is not our tragedy (Heather Gilmore, personal communication, December 1, 2015). We resist Disconnection and Enmeshment, enacting fluidity from Queer Theory where we move into and away from the work, like a dance. We co-create spaces where imperfection and need engender creativity. We can be messy with each other (Reynolds, 2014a). But it is also hope-filled, embracing our ethical obligation to be the bringers of hope, seeing a believed-in hope as an ethical stance; a "Relational hope, hope as something that happens in the space between us, rather than inside of me or you..." (Personal communication, Lizette Nolte, April 13, 2018).

We are connected to ourselves, our emotions, our bodies, our team members, and persons. In the Zone of Fabulousness we enact our collective ethics, shoulder up the team, engage collective accountability and respond with collective care versus self-care. We envision our work as useful and possible, and the person is at the centre.

Zone Slippage

One necessary assumption I make for my work as a clinical supervisor is the belief that no one came into this work to hurt people. It may not be an accurate assumption, but it is a useful assumption without which I could not work. From this analysis I see workers who slip into Disconnection or Enmeshment as workers we have let down. As fellow workers we witness these folks slipping, yet we side with the politics of politeness, gossip, and lack the moral courage to offer critique, smoothing other ethical issues. Collective care and collective ethics require that we offer critique when we witness peers slipping. As workers we do not simply become enmeshed or disconnected. I think of this as Zone Slippage, where we are in the Zone of Fabulousness and then we get exhausted, dis-heartened, broken-hearted, spiritually pained, and we slip into Enmeshment, or Disconnection. We need to consider what we are thinking, feeling, and doing that lets us know we are leaving the Zone of Fabulousness. When I start to get overwhelmed, tired, broken-hearted, I move towards Disconnection. When I am talking to co-workers, I start to think, "Damn, would they just get to the point? Could they just shut up?" When I start getting impatient, I know I am leaving the Zone of Fabulousness, moving towards disconnection. When I slip towards Enmeshment, I get heart-broken about one person, and I want to do things for them I could never do for others. Or I want our whole team to reorganize around somebody at the cost of the relational community.

We cannot keep ourselves Fabulous: Cultures of Critique, Collective Care and Solidarity Teams

Self-care is often prescribed as the antidote to Burnout, but it is individualized, positions workers as damaged and does not respond to the social determinants of health and contexts of social injustice in which persons suffer and workers struggle. Collective care invites us to shoulder each other up, work in solidarity, see our sustainability as a collective project and acknowledges that we are not going to stay with sustainability and be useful across the long haul individually. As individual workers we cannot keep ourselves Fabulous: We are meant to do this work together, and our sustainability in inextricably linked to our collective care. Solidarity Teams (Reynolds, 2011b) can be a useful practice for folks to intentionally structure support and decide who and what holds them up, sustains them, and how to access this heart-felt and spirited connection in responding to the darkness in our work and the heartbreak of unnecessary politicized deaths of vulnerable and oppressed people. We need to create relationships of respect and dignity and create cultures of accountability, appreciation and critique, to catch each other when we experience Zone Slippage, and offer ethical critique that brings us back to Fabulousness (Reynolds, 2014b). Despite discomfort we engage moral courage and offer critique to bring workers back to Fabulousness because, "We owe each other a terrible loyalty" (Janice Abbott, personal communication, January 8, 2012).

Conclusion

The Zone of Fabulousness is a frame to consider how are we centering persons, enacting collective ethics and fostering collective sustainability while working in contexts of social injustice, mean-spirited politics and oppression. How are we centering persons? How are we enacting connection; being collaborative, creative, messy, and imperfect? How are we connected to our bodies, emotions, the sacred, justice-doing, each other, and communities of struggle?

What is going on for workers in terms of 'vicariously traumatic experiences' might be better understood as acts of resistance and reasonable responses to politically desperate situations, and not symptoms of mental unwellness. When the measure is mental wellness, which is always influenced by privilege; more privileged workers will often be evaluated as more professional, having better self-care, boundaries, and more resilience against Burnout. I am humbled by community workers, who - despite struggling to do justice in harsh contexts of exploitation, oppression, and being broken-hearted - are able to show up, shoulder each other up, and hold other people at the center: That is the Zone of Fabulousness.

Acknowledgments

This writing and work took place on the traditional and unceded ancestral lands and territories of the Coast Salish – (xʷməθkwəy̓əm [Musqueam], Sḵwx̱wú7mesh [Squamish], and Səl̓ílwətaʔ [Tsleil-Waututh] – nations, which were never surrendered.

Revolutionary Love to my Solidarity Team who carry me back to the ZOF: Tara 'Danger' Taylor, Cori Kelly, Riel Dupuis-Rossi, Scott Kouri, Stephanie Saville, Sacha Médiné, Lana Fox, David Ng, Jen Sung, Prairie Chiu, Val Joseph, Janet Newbury, Wendy Wittmack and Stacy Leblanc. Mr. Peaslee helped again.

References

Manuel, A., & Derrickson, R. (2015). *Unsettling Canada*. Toronto, ON: Between the Lines Press.

Reynolds, V. (2011a). Resisting Burnout with justice-doing. *The International Journal of Narrative Therapy and Community Work*. (4) 27-45.

Reynolds, V. (2011b). Supervision of solidarity practices: Solidarity teams and people-ing-the-room. *Context*. August 2011. Association for Family and Systemic Therapy, UK, 4-7.

Reynolds, V. (2014a). A solidarity approach: The rhizome & messy inquiry. In Simon, G. & Chard, A. (Eds.) *Systemic Inquiry: Innovations in Reflexive Practice Research*. Farnhill, UK: Everything Is Connected Books.

Reynolds (2014b) Centering ethics in therapeutic supervision: Fostering cultures of critique and structuring safety. *The International Journal of Narrative Therapy and Community Work*. No. 1, 1-13.

Reynolds, V. & Hammoud-Beckett, S. (2018). Social Justice Activism and Therapy: Tensions, Points of Connection, and Hopeful Scepticism. In Audet, C. & Pare, D. (Eds.) *Social Justice and Counselling*. NY: Routledge.

Tuck, E. & Yang, K. W. (2012). Decolonization is not a metaphor. *Decolonization: Indigeneity, Education & Society*, 1(1), 1–40. Retrieved from https://jps.library.utoronto.ca/index.php/des

Inspiring Believed in Hope as an Ethical Position. Vicarious Resistance in Justice Doing

Vikki Reynolds, Riel Dupuis-Rossi & Travis Heath

Still 'Amazingly Alive'

My relationship to believed-in-hope and vicarious resistance has been nourished, inspired and shouldered-up by networks of social justice activists, communities of resistance, teams of practitioners, and people I aim to be of use to, across four decades of struggle, activism and community work. My work alongside people who are suffering has informed and transformed me. I owe a huge debt in particular to asylum seekers and refugees who have survived torture and political violence, people who were inmates on Death Row in the USA, and Indigenous people from Turtle Island (North America) who have survived and continue to resist the political violence of colonization, genocide and assimilation. Despite the darkness of this work, and the contexts of mean and hate-filled politics that create the structures of suffering I respond to, I still feel a spirited connection with activist/street poet Bud Osborne's (1999) poem: "Here we are amazingly alive, against long odds and left for dead" (p. 9).

In many ways this writing is a response to the many workers across time who have asked how I have resisted burnout and experienced both sustainability and transformation across decades of struggle in community work and activism. I have invited Riel Dupuis-Rossi and Travis Heath to offer critiques and reflections to this writing because of my respect for their ethics and work, and to invite accountability across domains of privilege and power, making space for multiple voices. I know Riel & Travis to have the moral courage to offer expansive critique and invitations to accountability. We did not write together because we do not want to conflate our important differences. I did not want us to speak harmoniously as that would conceal more than our separate but connected voices could reveal. Riel and Travis' solidarity in this project has allowed me to speak more vulnerably, from my broken-hearted places, and offers, I believe, an ethical container to hold witness alongside critique and a true reckoning with power.

I believe that as community workers we are ethically required to bring hope to our relational work with people. This is a recursive, un-ending project of engendering hope and bringing hope to the helping relationship. Hope, as I mean it here, is not optimism or positivity, but a believed-in-hope that is required for an ethical relationship with our work. Three decades of supervising teams working and living in the margins with people struggling against structural oppression and exploitation has also taught me that justice-doing, and enacting our collective ethics, is a necessary foundation for hope and a possible path for sustainability in our work. Building solidarity teams, and creating practices for our collective care have proved to be useful tactics across time and struggles. Sustainability is so much more than resisting vicarious-trauma or burnout; it speaks to the transformations and vicarious resistance we have witnessed and engaged with in relationships with people struggling for dignity, safety, and justice in contexts of structural oppression and hate (Reynolds, 2010; Reynolds, 2011a).

As an activist, therapist and clinical supervisor, my work across time has been to bridge the worlds of social justice activism with community work (Reynolds, 2019; Reynolds & Hammoud-Beckett, 2018). The context of my work is supervision and therapy with peers, activists, and other workers responding to the opioid catastrophe, torture and political violence, sexualized violence, mental health, substance misuse, homelessness, legislated poverty and working alongside gender and sexually diverse communities.

My people are from Ireland, Newfoundland, and England, and I am a white settler with heterosexual and cisgender privilege. I am still immersed in the on-going work of un-settling myself as a white settler (Regan, 2010), despite my intention to be decolonizing in all of my paid and unpaid work. Tuck and Yang (2012) teach that decolonization is not a metaphor, and means commitments to Indigenous land return and Indigenous governance. I aim to be directed in all my activist work and organizing by Indigenous people (Manuel & Derrickson, 2015). As a settler I have set intentions to stay implicated in the ongoing catastrophes (Kouri & Skott-Myers, 2016) of colonization and genocide (Brave Heart, & DeBruyn, 1998) and committed to taking actions.

I position my work as an anti-perfection project to acknowledge that working towards just relations is going to be imperfect because we have not co-created a just society. Engaging in this purposefully messy and imperfect process (Reynolds, 2014a) is informed by queer theory (Butler, 1990), critical trans theory (Spade, 2011), and anti-authoritarian social justice activism (Chomsky, 2005; Buechler, 2005; Shantz, 2011) where we aim to respond immediately to all oppressive and abusive acts. It requires that we take overt positions for justice-doing, defy neutrality, and have the moral courage to face up to and repair the consequences of imperfect actions.

Believed-in-Hope

Fostering believed-in-hope is hard, intentional work. Discerning believed-in-hope from optimism and positivity is important in order to maintain an ethical stance for justice-doing. Hope is not synonymous with optimism (Weingarten, 2000). I am not optimistic; I am very realistic about what is going on in this world, and I am terrified by it. But my terror does not get me stuck, it activates me, as feminist poet Marge Piercy (1982, p. 88) names it, towards a 'just anger':

"A good anger acted upon
is beautiful as lightning
and swift with power.
A good anger swallowed,
A good anger swallowed
clots the blood
to slime."

I can appear cloyingly hope-filled, but that is because I have learned that believed-in- hope is a useful and necessary tactic against despair. Our job, as the bringers of hope, is not to throw up our hands, but to roll up our sleeves. This requires the development of a finely attuned sense of hope, and a tenacious commitment to the moment-to-moment intention to seek out the acts of resistance (Reynolds, 2010; Richardson & Wade, 2008) and moments of justice-doing, no matter how small and trace those may be, and amplify them into a believed-in-hope.

Hopelessness can be a site of privilege. This was a humbling learning for me as a younger activist. I was devastated and empty following my active participation in solidarity struggles with Central and South American countries responding to the dirty wars of the 1980s, which were backed by American imperialism and capitalism. I was bereft, de-energized, hopeless. Then I came across these words from Brazilian scholar and popular educator Paulo Freire (1970): "Hopelessness is a form of silence, of denying the world and fleeing from it. The dehumanization resulting from an unjust order is not a cause for despair, but for hope, leading to the incessant pursuit of the humanity denied by injustice" (p. 72-73). I was confronted with an awareness of how my relationship to hopelessness was inextricably linked to my privileges, especially as a white citizen in the global north. Global south activists, coming from less privileges than I hold, were responding to the darkness as a call to action, requiring them to maintain a hold on hope in precarious contexts. This absolutely inspired me, and lit a fire in me that has kept me of use—a fire I must guard against the systemic privileges that work to extinguish it.

Resisting Despair

The etymology of the word 'despair' comes from Latin for 'without hope', and is related to spīritus, which means breath or spirit. From this, 'despair' can be understood to mean: an absence of spirit. I believe bringing a relational self and a spirited presence to the people we work alongside is an ethical requirement of the work. Un-spirited work is more than merely problematic: it calls to question our ability to do our work ethically, or at all.

Psychology and the helping professions' commitments to objectivity and neutrality can lead to despair. Professionalism can bring a silencing of all things 'political' and 'religious'. This can easily morph into designing helping relationships that are silent about both power and the sacred. This silencing stance bolsters and reinforces the very conditions of an unjust society that are the root of many people's suffering. Taking an overt position for justice is itself an act of resistance against despair; I have found that this is required to care for my own tender relationship with hope.

I spent a decade across the 1980s and 1990s immersed in the death penalty abolitionist struggle; I was involved with multiple groups' efforts to organize international campaigns and direct actions against the death penalty in the USA and internationally. I worked for over twenty men on death row in the USA. All of these men were executed by the state. Many people commiserated with me about these men's deaths, but some of the messages I received implied that I had wasted a decade, or that I could have done more effective and useful work. These invitations to despair were compelling. But I was transformed by my work with those men on death row, those men who offered me two powerful teachings, without which I would not be able to do any of my work that followed. The first is an adage from Death Row activism, that everyone is so much more than the worst thing they have ever done. I did not know this, but twenty men on death row taught me this because they had the courage to reveal themselves to me as human beings: as persons, artists, relational beings, spirited persons, *and* as men who have enacted violence against women. The fact that I am a woman who has survived violence at the hands of men positioned me as a meaningful witness to these men's connections and belongings to humanity. The fact that I resisted their deaths, not because they were innocent, but because I did not believe any state should allow itself to kill people, held meaning for these men.

Resistance to the death penalty also taught me that the binary of winners and losers is a hope-destroying approach to doing-justice. I do not mean that I had no hope of saving a man's life or that I have abandoned hope of ending the death penalty worldwide; I was adamantly resisting state killings until the last moments of each man's life. But I was not judging the usefulness of our collective resistance on whether or not we were able to stop the oppressive power of the American government's killing machine. Our work was meaningful and useful because we treated people who were deemed inhuman with dignity and respect, and for many of these men that relationship made a significant difference in how they faced death. They knew they were not entirely abandoned, but accompanied by others thus maintaining their connection to humanity, if not to life. Despite the invitation to despair and hopelessness, resisting the death penalty amplified my commitment to resisting despair itself and bringing hope against the darkness, against long odds.

Bringers of hope

It is our collective ethical obligation as practitioners to bring reasonable hope, a believe-in-hope, an embodied hope to our relational work with clients, and not to steal the hope they have. When services and individual workers transgress against people, we actually steal hope from them: either through being 'the help that doesn't help', or transgressing in oppressive ways, such as unethical practice that leads to child apprehension. When we do poor work in a helping profession, the consequences are not just that we are not useful. Our poor actions make it prudent and intelligent for people to resist further connections with professionalized help, and thereby create barriers to getting life affirming services they need. Our response to the harms caused by other workers has to resist blaming individuals and move into collective accountability. We then act to make repair of the ruptures we have caused as professionals, both individually and structurally. Our job is to step up and create a space in which there is a possibility for hope to grow.

Bringing hope is not the sole realm of workers, as people inspire and transform workers in reciprocal hope-inspiring relationships. When we track ethics in community work we centre the most vulnerable person in the relationship, which is the person we work alongside. At this intersection of power, it is the role of workers to bring hope. Simultaneously, workers need to resist invitations to what Teju Cole (2012) calls the "white saviour industrial complex" which elevates workers and disappears and makes invisible the resistance, wisdom and work of people. As workers we are not the victims or heroes of our work, but required to have enough-access to hope in our lives so that we can be the bringers of hope. This is hard work that requires collective care and practices of sustainability beyond self-care.

Shouldering up workers as they respond to peoples' suffering that is connected to exploitation and oppression requires that I bring hope to the supervisory relationship. My approach to this has been inspired by a teaching I received from a Tibetan monk, who was himself a survivor of torture and political violence. I was working in Dharmsala, India with the exiled Tibetan community at a Centre for Survivors of Torture; my role was to bring innovative practice, and help workers amplify people's acts of resistance as part of our own resistance, as practitioners, to Psychology's portrayal of people who have survived torture as traumatized and broken people (Reynolds et al, 2014b). We were constantly responding to tragic losses of life, human suffering, genocide, and torture. In the darkest moments I was flirting with despair, and asked this monk-brother how he kept his hope alive in the darkness, especially when a statistical analysis of our work would say we were not meeting any outcomes and were in fact losing ground. He referenced an adage from his tradition that went along these lines: Things are not this bad because we are doing nothing or are ineffective. Things are this bad and no worse because we are doing everything humanly possible to not have things be worse. I hold this teaching close as a resistance against the tyranny of measurable outcomes and a scarcity of resources amidst an abundance of need. This is especially poignant where I live, in British Columbia: one of the richest Canadian provinces, which has the second highest rate of child poverty and hunger in the country. Shame.

Justice-Doing as a Foundation for Hope

Enacting hope requires an ethical stance for justice-doing, otherwise we might be merely performing optimism, positivity, naivety, or charity. Justice-doing entails more than not replicating oppressive practices in our relationships with people. It requires the doing of justice with people, engaging the activist project to transform the social contexts in which suffering and oppression occur, and to do this in ways led by people and with accountability to their communities.

Justice-doing means doing dignity with people and witnessing their resistance to abuses of power, both structural and interpersonal. We resist accommodating suffering others to oppressive lives. I remind myself that no one came to this work to harm people, and yet our work can often result in people being trained up to accommodate themselves to poverty, disrespect or racism. To resist accommodating people to oppression, we have to use our collective power to transform the social contexts that make the horrors of oppression and suffering possible (Reynolds, 2019).

When we work in ways that enact our collective ethics for justice-doing— even though the work is hard and heart-breaking—we can have sustainability. The goal of our work is not to avoid heartbreak, but to be able to hold the person we work alongside at the centre even when we are heartbroken. When we work in ways that are unethical, no amount of self-care will keep us sustained, as we will experience spiritual pain, or ethical pain. When we transgress the values and ethics that are the heart of our work, and that drew us to the work, it is not burnout or vicarious trauma we experience, but ethical pain. A collective ethic of justice-doing makes it possible for us to be the people who can bring hope to the helping relationship (Reynolds, 2011).

Solidarity Teams & Sustainability

When I began work with people who had survived torture over three decades ago I knew that I could not keep myself hope-filled, useful and ethical alone. I knew I would need solidarity and I built a Solidarity Team (Reynolds, 2011b) with the intention of keeping me sustained, ethical, spirited, hopeful, and able to practice in alliance with our collective ethics for justice-doing. Solidarity speaks to the interconnectedness of our collective movements towards social justice, and our commitments to resisting oppression on all fronts. A spirit of solidarity makes the interconnectedness of our justice-doing work visible, and speaks to our ethical commitments to recursively carry and sustain each other, and our collective connection to hope.

A Solidarity Team is an intentional group of folks who work as a networked community (Lacey, 2005) that holds the worker up and accompanies them in the sites of ethical struggle and suffering in the work. We bring our solidarity team members into our work in actual and imagined ways. Being held by a networked community allows workers to access more resources and wisdoms on how they can be most useful to people. Instead of thinking of how an 'expert practitioner' would intervene, workers can imagine how *they* might be more useful to this person, and reconnect with their own hope, if a member of their solidarity team was accompanying them with a spirited relationship of solidarity. The role of the Solidarity Team is to help us resist despair, make ourselves useful, and be the bringers of hope: and no one can do this alone. The Solidarity Team needs to be peopled with folks who have the moral courage to lean in, across our histories of struggle and relationships of respect and dignity, and offer critique. I could not do my work sustainably, or maintain my relationship with hope, without the solidarity of impassioned, brilliant, ethical people who have had the moral courage to lean in and invite me to accountability for the ethics we hold collectively.

Vicarious Resistance and Transformations

Working with people who have survived torture for three decades has not burned me out, and I do not suffer vicarious trauma from it. I sometimes have dark dreams. The world is a dark place, my heart is broken. I have struggled alongside people who are asylum seekers and who have been refused refugee status by my Canadian government. I have been one of the people who has given someone their last hug before they got on a plane to be deported, to be tortured and murdered by their state. That has broken my heart. But that person who survived torture did not break my heart, Canada did. We have denied people refuge in this country, despite the fact that Canada should not be deciding who can seek refuge here (Dupuis-Rossi, 2020). As a nation we have not addressed our own presence as a diversity of settlers on Indigenous territories, which have been unceded and ancestral territories from time immemorial. The Canadian state and its agents have perpetrated political violence and torture and are complicit in race-based genocide of Indigenous women according to the Final Report of the National Inquiry into Missing and Murdered Indigenous Women and Girls (2019). It is not that I do not have a broken heart from working with communities of people who have survived torture and political violence, I do. But I do not believe the notion of vicarious trauma speaks ethically or meaningfully to my experience. The talk, resources, and investment into vicarious trauma are massive, but it makes me question where is the ongoing dialogue about vicarious resistance?

I have had the honour to witness stories of resistance from people who have survived torture and political violence, both abroad and in Canada. These dialogues have moved me, inspired me, transformed, educated, and challenged me. People have moved me to political action. People have made me question my education in psychology and the trauma trainings that label people as damaged on the inside. People have required me to show up for them and with them in ways that stretched my trainings and knowledge. The Chilean community has sharpened my political analysis. The Ogoni men I have worked alongside, who were tortured for environmental activism resisting the international resource extraction industry's pipelines in their territories in Nigeria, expanded my analysis of what activism was and can be. They forced me to make intersectional connections between social justice activism and what Indian physicist and activist Vandana Shiva (2005) calls Earth Democracy. This was breaking new ground three decades ago. These teachings and spirited connections have transformed me and made me more useful as an activist, worker, supervisor, and professor. Witnessing decades of people's resistance against state and capitalist power has moved me and ignited my own fire for justice-doing. My own relationship with hope has also been enriched by people I work alongside who have been the bringers of hope for me, as our relationships are reciprocal, and I acknowledge that people have also changed and shouldered me up. These are the benefits and gifts I have received from Vicarious Resistance.

As a supervisor I am curious about the ways our work amplifies our hope and transforms us. This has engendered a series of questions:

- How has this work amplified your hope: In yourself as a worker? In community? In the possibilities for a more just society?
- How are you transformed for having done this work?
- What have people contributed to your life, your relationships?
- What practices of gratitude and 'giving it back' (AA, 2001) has this work engendered in you?
- How are you different in this world for having done this work?

Collaborative Therapy innovator Harlene Anderson (1997) teaches that if we are truly in relationships with people, then we, as practitioners, are also at risk of being transformed. Our work is supposed to transform us, and not leave us untouched or unchanged. This transformation is not best understood as vicarious trauma or burnout, but holds the possibility for bringing us closer to our collective vision for how we need this world to be. We do not want to accommodate people to lives of oppression, and thereby hold up systems of exploitation and oppression. Our vision, as Paulo Freire (1970) unapologetically claims, is to transform ourselves, our societies, and this world in hope-filled ways that are just and sustainable.

A story of hope in unexpected places

I had just returned from a cross-country tour speaking about the opioid catastrophe and trying to promote harm-reduction and dignity-driven practice across many communities in Canada. I was exhausted and stretched. I had a desperate call to meet with a team of Aboriginal workers, who were working alongside Aboriginal mothers to help them navigate the oppressive structures required to maintain their housing and resist the apprehension of their children (Gerlach, Browne & Elliot, 2017). I was honoured to be invited in, and despite jet lag and being very tired I knew I had to respond with action and 'showing up'. People who have survived torture and political violence have taught me that the worst thing is not the torture itself, nor the need to seek refuge and leave their homelands: the real torture is living without your children. Canada has more Indigenous children in state care than during the period of Residential schools, and this contravenes the United Nations Declaration on the Rights of Indigenous Peoples (2007, p.5 Article 7, 2). To enact my commitment to a (trying to be) decolonizing stance, I knew I needed to respond to this team of Aboriginal workers and the mother-led families they support. But I was not just tired, I was also devastated. I am also connected to a team working in a live-in program for youth of all genders struggling with substances, exploitation and oppression in their lives. A youth who was in the program the previous year had died this day of an overdose. This youth died because recovery is not linear, and because there was no Overdose Prevention Site in their community. Donald MacPherson, the Executive Director of the Canadian Drug Policy Coalition, would say this youth died by bad drug policy (personal communication, 2015). The team was overwhelmed with grief. I was trying to respond on many fronts. It was a long, dark, sleepless night.

I awake fitfully, and as I am preparing to meet with the Aboriginal workers, I am straining to be the bringer of hope. I do my self-care practices of plank and stretching as I try to become embodied. I drink decaffeinated coffee and water. The program's workers are dedicated and skilled, but they have also caused harm to each other and to the Aboriginal mothers. I have no prior relationships with these workers, and I am very aware I am yet another white woman professional showing up with a PhD and prestige bolstered by white supremacy. Hope is hard to find. I arrive early and over-prepared.

To my surprise I am met with a circle of about fifteen workers, all earlier than me, and they are nearing the end of a smudge ceremony. They are already enacting the willingness and vulnerability I will need to be able to invite responsibility and enact repair, which gives my believed-in-hope a place to start. A young worker approaches me and non-verbally invites me to smudge. I am hesitant to engage in spiritual practices not my own, but I have also been mentored to participate accountably when invited in to sacred spaces, and to be careful what I take out. When the young worker has finished brushing me down with an eagle feather, she puts everything aside. Then she comes to me and says kindly, "Do you know who I am?" I say she is familiar but I don't remember where we know each other from, or her name. She says, "You were my therapist" (on the team where we had just lost the youth to the opioid catastrophe). She introduces herself as Sarah-Anne Mitchell (her real name, as she wants to be identified in this writing). She tells me she has twenty years free from drugs, that our program and workers are part of how she got her life together. She also says she has five children, and none of them are apprehended by the government. I feel elated, joyful: full of hope. I ask if we can take a selfie on my phone, and we do. I send it to the youth substance misuse program, where the workers share this story of hope, of how youth can and do find liberation and meaningful lives. We can hold this hope in a tension alongside the heartbreak and rage of the youth who has died. Sarah-Anne says to me, "The creator sent you to us and our families today". I say, "The creator also sent you to me today".

Borrowing the hope of others

Acts of hope-filled solidarity continue to humble me and shoulder me up for this work. We are not meant to do this work alone, nor are we required to rely on self-care and individual resilience, or some equally obscure personal trait, to keep us alive in the work. There is a fluidity in our collective work that allows for and requires an ebb and flow of hope around and between us. In moments when hope is hard to grasp, it is possible to borrow the hope of others.

When it became undeniable that the present opioid catastrophe was more than a bad run of drugs, and that it was going to be reminiscent of the AIDS pandemic, where people died because they were not dignified as human, I despaired. I was thinking that I could not do this again. I met with a beloved friend from decades-past AIDS activist days. My friend held space for my pain and heartache, but resisted my despair by lending me his hope. He said, "yes Vikki, you can do this again, and you will do this again". That night he sent me this writing from the Talmud, which is the central text of Rabbinic Judaism and the primary source of Jewish religious law and theology (Steinstaltz, 2009):

> "Do not be daunted by the enormity of the world's grief.
> Do justly now.
> Love mercy now.
> Walk humbly now.
> You are not obligated to complete the work,
> but neither are you free to abandon it."

Dedication

To Trey Helton, Tara Taylor, Sarah Blythe and the team at the original Overdose Prevention Site, OPS in Vancouver; to Zoe Dodd in Toronto, Stan Kupferschmidt in Ottawa, and all good folks responding to the opioid catastrophe and deaths by bad drug policy who continue to enact and re-create fierce, creative, life-saving acts of resistance that amplify my hope.

Acknowledgments

This writing and work took place on the traditional and unceded ancestral lands and territories of the Coast Salish (xʷməθkwəy̓əm [Musqueam], Sḵwx̱wú7mesh [Squamish], and Səl̓ílwətaʔ [Tsleil-Waututh] nations, which were never surrendered.

Gratitude and respect for my Solidarity Team who shoulder me up: Cori Kelly, Tara Danger Taylor, Wendy Wittmack and Janet Newbury. Humility and gratitude to Riel Dupuis-Rossi, and Travis Heath, for their willingness to offer generative and expansive reflections. Kim Stefanie Krasnow, Bupie Dulay, Stephanie Saville, Jill Faulkner, Liv Henry, Cori Kelly, Sacha Médiné and Donald MacPherson contributed generous and thoughtful critiques to this writing. Gratitude and respect to Sarah-Anne Mitchell for sharing her story and inspiring hope. Mr. Peaslee helped again.

Vikki Reynolds is an activist/therapist from Vancouver, Canada, who works to bridge the worlds of social justice activism and therapy. Vikki is a white settler of Irish, Newfoundland and English folks, and a heterosexual woman with cisgender privilege. Her experience includes supervision and therapy with peers, activists, and other workers responding to the opioid epidemic/poisonings, torture and political violence, sexualized violence, mental health and substance misuse, homelessness and legislated poverty and working alongside gender and sexually diverse communities. Vikki is an Adjunct Professor and has written, keynoted and presented internationally: **www.vikkireynolds.ca**

****

Riel Dupuis-Rossi is a Two Spirit therapist of Kanien'kehá:ka, Algonquin and Italian descent. Riel grew up in their traditional territories, off reserve in Hamilton, ON and Montreal, QC.

Riel has been providing decolonizing and culturally-centered Indigenous trauma therapy to Indigenous adults in the unceded Homelands of the Coast Salish Nations since 2011. Riel holds both a Masters in Curriculum Studies and a Master of Social Work. Riel's clinical specializations are in historical, transgenerational, complex and shock trauma therapy.

Reflection by Riel Dupuis-Rossi

As an Indigenous person, my hope lies in what I have inherited from my Onkwehon: we Ancestors and relatives. As an Indigenous person, my hope lies in the fact that under the layers of collective grief is sacred knowledge of a way of life that upholds, centers, respects and lives in harmony with All of our Relations: the Earth, the Sky, the waterways, the forests, plants, sacred medicines, the mountains, the animals, the water life and the winged ones/birds.

My hope is born of reclamation: the subtle yet powerful act of reclaiming one's right to love as an Indigenous person and of those acts of greater magnitude which include our communities' defense of our lands. These acts, whether they be deeply intimate or greatly political, are the equivalent of moving mountains and changing tides. I see Indigenous Peoples' courage in this respect and this courage unfolds on a moment to moment basis.

My hope is alive in the knowledge that as Indigenous Peoples we have complex governance and kinship systems that are based in philosophies and language systems that reflect deep respect and care for all living things. My hope lies in the fact, that as the Original Peoples of this land, we have the skills, competence, insight, wisdom and the time-honoured experience of how to live in our Homelands in a way that is peaceful, honourable, kind, loving and deeply generous. We are a healthy people and we live this health-despite being subjected to relentless and brutal systemic attack by the Settler State.

The poverty, homelessness, domestic violence, addiction, child abuse, chronic disease, high rates of suicide and chronic suicidality, cultural dislocation, disproportionate rates of incarcerations and alarmingly high rates of child apprehensions are all forms of violent oppression under colonial rule but it is not who we are. They are the impact of 500 years of colonial war against our Peoples: genocidal warfare, forced relocation, reservations, residential schools, criminalization of our ceremonies, dislocation of our traditional governments, the intentional flooding of

Indigenous communities with alcohol and drugs, imposed poverty, police brutality and the ongoing abductions and murder of Indigenous women, girls and trans peoples. These symptoms of colonial violence are not ours to own. Our Indigenous histories, philosophies, governance structures, our songs, ceremonies and medicines contain within them knowledge of who we are and it is hopeful and prideful.

Even those who purport to practice anti-oppressive approaches often do not take the time to see us for who we truly are. The directionlessness of settler society, the poverty of capitalism, the emptiness of a market economy, the darkness of institutionalized settler religion, the incompetence of settler governments-all of these get projected onto us as Indigenous Peoples. We are forced to bear the misery, the suffering, the poverty and the criminality of colonial oppression. All of this stands in sharp contrast to the wisdom, wealth and grace of our traditional governance structures, economies, cultures and spiritualities which exist in respectful alignment with All of Our Relations. It is in the inheritance of ancestral knowledge and in the care that it took to pass it down over generations, despite over 500 years of genocidal attack, that I find hope. It is here that I also find truth, courage, integrity, strength, humility, reverence and honour.

We, Indigenous Peoples, are not souls lost in a sea of pain, darkness and despair. We are Onkwehon: we, the Original Peoples of our vast and most sacred territories. We are the inherent and rightful Leaders, Knowledge Keepers, Healers and Ceremonialists of these lands. And the lands upon which we have lived since time immemorial recognize, claim, care for and protect us even as we live, survive and resist the unspeakable violence of ongoing attempted genocide. But the desecration has nothing to do with us and everything to do with how the settler state and its benefactors live and govern. The oppression to which we are subjected *is* the disease and the criminality of the settler state. Violence, theft, desecration, oppression, darkness and despair is the history of the settler state and its citizens. It is not our history. As Indigenous Peoples, we have histories as old as time itself and it is in this history and its continuity that my hope is inspired.

My hope also lies in the possibility that one day settlers will turn their gaze, with all its unconscious abuse of power, away from us, Indigenous Peoples, and begin to take a good hard look at themselves. My hope lies in the possibility that one day, settlers may realize that their nation and their governments are illegitimate and that no amount of anti-oppressive practice will ever justify their existence. To Indigenous Nations, Canada is an illegitimate, illegal occupying force. It is not an entity that has potential for redress or reconciliation. It is a presence that is inherently violent and unjust. It is from this clarity that hope can be created. But this will require that even those with anti-oppressive commitments take an honest look at themselves and be truthful about all of the ways that the unearned privileges bestowed upon them by the Settler state are still held onto tightly and with great force.

****

Travis Heath is an adopted, cisgender man from United States of America of mixed racial background (birth father was Pardo, from Brazil, and birth mother of German and Polish descent). Travis works as a psychologist and professor in Denver, Colorado. Travis has a therapy practice that operates on a radical sliding fee scale, and he works with many people on the margins.

Reflection by Travis Heath

For some time, I have felt exasperated and exhausted by what I've started to referring to as "the cult of positivity." Don't like how you feel? Well, only you can choose your attitude. Do you weigh too much? Look at this diet or workout plan. Feeling the stress of your job? Just engage in self-care. This reduces the idea of hope to nothing more than a commodity to be bought and sold. It also positions happiness as the highest end. And it sets up those of us on the margins to feel as though we're never quite good enough.

I'm not interested in finding hope, at least not the way they have defined it. Hope becomes a tool of the colonizer that pulls the wool over our eyes and tries to make us believe we are actually pawns in the neoliberal game of life. If we just work hard enough and study well enough, we too, can make our own luck and cultivate the skill of happiness.

I've discovered their hope to be at worst a lie and at best a mirage. It's based on the idea of a republic and a constitution that was never created for me. Hope, just like so many other things, has been coopted by the machine. How do we take it back? Or is it time to blow it up and start all over again? How do we find hope we can believe in? Might hope be something we have to construct anew with each person we are in conversation with? How does hope on the margins look different than hope in the middle?

As Vikki pointed out, this is certainly not a project that can be successfully navigated from a place of neutrality under the guise of professionalism. People I've been in conversation with have taught me that it takes a kind of fierce humility to locate and elevate the hope we find on the margins. This brings me to a story of a person I share with his consent. He asked that I call him by the pseudonym "Julio." Specifics of the story will also be omitted per his request.

Julio is a 23-year-old man of Mexican descent. His parents came to the United States shortly before he was born. As such, he was a citizen of United States by birth. He experienced violence in his home growing up as well as overt racism in the small town in which he lived most of his life. This began to try and steal hope and a lot of other things from him relatively early in life. When he turned 18, he enlisted in a branch of the military. He was off to combat a short time later. He told me, "I had no idea what the fuck I was getting myself into. I thought it would be like a videogame or something."

Someone who had seen me in the past sent Julio my direction because he was having thoughts of no longer wanting to live, and he was on a waiting list still months long at the local VA Hospital. He was concerned about not being able to pay, which I told him was of no concern since I work on a radical sliding fee scale. We made an appointment for the next week.

Upon his arrival, he told me some stories about things that happened while he was in combat. He said, "I'm a piece of shit. Look at what I've done. There's no other way to say it. I'm a piece of shit. Everything that everyone said about growing up must be true. I'm just a Mexican piece of shit." It was as if in this moment any remaining hope separated itself from his body.

Without giving it too much thought, I asked, "Do you think sometimes groups that are capable of behaving badly like the military can mandate that otherwise good people do bad things?" He stared back at me and declared, "What?" I repeated the question. After 30 seconds or so of silence, he replied, "I don't know. I mean, no one has ever asked me a question like that before." We decided that this was the kind of question he might be better served to live with for a while rather than just answer outright.

He came back to our next meeting with a sense of urgency in his speech as well as in how he was holding his body. "You remember that question you asked me last time? I couldn't get it out of my head. Every time I started to think I was a piece of shit, I was like, nah, good person, bad group. It's not like the whole military is bad, but it can go bad. Really bad." I asked, "When you said to yourself good person, bad group, what started to happen in your life?" He had an answer at the ready, "I started to feel like there was hope for me again. I thought, maybe I can live this life."

Obviously, this conversation continued over a period of months and contained quite a number of twists and turns, but when I recently asked Julio what moment he thought was most important in our work, he relayed the story I just shared. For the purpose of this writing, I want to propose that we co-created a believed-in-hope that resided on the margins. The politics of hope at the center had been trying to squash Julio's believed-in-hope ever since he was a boy. As a young adult, the system mandated that he behave in a way that betrayed his own ethics and values and then had the audacity to try and blame him for it. If dominant systems are too often the thieves of hope, perhaps conversations committed to justice-doing, however imperfect they may be, are one potential antidote.

References

Alcoholics Anonymous. (2001). *The Big Book* (4th ed.). New York: Alcoholic Anonymous World.

Anderson, H. (1997). *Conversation, language, and possibilities: A postmodern approach to therapy.* New York, NY: Basic.

Brave Heart, M. Y. H., & DeBruyn, L. M. (1998). The American Indian holocaust: Healing historical unresolved grief. *American Indian and Alaska Native Mental Health Research*, 8(2) 60-82. http://doi.org/10.5820/aian.0802.1998.60

Buechler, S. (2005). New social movement theories. *Sociological Quarterly*, 36(3), 441-464. http://doi.org/10.1111/j.1533-8525.1995.tb00447.x

Butler, J. (1990). *Gender trouble: Feminism and the subversion of identity.* New York, NY: Routledge.

Canada (2019). *Reclaiming power and place: The final report of the National Inquiry into Missing and Murdered Indigenous Women and Girls* (2019). Retrieved from:
https://www.mmiwg-ffada.ca/wp-content/uploads/2019/06/Final_Report_Vol_1a-1.pdf

Chomsky, N. (2005). *Chomsky on anarchism.* B. Pateman (Ed.). Edinburgh, Scotland: AK Press.

Cole, T. (2012). *The white savior industrial complex*, available at:
https://www.theatlantic.com/international/archive/2012/03/the-white-savior-industrial-complex/254843/

Dupuis-Rossi, R. (2020). *The trauma of colonization and the importance of decolonizing therapeutic relationship: The role of helper in centering indigenous wisdom.* Manuscript submitted for publication.

Freire, P. (1970). *Pedagogy of the oppressed.* New York: Continuum.

Gerlach, A., Browne, A., & Elliot, D. (2017). Navigating structural violence with Indigenous families. *The International Indigenous Policy Journal, 8(3),* http://doi.org/10.18584/iipj.2017.8.3.6

Kouri, S., & Skott-Myers, S. (2016). Catastrophe: a transversal mapping of colonialism and settler subjectivity. *Settler Colonial Studies*, 6(3), 279–274, http://doi.org/10.1080/2201473X.2015.1061967.

Lacey, A. (2005). Spaces of justice: The social divine of global anti-capital activists' sites of resistance. *The Canadian Revue of Sociology and Anthropologie/Revue Canadienne de sociologie et d'anthropologie*, 42(4), 407.

Manuel, A., & Derrickson, R. (2015). *Unsettling Canada*. Toronto, ON: Between the Lines Press.

Osborn, B. (1999). *Hundred block rock.* Vancouver, British Columbia, Canada: Arsenal Pulp Press.

Piercy, M. (1982). *Circles on the Water*. New York: Knopf

Regan, P. (2010). *Unsettling the settler within: Indian residential schools, truth telling, and reconciliation in Canada*. Vancouver, BC: UBC Press.

Reynolds, V. (2010). *Doing Justice as a Path to Sustainability in Community Work.* http://www.taosinstitute.net/Websites/taos/Images/PhDProgramsCompletedDissertations/ReynoldsPhDDissertationFeb2210.pdf

Reynolds, V. (2011a). Resisting burnout with justice-doing. The International Journal of Narrative Therapy and Community Work. (4) 27-45.

Reynolds, V. (2011b). Supervision of solidarity practices: Solidarity teams and people-ing-the-room. *Context*. August 2011. Association for Family and Systemic Therapy, UK, 4-7.

Reynolds, V. (2014a). A solidarity approach: The rhizome & messy inquiry. In Simon, G. & Chard, A. (Eds.) *Systemic Inquiry: Innovations in Reflexive Practice Research*. Farnhill, UK: Everything Is Connected Press.

Reynolds, V., "Bahman", Hammoud-Beckett, S., Sanders, C.J., & Haworth, G. (2014b). Poetic Resistance: Bahman's resistance to torture and political violence. *The International Journal of Narrative Therapy and Community Work*. No.2, 1-15.

Reynolds, V., & Hammoud-Beckett, S. (2018). Social justice activism and therapy: Tensions, points of connection, and hopeful scepticism. In C. Audet & D. Paré (Eds.), *Social justice and counseling: Discourse in practice* (pp. 3-15). New York, NY: Routledge.

Reynolds, V. (2019). Setting an Intention for Decolonizing Practice and Justice-Doing: Social Justice Activism in Community Work and Therapy. In Collins, S. (Ed.) *Embracing Cultural Responsivity and Social Justice: Re-Shaping Professional Identity in Counselling Psychology*. Victoria, British Columbia: Counselling Concepts, pp. 615-630.

Richardson, C., & Wade, A. (2008). Taking resistance seriously: A response-based approach to social work in cases of violence against Indigenous women. In S.

Strega & J. Carrière (Eds.), *Walking this path together: Anti-racist and anti-oppressive child welfare practice*. Winnipeg, MB: Fernwood.

Shantz, J. (2011). *Against all authority: Anarchism and the literary imagination*. Exeter, UK: Imprint Academic

Shiva, V. (2005). *Earth democracy: Justice, sustainability, and peace*. Cambridge, England: South End Press.

Spade, D. (2011). *Normal life: Administrative violence, critical trans politics, and the limits of law*. Brooklyn, NY: South End Press.

Steinsaltz, A. (2009). *What is the Talmud?* The Essential Talmud (30th Anniversary Ed.). New York: Basic Books.

Tuck, E. & Yang, K. W. (2012). Decolonization is not a metaphor. *Decolonization: Indigeneity, Education & Society*, 1(1), 1–40. Retrieved from https://jps.library.utoronto.ca/index.php/des

UN General Assembly, *United Nations Declaration on the Rights of Indigenous Peoples: resolution / adopted by the General Assembly*, 2 October 2007, A/RES/61/295, available at: https://www.un.org/esa/socdev/unpfii/documents/DRIPS_en.pdf [accessed 1 March 2020]

Weingarten, K. (2000). *Witnessing, wonder and hope*. Family Process, 39(4), 389-402.

Everything is Connected Press Publications

Systemic Inquiry. Innovations in Reflexive Practice Research
Gail Simon & Alex Chard (Eds.)
ISBN 978-0-9930723-0-7

Systemic Therapy and Transformative Practice
Imelda McCarthy & Gail Simon (Eds.)
ISBN 978-0-9930723-2-1

Speaking, Actually: Towards a New 'Fluid' Common-Sense Understanding of
Relational Becomings
John Shotter
ISBN 978-0-9930723-4-5

A Wild Impatience. Critical Systemic Practice and Research. Selected Papers.
Gail Simon
ISBN 978-0-9930723-6-9

Rewilding Therapy. EcoSystemic Theory and Practice
Chiara Santin
ISBN 978-1-7397733-0-4

The EcoSystemic Return. An Anthology for Now
Hugh Palmer & Lorna Edwards (Eds.)
ISBN 978-1-7397733-4-2

Creating Relational Ripples
Marilena Karamatsouki
ISBN 978-1-7397733-2-8

To Be of Use. Selected Papers. Vikki Reynolds
Vikki Reynolds
ISBN 978-1-7397733-6-6

Murmurations: Journal of Transformative Systemic Practice
www.murmurations.cloud
ISSN 2516-0052

www.eicpress.com

everything is connected

www.ingramcontent.com/pod-product-compliance
Lightning Source LLC
Chambersburg PA
CBHW050334270326
41926CB00016B/3449